Preaching That Comes Alive is a boo........................y
and well. Using the analogy of a hu........................e
different facets of crafting a sermon........................',
nervous, and muscular systems – in a \.....................1
experienced preacher alike. Blending .... of the classroom and the
pulpit, brimming with worked examples, and rooted in her own Singaporean
context, this is warmly commended for all those seeking to bring to people a
life-giving word from the Lord.

Antony Billington, PhD
Head of Theology, London Institute for Contemporary Christianity, UK

Preaching That Comes Alive will provide all readers, not just those with Dr Low's own Asian slant, tips for effective preaching and helpful summaries of approaches which are espoused by preaching professors in the West. This makes her book an excellent introduction to the science and art of preaching. Thank you, Dr Low!

Rev Gordon Wong, PhD
President, Trinity Annual Conference,
The Methodist Church in Singapore

Dr Low's treatise on the homiletic discipline is a delightful smorgasbord of theological reflection and practical delineation. She has strenuously and delicately illustrated the relationship between biblical scholarship and homiletical craftsmanship. Using her students' and other practitioners' sermons as working examples, she skillfully explains the intricacies of sermon preparation and its accompanying sentinels of exegesis, context, forms, functions and structure. A timely book which will prove indispensable for both aspiring and seasoned preachers alike.

Rt Rev Steven Gan, DMin
Synod Moderator, The Presbyterian Church in Singapore

Rooted in Scripture, practiced in a community of preachers and welling from a deep sense of personal calling, Maggie Low's *Preaching That Comes Alive* is an important contribution to the ongoing conversations and reflections on what effective preaching may mean today.

Rev Canon Terry Wong
The Anglican Diocese of Singapore

This is more than a how-to book on preaching; it is preaching itself! It is grounded in sound, biblical theology, well-structured, clearly argued, and spiced with homely illustrations and real-life examples. Students from the Majority World will likely find something in it with which they can identify. But it is by no means parochial. Maggie Low interacts with a wide range of homileticians from around the world giving her book a universal appeal.

Rev Simon Chan, PhD
Trinity Theological College, Singapore
Editor, *Asia Journal of Theology*

Here is a treasure trove of helpful homiletical insights for all who preach God's Word. Birthed in the author's nurturing of budding preachers and seminarians, the book is peppered with practical guidelines and seasoned with biblical examples. Particularly salutary are the emphases on preaching as a transformative encounter with God, and the preacher's need to hear from God before speaking for God.

Rev Mark Chan, PhD
Director, Centre for the Study of Christianity in Asia (CSCA),
Lecturer in Theology and Homiletics, Trinity Theological College, Singapore

I wish this helpful book had been available when I studied homiletics at theological school. It is a delightful resource for learning and growing in the preaching ministry. I appreciate the systematic process in which the author guides the homiletical student "from head to toe" in having the necessary heart and understanding the practical skills needed in preparing and delivering a sermon that the Holy Spirit can use to minister deeply in the hearts of the listeners.

Rev John Lin
Dean of Vietnam, The Anglican Diocese of Singapore

Rev Dr Low is driven by a passion for the church to be fed by the Word so it can change the world. Here is a book that will inspire preachers everywhere to understand the weight of their calling and raise the quality of their sermons. Offering both warm, deeply grounded practical guidance and a solid theoretical framework, Maggie Low is the preaching mentor you always hoped to find.

Jo Swinney
Editor, *Preach Magazine*

Preaching That Comes Alive

Langham
GLOBAL LIBRARY

Preaching That Comes Alive

Delivering a Word from the Lord

Maggie Low

Langham
GLOBAL LIBRARY

© 2017 by Maggie Low

Published 2017 by Langham Global Library
An imprint of Langham Creative Projects

Langham Partnership
PO Box 296, Carlisle, Cumbria CA3 9WZ, UK
www.langham.org

ISBNs:
978-1-78368-244-7 Print
978-1-78368-246-1 Mobi
978-1-78368-245-4 ePub
978-1-78368-247-8 PDF

Maggie Low has asserted her right under the Copyright, Designs and Patents Act, 1988 to be identified as the Author of this work.

All rights reserved. No part of this publication may be reproduced, stored in a retrieval system or transmitted, in any form or by any means, electronic, mechanical, photocopying, recording or otherwise, without the prior written permission of the publisher or the Copyright Licensing Agency.

Unless otherwise stated, Scripture quotations are from the New Revised Standard Version Bible, copyright © 1989 National Council of the Churches of Christ in the United States of America. Used by permission. All rights reserved.

British Library Cataloguing in Publication Data
A catalogue record for this book is available from the British Library

ISBN: 978-1-78368-244-7

Cover & Book Design: projectluz.com

Langham Partnership actively supports theological dialogue and an author's right to publish but does not necessarily endorse the views and opinions set forth, and works referenced within this publication or guarantee its technical and grammatical correctness. Langham Partnership does not accept any responsibility or liability to persons or property as a consequence of the reading, use or interpretation of its published content.

CONTENTS

Acknowledgments xiii

Prologue. xv

Part I: Foundations for Preaching

1   The Call to Preach: Biblical Foundation 3
        1. Preaching as Heralding (*kerysso* and *euangelizo*) 4
           Euangelizo (Bringing Good News) 10
           The Result of *Kerysso* and *Euangelizo* 12
        2. Preaching as Teaching (*didasko*) 13
        3. Preaching as Exhorting (*parakaleo*) 17
        4. Preaching as Witnessing (*martyreo*) 20
        5. A Framework for Preaching 22
    Conclusion 25

2   The Crux of Preaching: Homiletical Foundation. 27
        A. Why Have "A Word from the Lord"? 28
          1. Purpose of Preaching 28
          2. Rhetoric of Preaching 32
        B. How to Formulate "A Word from the Lord" 35
          1. Haddon Robinson 35
          2. Paul Scott Wilson 35
          3. Bryan Chapell 37
          4. Fred Craddock, Thomas Long, and Stephen Farris 38
    Conclusion 39

3   Seeing the Bones: Exegetical Foundation 41
        1. Determine the Limits of the Text 43
        2. Dig Up the Historical Context of the Text 44
        3. Delineate the Literary Context of the Text 46
        4. Discern Genre, Form, and Structure 47
        5. Dissect the Syntax and Grammar 49
        6. Define Key Words 51
        7. Discuss Biblical Theology 52
    Conclusion 55

4   The Heart of Preaching: *Lectio Divina*........................ 59
     A. The God Who Speaks 60
          1. Through the Old and New Testaments 60
          2. Through Church History 62
     B. *Lectio Divina*: Hearing a Word from the Lord 64
          1. Attitudes for the *Lectio Divina* 65
          2. Acting on the *Lectio Divina* 67
     C. Writing Out a Word from the Lord 72
          1. Be Clear 72
          2. Be Coherent 73
          3. Be Concise 74

Part II: Shaping the Skeleton

5   Shaping the Skeleton I: Deductive Forms..................... 79
     A. Why Deductive Forms? 81
     B. How to Shape Deductive Forms 82
          1. Write the Main Points in Complete Sentences 82
          2. Connect the Main Points to the Word from the Lord 83
          3. Connect the Main Points to Each Other 84
          4. Connect the Main Points to the Hearers 86
     C. Examples 87
     Conclusion 89

6   Shaping the Skeleton II: Inductive Forms..................... 91
     A. Why Inductive Forms? 91
     B. How to Shape Inductive Forms 95
          1. Inductive Propositional Forms 95
          2. Inductive Narrative Forms 98
     Conclusion 106

7   Shaping the Skeleton III: Textual Forms..................... 109
     A. Why Textual Forms? 109
     B. How to Shape Textual Forms 110
          1. Prophetic Literature 110
          2. Apocalyptic Literature 112
          3. Psalms 114
          4. Epistles 116
     Conclusion 117

Part III: Building the Body

8 The Digestive System: Explanations (What?) 121
    A. Why Explain? 121
    B. How to Explain? 123
        1. Explain the Problematic 124
        2. Explain the Passage 124
        3. Explain to the People 125
        4. Explain the Perspectives 127
    C. Concluding Examples 128

9 The Nervous System: Illustrations (Really?) 131
    A. Why Illustrations? 131
        1. Prove by Facts 133
        2. Persuade by Examples 134
    B. How to Tell Illustrations? 137
        1. Tell It Relevantly to the Text 137
        2. Tell It Relevantly to the People 138
        3. Tell It Relevantly to the Illustration 142
    C. Where to Find Illustrations? 145
        1. The World Within: Personal Experience 145
        2. The World Around: Popular Culture 146
        3. The World Behind: History 148
        4. The World of Nature 148
        5. The World Online 148

10 The Muscular System: Applications (So?) 151
    A. Why Apply? 152
    B. Who to Apply To? 153
    C. What to Apply? 156
        1. Apply to the Congregant 156
        2. Apply to the Church 157
        3. Apply to the Community 159
    D. How to Apply? 160
        1. Apply to Specific People 161
        2. Apply in Specific Situations 161
        3. Apply through Specific Actions 162
        4. Apply with Suitable Motivations 164

      E. An Example 165
      Conclusion 167

Part IV: Connecting the Head, Feet, and Ligaments

11   The Head: Introduction.. 171
      A. Why Introduction? 172
      B. How to Introduce 174
          1. Make It Relevant to the Central Word 174
          2. Make It Relevant to the Contemporary Context 176
          3. Make It Relevant to the Congregation 182
      C. Examples 183
          Worked Example 183
          Practice Example 184

12   The Feet: Conclusion 187
      A. Why Conclude? 188
          1. Recall the Word of the Lord 188
          2. Call to Respond 190
      B. How to Conclude 192
          1. Tell an Illustration 192
          2. Give Directions 197
          3. Inspire a Vision 199
          4. Extend an Invitation 204
      Conclusion 209

13   The Ligaments: Transitions 211
      A. Why Transition? 212
      B. How to Transition? 213
          1. Reason for Connections 213
          2. Raise Questions 215
          3. Review and Preview 216
          4. Repeat the Central Word 217
      C. An Example 218

Part V: Delivering with Ears, Eyes, and Voice

14   The Ears: Oral Style 223
      A. Why Words? 223
      B. How to Use Words? 224
          1. Be Plain 224

	2. Be Poetic	225
	3. Be Personal	228
	4. Be Powerful	231
	C. An Example	232
15	Eyes and Voice: Delivery	235
	A. Why Deliver?	235
	B. How to Deliver?	236
	1. Deliver with Your Eyes	236
	2. Deliver with Your Voice	240
	3. Deliver with Your Heart	245
Epilogue		249
	Pre-Sermon Prayer	249
	Post-Sermon Prayer	250
Bibliography		255
Author Index		263
Scripture Index		265

Acknowledgments

Thanks are due to my preaching students who provided the raw material for this book. They hail from all over Asia: Hong Kong, Indonesia, Mongolia, Myanmar, Nepal, Singapore, and Vietnam. Although identified only by nationalities in the book, I list their names below in alphabetical order:

Abraham Yap	Jessica Abraham
Anthony Phua	Kang Choon Pin
Benjamin Lee	Lam My An
Byron Teo	Mak Zhe Hao
Cathy Law	Moe Nilar
Charles Tewer	Peter Ticoalu
Chua Likai	Prem Bahadur Tamang
David Ho	Pua Eeli
Dino Thangamany	Susanty Parsaoran Manullang
Do Thi Thanh Phuong	Suseelah Isaac
Eddie Ho	Than Hue Anh
Edmund Koh	Tran Thi Thanh Nhan
Elaine Lim	Urjinkhand Namgar
Goh Wei Ming	Yvonne Chia
How Choon Onn	

I'm grateful to Trinity Theological College for granting me a six-month sabbatical to work on this book. To my colleagues, thanks to Simon Chan for first asking me to teach homiletics when he was Academic Dean and to Roland Chia for connecting me with Langham Partnership. Jeffrey Truscott and Mark Chan, both of whom teach homiletics, gave invaluable feedback on my manuscript. Michelle Oh-Tan generously gave her time and journalistic skills to help edit my manuscript.

To my husband David who believed in me more than I did in myself: I would not have grown to be the preacher I am today without your loving critique and constant stirring up of God's gift in me.

It is a joyful privilege to sow and water with the Word, knowing that ultimately, God is the one who gives life and growth. May you, my fellow preachers, experience more of that joy as you deliver a word from the Lord!

Maggie Low

Prologue

This is the first book on my bucket list. When a friend passed away of cancer and another had a near fatal stroke, it gave me the clarity to realize that this is the one book that I want to write during my sabbatical. Even though I am an Old Testament lecturer, preaching has always been my burning passion.

When I sit in various church services, I am often torn between hope and despair. Hope when I see congregations attending faithfully to hear a word from the Lord, and despair if they are given only emotional scraps or intellectual indigestion. People are hungry to learn the Word and to meet with God so that they can be strengthened to go back and live their lives in the world. It is when people are spiritually fed that the church can minister to the rest of the world.

So as I taught Old Testament courses in Trinity Theological College, I also mentored graduating students who were assigned to preach in our weekly chapel services. Although they have learned the basic principles in the homiletics courses taught by my respected colleagues, it is when they stand in front of a congregation that they wrestle with the theory. They know they are to have one main idea when drafting a sermon, but many flounder about to find that idea. They know how to interpret a text in its context, but they can't connect the dots between past revelation and present relevance. I would work through several drafts with each student, and it was in tending this nursery of preachers that this book was conceived. Many of my students encouraged me to compile my instructions to help them and others preach the Word more effectively.

Of the making of books on preaching, however, there is no end. What makes mine unique? First, for both the beginning student and busy pastor, I share proven practices. I include many "before" and "after" versions of students' examples that demonstrate how specific guidelines can improve each segment of a sermon.

Second, for the more thoughtful reader, this book integrates theory with practice. Because I write as a biblical scholar, I begin with a scriptural model for preaching that will give the preacher confident ground to stand on at the pulpit. I critique homiletical theory from the perspective of biblical scholarship: There are different views about whether a sermon should be text-, author-, gospel-, or experience-centered, but there is a theological breadth in our canon that points to a multiplicity of approaches. In terms of practical skills, I help the reader to be aware of current psychological and sociological studies that provide insights into communication skills.

Third, this book is written from an Asian perspective. Specifically, I write in the Singapore context, a melting pot of Western and Asian thinking and lifestyle. Furthermore, Trinity Theological College has many students from countries such as Indonesia, Malaysia, Thailand, Myanmar, Vietnam, China, India, Nepal, Mongolia, Philippines, etc. Their sermons reflect Asian challenges: pluralism, persecutions, and migrant workers, although there are also universal issues, such as materialism, ministry, and family. I discuss preaching with reference to both the Asian and globalized contexts.

The fourth and last reason why I am compelled to write this book is because I have learned what makes preaching come alive. The heart of this book is contained in the subtitle: "Delivering a Word from the Lord." When I started preaching about thirty years ago, first as a Varsity Christian Fellowship staff worker in Singapore and then as a newly minted pastor, I would take two weeks to prepare for a sermon by reading every commentary and book I could get my hands on. After delivering the sermon, I would take another two weeks to recover from the exertion. People affirmed my gift, but I was driven in my perfectionistic pursuit out of a lethal mix of insecurity and a constant comparison with others. I almost burned out till a sabbatical at Regent College, Vancouver, rescued me. While there, I rediscovered the simple yet difficult truth of accepting myself for who I am before God. It is a difficult truth because it means peeling off my own ingrown ambitions, but it was oh-so-freeing because I don't have to prove myself to anyone anymore. I only need to focus on what God wants me to say and do, without worrying about responses and results. I learned to listen to God.

After my sabbatical, my church members would say, "There's something different about the way you preach now; we don't know what it is, but we like it better!" That difference was that they heard less of me and more of God. There was less of me trying to dazzle with my intellect and more of simply preaching what God wants to say to his people – nothing more and nothing less. I still did my exegesis, but I no longer overdid it. Just as vital was the practice of *lectio divina* and listening to the Spirit. The sermon came alive and so did the congregation because they heard the life-giving word of the Lord.

This concept of preaching that comes alive draws my attention to Ezekiel's well-known valley of dry bones (Ezek 37). While that vision was about the restoration of the Jewish nation after the Babylonian exile in 536 BCE, it struck me that it is also a parallel for the construction of a sermon that builds from the dry bones of exegesis to a living message. Hence I use the anatomical metaphor of a human body to link all the different aspects of sermon crafting. Part I starts with biblical, homiletical, and exegetical foundations (chs. 1–3). The heart of the book and of the sermon is in the fourth chapter on listening to a word from the Lord through the *lectio divina*. It is the heart that will pump blood to oxygenate the rest of the body.

Part II of the book is when the bones rattle and come together (Ezek 37:7). The skeleton provides the structure that holds the sermon together, and while there is only one arrangement for the human skeleton, a sermon can have three possible forms: deductive (the traditional 3-point sermon), inductive, and textual (based on biblical genres). Chapters 5, 6, and 7 discuss the rationales and methods for each of these respective outlines.

After constructing the skeleton, Part III builds the body. While Ezekiel 37:8 has sinew, flesh, and skin coming together, I compare the explanations, illustrations, and applications of a sermon to the digestive, nervous, and muscular systems respectively. Chapters 8, 9, and 10 discuss the theoretical whys and practical hows of each segment.

In Part IV, the head (Introduction), feet (Conclusion), and ligaments (Transitions) are attached to the body. They are attached last so that the overall message can be previewed and reviewed clearly. Chapters 11, 12, and 13 give step-by-step guidelines in writing introductions that arrest attention, conclusions that inspire people to live out the sermon, and tight transitions that engage the hearers from the beginning to the end.

Finally, chapters 14 and 15 in Part V deal with the delivery in terms of writing for the ears and speaking with the eyes, voice, and emotions. The delivery is comparable to the breath that came into the lifeless bodies in Ezekiel's vision (37:9–10). Unless the preacher speaks the sermon effectively with his breath, it remains a lifeless piece of paper. At the same time, the Hebrew word for breath is the same word for S/spirit (*ruah*). It is God who creates life by giving a new heart and spirit (Ezek 36:26). Having prepared the sermon and practiced the delivery, the preacher needs to pray that the Spirit speaks to the hearts of the hearers, calling them to come alive and to live for God. It is my prayer, dear reader, for the sake of the church and for the glory of God, that your preaching will come alive as you deliver a word from the Lord!

Part I

Foundations for Preaching

1

The Call to Preach: Biblical Foundation

I am alive because someone preached.

That someone was a genial Texan giant, and I was a 12-year-old attending my very first church camp. Dr E. N. Poulson, then Dean of Singapore Bible College and also the Acting Senior Pastor of my church, was the speaker. He was preaching on the last night of the retreat, and as he expounded the Word, God jolted my heart. Today I can't remember exactly what he said, but I do remember standing up with trembling conviction to make a commitment. Though I grew up in a Christian family, God had stayed between the covers of the Bible, and prayer was just a shopping list for blessings. But that night, God became real – "in-your-face" kind of real. I awoke to the fact that if God is God, then I can no longer live life my own way. I have to live for him.

Fast-forward eighteen years, and I was a seminary student about to preach my first evangelistic message. My husband was serving in a Boys' Brigade Company that was having a Gospel Camp over the Easter weekend, and he had asked me to deliver the message. It was not my maiden sermon, having been a Varsity Christian Fellowship staff worker for three years before that. But it was the first time I was going to give an invitation to the audience to receive Christ. While I was used to addressing undergraduates, keeping the attention of some thirty energetic 12- to 16-year-old boys was a new challenge. I got down on my knees, prayed, and sweated.

On Easter morning, I explained the reality of the resurrection through historical evidence and the testimonies of changed lives. Then, I began the altar call. Doubts crept into my mind: *What if no one responded? Would I be a failure? Would I let people down?* But I knew I had to step off the cliff of safety and simply let the Spirit do as he willed. At least, I would have sown the seeds of the gospel.

I looked at all the bowed heads as I spoke, and to my utter surprise, one hand shot up as soon as the invitation left my mouth. I acknowledged that boy, and feeling a little more confident, asked if there was anyone else who wanted to receive Christ. Two more hands went up. Not daring to prolong the wait lest the boys got restless, I gave a final call, closed in prayer and invited those who wanted to receive Christ but had not raised their hands to repeat the sinner's prayer with the others.

I was still in a daze when the boys were dismissed. My husband was smiling broadly. God had answered our prayers and graciously allowed us to see the fruit of our labor. The church helpers followed up with the boys who had responded that Easter, and later, we heard that one of them had gone on to serve as a Boys' Brigade Officer. What a privilege it is when we get to see hearts come alive through the act of preaching.

Why and how does preaching transform lives? The Bible has several different words for preaching, and I will present four models: (1) Heralding (based on *kerysso* "proclaiming" and *euangelizo* "evangelizing"), (2) Teaching (*didasko*), (3) Exhorting (*parakaleo*), and (4) Witnessing (*martyreo*). Each model shares four qualities about preaching in varying degrees: Preaching is authoritative, transformative, authentic, and relevant. At the end of the chapter, I will integrate the four models into a holistic framework for preaching.

*1. Preaching as Heralding (*kerysso *and* euangelizo*)*

Kerysso and *euangelizo* are closely associated and almost synonymous, so I will consider both under the heralding model. In the Septuagint (Greek translation of the Old Testament), *kerysso* usually translates the ubiquitous Hebrew *qara'*, meaning "to call." The usage of this word shows four emphases.

a. Heralding is authoritative

In the Greek world, the herald has a place at the royal court, and his status depends on that of the one who commissions him.[1] In fact, a herald is also regarded as being under the special protection of the deity and must be left unharmed, even if he commits violence in a foreign land. In comparison, Christian heralds are sent out like sheep in the midst of wolves and should

---

1. Gerhard Friedrich, "κῆρυξ," *TDNT* 3: 683–689.

expect persecution (Matt 10:16). However, Jesus assures them that the Father watches over them, having counted the number of hairs on their head, and that the Holy Spirit will also enable them to speak in times of trials (Matt 10).

In other words, the Christian herald is sent with the prerogative of God who is king over all creation. He or she is sent to proclaim that the kingdom of God has come. This is what John the Baptist came for (Matt 3:1), what Jesus went about doing (Matt 4:17, 23, 35; 11:1), and what the disciples were sent out to do (Matt 10:7). It is a message that will be brought to the whole world (Matt 24:14).

The herald's message is validated by signs of deliverance and healing, performed first by Jesus (Matt 4:23; 9:35; Mark 1:38), then by his disciples (Matt 10:8; Mark 3:14; 6:13; Luke 9:2), and by other disciples after Pentecost (Acts 8:6). These are the inaugural signs of the presence and power of the kingdom. However, as Gerhard Friedrich points out:

> It is not that miracles usher in the new age. Miracles take place because the efficacious Word of God has declared the divine rule, and in it everything is sound and well. . . . Their office is simply to confirm what is proclaimed. . . . The miracle is not an event compelling those who see it to believe. It is exposed to the same ambiguity as Christian preaching. Jesus does not lay too great stress on His miracles (Mark 5:43; 8:26).[2]

From the broader perspective of biblical theology, God sometimes does not heal. Paul preached to the Galatians when he was ill (Gal 4:13), he left Trophimus sick in Miletus (2 Tim 4:20), and advised Timothy to take a little wine for his stomach and frequent ailments (1 Tim 5:23). Nonetheless, God's kingdom has come, evidenced by Christ's death and resurrection, and we can still see gracious evidence of healing and deliverance today.

Christ is the divine preacher who speaks through the human preacher.[3] "Faith comes from what is heard, and what is heard comes through the word of Christ" (Rom 10:17). It is usually not fruitful to split hairs over whether "the word of Christ" is the Greek objective genitive (so that it is the word *about* Christ) or the subjective genitive (that is, the word that comes *from* Christ) because both are true. The preacher can stand confidently at the pulpit knowing that the full authority of God is behind him. We do not stand upon

---

2. Friedrich, *TDNT* 3:714.
3. Friedrich, *TDNT* 3:696.

our exegetical skills or eloquence or extensive research. These may impress, but they do not give life. We deliver the message we have heard, trusting that God will bring its effect in the hearers' life, which leads us to the next point.

b. Heralding is transformative
The herald declares an event, and when that message is received by faith, lives are transformed; there is a transferal from the kingdom of darkness to the kingdom of light. In Luke 4:18–19, Jesus preached from Isaiah 61 that he has been sent "to proclaim (*qara'*) liberty to the captives . . . and to proclaim (*qara'*) the year of the Lord's favor." Isaiah delivered this oracle after the exile had ended, but Zion was still under Persian rule. The people mourned their devastation and longed for the day when God will establish his kingdom and restore full liberty. A few centuries later, in a synagogue under Roman rule, Jesus proclaimed that this promise is fulfilled – liberty is now here!

This "liberty," translated from Hebrew *deror*, refers to the liberty of the sabbatical or Jubilee year (Lev 25:10; Jer 34:8, 15, 17; Ezek 46:17). It is not so much about political liberation as it is about social and economic restoration where debts are cancelled, slaves are released, and lands returned. This is life in the kingdom of God. It is translated in the Septuagint as *aphesis*, meaning forgiveness or cancellation of sins, an apt description of the Sabbath intended by God. When people experience God's forgiveness, they are to forego the debts of others. Preaching proclaims that the Sabbath has arrived, the door has been thrown open, and we can walk out into fullness of life. Real change, real liberty, is possible now!

Another significant text is Romans 10:13–15, 17:

> For, "Everyone who calls on the name of the Lord shall be saved." But how are they to call on one in whom they have not believed? And how are they to believe in one of whom they have never heard? And how are they to hear without someone to proclaim him? And how are they to proclaim him unless they are sent? As it is written, "How beautiful are the feet of those who bring good news!" . . . So faith comes from what is heard, and what is heard comes through the word of Christ.

Preaching is not a mere impartation of facts; it is an event that imparts life. It is an event based on *the* event: the incarnation, life, crucifixion, and resurrection of Christ. "This is a fact that cannot be apprehended like other historical events. It has to be continually proclaimed afresh."[4] It is to be proclaimed both to those who have not heard and to those who have already believed it.

Darrell W. Johnson argues that *kerysso* applies to the congregation as well because believers are a forgetful lot and the Sunday worship service is also a public event at which anyone is welcomed.[5] In 2 Timothy 4:2-3, Paul commands Timothy to preach the word, in season and out of season, "for the time is coming when people will not put up with sound doctrine, but having itching ears, they will accumulate for themselves teachers to suit their own desires." Preaching, then, is also a vaccination against the infection of heresies, for those who are saved by faith must continue to live by faith. Even if the faithful were not forgetful, we have not yet reached perfection but are journeying along the way of sanctification towards full liberty (Col 1:22-23).

The Christ event took place nearly two millennia ago, but the news has not reached all captives. While I was writing this book, Asia commemorated VJ Day (Victory over Japan Day) on 15 August 1945, the day Japan surrendered to the Allied Nations in World War II. Unfortunately, one Japanese lieutenant, Hiroo Onoda, never got the news. In the preceding year, he was sent by the Japanese army to the remote Philippine island of Lubang, assigned to undertake guerrilla warfare and to gather intelligence. When the Allies took control of the island, the remaining Japanese soldiers retreated into the jungle to continue their mission. This continued for a year until the war was over. Leaflets were dropped into the jungle to announce the end of the war, but the covert Japanese soldiers thought they were Allied hoaxes. The years dragged by and thirty years later, Onoda was the only soldier left in his group after defection, illness, and skirmishes claimed the lives of the rest. Finally in 1974, a Japanese traveller, Nono Suzuki, found Onoda and tried to convince him that the war was really over. Onoda still refused to give up his position. He said he would only do it when his commander ordered him to do so. Incredibly, Suzuki went back to Japan and found Onoda's former commander. The commander met with Onoda in the Philippines and read him the original orders stating that all combat activity was to cease. Onoda was shocked. He later recounted that moment in his biography:

> We really lost the war! How could they be so sloppy? Suddenly everything went black . . . What had I been doing for all these

---

4. Friedrich, *TDNT* 3:711.
5. Johnson, *Glory of Preaching*, 86.

years? Gradually the storm subsided, and for the first time I really understood: My thirty years as a guerrilla fighter for the Japanese army were abruptly finished. This was the end.[6]

After formally surrendering to Philippine President Ferdinand Marcos, Onoda was pardoned for his crimes (having killed thirty Filipinos while in hiding).[7]

Onoda found freedom only when someone with authority declared to him that the war was over. Similarly, heralding makes the difference between life and death, joy and despair. Preachers are to call for a response, whether of repentance or restoration. It is a call by one who knows the transformative power of the message.

c. Heralding is authentic

There are three incidents in the Gospel of Mark when those who experienced or witnessed Jesus's healing could not help but proclaim the word. The cleansed leper broadcasted it so freely that Jesus could no longer go into a town (Mark 1:45; Matt 8:4; Luke 5:14). Those who saw Jesus heal the deaf mute were ordered to tell no one, but they proclaimed it anyway (Mark 7:36). The delivered Gerasene demoniac, though turned down from following Jesus, went and testified throughout the Decapolis (Mark 5:20; Luke 8:39). The herald is one who has so experienced the goodness of God that he cannot hold his tongue. Jesus's disciples were sent out to preach only after they had been with Jesus (Mark 6:7) and witnessed his miracles and healing.

As a preacher, you can only preach when you have experienced the reality of the kingdom in your own life. You may have known it at your conversion five, ten, or twenty years ago, but every time you deliver a message, you need to hear Christ speaking it to you. Do you need victory over some present sin, pride, addiction, anger, bitterness? Phillips Brooks's definition of preaching as "truth through personality" applies here. A preacher who merely delivers the gospel "reaches us tinged and flavoured with his superficial characteristics, belittled with his littleness." But when the gospel comes *through* a preacher, then "we receive it impressed and winged with all the earnestness and strength that there is in him."[8] Heralds must live the life they preach; at the

---

6. Hiroo Onoda, *No Surrender*, 14–15.
7. Jennifer Rosenberg, "The War is Over . . . Please Come out." Online.
8. Brooks, *Lectures on Preaching*, 8.

same time, they are to be aware of their hearers' lives as well, which leads us to the next point.

d. Heralding is relevant

Preaching calls for different responses from different people. We see this from two prophetic events in the Old Testament. Jonah was commissioned to go to Nineveh to cry out (*qara'*) *against* it, "for their wickedness has come up before God" (Jonah 1:2). We know the story: Jonah runs away, nearly drowns and repents, God re-commissions him, and then tells him to proclaim *to* (not against) Nineveh. The message now comes with a grace period: "Forty days more, and Nineveh shall be overthrown" (Jonah 3:4). God softened Jonah's heart in salt water long enough for him to bear this message. It was a message of judgment for Nineveh's wickedness, but it was also one that held out hope since they are given a grace period of forty days. The people of Nineveh grasped this hope, crying out to God who had sent Jonah to cry out to them.

In contrast, the book of Isaiah has God commissioning messengers to "cry to" Jerusalem that "she has served her term, that her penalty is paid, that she has received from the LORD's hand double for all her sins" (Isa 40:2). The Hebrew for "cry to" is exactly the same as in Jonah 3:2,[9] but to the exiles, the message is not one of punishment but of restoration. The herald today is likewise sent to people in different contexts. He needs to bring the right word at the right time. He cannot speak softly to sinners nor blast judgment at those in pain. The herald needs to deliver the king's particular message on each occasion.

Thomas G. Long points out the strengths and weaknesses of the herald model for preaching. Positively, it holds that "preaching is not about the preacher, it is about the voice of God," but Long decries it for de-emphasizing the personality of the preacher and ignoring the context of preaching. He warns that "the herald is encouraged to deliver the biblical word as is, somewhat oblivious to whether the hearers are rich or poor, Korean or African American, single mothers or corporate CEOs, residents of a nursing home or youth on a retreat."[10] Long was probably thinking of preaching that has grown out of touch with the world, but this is not the biblical understanding of *kerysso*. No doubt, we have heard sermons droning through a doctrinal

---

9. The Greek translation of Isaiah 40:2, however, has *parakaleo*, meaning comfort or encourage, rather than *kerysso*.

10. Long, *Witness of Preaching*, 20, 26.

haze, and out of respect for the ordained office, we attribute the dullness to our own incompetence. However, as we have seen above, *kerysso* emphasizes not only the authority of the message, but the relevance of that message.

Euangelizo *(Bringing Good News)*

Although *euangelizo* means "to evangelize," I prefer to translate it literally as "bringing good news" because "evangelism" is usually applied exclusively to unbelievers, with overtones of coercion. However, we need to recapture the joy that comes with the original verb. In the Greek world, the evangelist and the herald have much in common – both are crowned with a laurel wreath, and the herald may himself announce victory over enemies. The *euangelion* (good news or gospel) can refer to news of victory in battle or winning in the games. Friedrich notes that in the poetic parallelism of Isaiah 61:1, *kerysso* is the more concrete form of *euangelizo*.[11]

> The spirit of the Lord God is upon me,
>   Because the LORD has anointed me;
> he has sent me to bring good news (Heb. *bisser*; Gk. *euangelizo*)
>   to the oppressed,
>   To bind up the broken hearted,
> To proclaim (Heb. *qara'*; Gk. *kerysso*) liberty to the captives,
>   And release to the prisoners.

In Hebrew poetics, the second parallel line usually presents the same idea in a more emphatic way. So, the good news of victory is first delivered to the oppressed, and then the proclamation of liberty makes that news a reality by swinging wide the prison doors for the captives.

In the New Testament, *euangelizo* and *euangelion* occur frequently with *kerysso*. In Matthew 4:23 and 9:35, Jesus went about preaching (*kyrusso*) the good news (*euangelion*). In Matthew 24:14 and 26:13, the good news of the kingdom is to be proclaimed to the whole world. Paul also describes his ministry as proclaiming the good news (Gal 2:2; Col 1:23; 1 Thess 2:9), and the church is to proclaim Christ, for it is written: "How beautiful are the feet of those who bring good news!" (Rom 10:15).

Therefore, we can expect *euangelizo* to share the same four qualities as *kerysso*. First, *euangelizo* is authoritative, evidenced by healing and deliverance

---

11. Gerhard Friedrich, "εὐαγγελίζομαι" *TDNT* 2:712.

(Matt 9:35; Luke 9:6; 1 Cor 2:4; 1 Thess 1:5). Second, it is transformative: "It does not merely declare salvation; it effects it."[12] In the Roman imperial cult, the birth and ascension of the emperor is good news because he is the godman who brings peace to the world and salvation for all. Similarly, the birth of Jesus is good news of great joy and peace to all people (Luke 2:10, 14) because of his Davidic kingship (Acts 13:32) that brings salvation for all (Rom 1:16). Preaching is not informing people about an article of news, like the endless posts on Facebook, Instagram, and Twitter. One can read such a message, like it, ignore it, or trash it without consequence. But the bearer of good news is more like Morpheus in the Matrix movie franchise.

Morpheus is a leader of the last remaining bastion of humanity in an apocalyptic world where humans are grown by sentient machines as an energy source while their minds are imprisoned in a virtual reality created by the machines. He appears to the protagonist Neo in the virtual world and tries unsuccessfully to explain the truth to him. He then offers Neo a choice of taking one of two pills, "You take the blue pill, the story ends. You wake up in your bed and believe whatever you want to believe. You take the red pill, you stay in Wonderland, and I show you how deep the rabbit-hole goes." Neo takes the red pill and wakes up to reality. In the movie, it is a horrifying existence where humans fight desperately for freedom. In the Bible, it is waking up to a glorious reality where the fight has already been won by Christ. Like Morpheus, the preacher presents listeners with a choice[13] – either stay in the temporal world, or take the pill of good news and wake up to God's eternal kingdom whose height and depth the preacher will lead them to know.

Third, the messenger is authentic for he comes from the battlefield having witnessed the victory. Friedrich records that the appearance of the messenger already gives away the news: "His face shines, his spear is decked with laurel, his head is crowned, he swings a branch of palms . . ."[14] So also the apostles proclaimed the good news after their experience of Pentecost (Acts 5:42), and despite persecutions, the scattered believers went about preaching the good news (Acts 8:4). Preachers who bring good news today must also reflect its jubilant truth, for it is the basis for growth and fruitfulness (Rom 16:25; 1 Cor

---

12. Friedrich, *TDNT* 2:723.

13. Whether one understands making a choice in the Arminian or Calvinist sense, the preacher is still tasked to call for a response.

14. Friedrich, *TDNT* 2:722.

15:12; Phil 1:27; Col 1:5–6). We need to hear the good news afresh lest the flood of bad news drown out our joy.

Fourth, good news should be relevant to the hearers. Philip, for example, explained the good news to the Ethiopian using Isaiah 53, since the eunuch was struggling with that text (Acts 8:35). In a different context when dealing with the fractious Philippian church, Paul exhorted the hearers to live out the good news (Phil 1:27) in a spirit of humility and unity as exemplified in a christological hymn.

The Result of Kerysso *and* Euangelizo

The authoritative and transformative word of God gives preachers hope that despite themselves, the sermon will touch lives. Without this hope, preachers simply grind through a weekly routine, with their own and the congregation's passion dying a slow death. However, this is a hope that the preacher must leave to God's sovereign will. I think that Johnson, and other homileticians, overstates the claim for preaching that "something always happen."[15] At least, it is not something that we can see or something that happens according to our expectations or timing.

Johnson bases his claim on two passages: Ezekiel's vision of the dry bones in chapter 37 and the parable of the four soils in Matthew 13. Ezekiel was instructed by God to speak to the bones, and Johnson points out that the bones came to life not because they heard the message but simply by the fiat of God's word. However, in the historical context of that vision, the bones represent the house of Israel that has been destroyed by Babylon. God had promised to bring them back to their homeland (Ezek 37:10), and this is something that God alone can do. So, dry bones' coming alive is not so much about the work of preaching but about God fulfilling the post-exilic restoration of Israel as a nation. Nonetheless, the text has a broader christological fulfillment when the Holy Spirit gives life to the spiritually dead through the preaching of good news. For this, people do need to respond by faith (Rom 10:14–17). From a Reformed perspective, faith itself is the work of the Spirit, and therefore, the hearers' response is in God's hands. This saves us from undue expectations and anxieties when we do not see something happening, but neither should it dampen our anticipation because our confidence lies not in seeing results but in the power of the Spirit.

---

15. Johnson, *Glory of Preaching*, 7.

What about the parable of the four soils? Do we expect at least one-quarter of the congregation to respond fruitfully? Johnson is right that the question provoked by the parable is not "Which of the soils am I?" Rather, it should be "How can I be the good soil?"[16] The task of the preacher is to help people listen like the good soil, but Johnson acknowledges that this is paradoxically the work of the Spirit. In fact, he notes the difficulty of Isaiah 6:9–10, which Jesus quotes regarding this parable (Matt 13:14; Mark 4:12; Luke 8:10; John 12:40).[17] The prophet Isaiah was told to preach that people may hear but not understand lest they turn back to God and be healed. In Isaiah's context, he was sent to deliver a word of judgment. Jesus cites this text to describe the hardness of the people, but in contrast to Isaiah's context, his parables are designed to pry open closed ears: "Let anyone with ears listen!" (Matt 13:9). Thus the preacher sows in all kinds of soil and trusts that God will work in his own time and in his own way.

The prophet Jeremiah preached through tears and persecutions but failed to turn the nation back to God in his lifetime. Despite feeling hopeless, he delivered God's warnings simply out of obedience to his prophetic calling. But his words were eventually recalled by the people when they were exiled into Babylon. There, his oracles of judgment and salvation turned the people back in faith. There are times when my preaching seems to catch fire and times when I get a cold reception. Occasionally, God encourages me by letting me find out years later what he has done, as when someone shared about becoming a missionary because of a sermon I had preached before. I have learned that if something happens, thank God; if nothing happens, trust God. Both *kerysso* and *euangelizo* accentuate the qualities of preaching as authoritative and transformative. The other two aspects of being authentic and relevant will be brought out more by the following models.

2. Preaching as Teaching (didasko)

People usually find it hard to explain the difference between preaching and teaching. Fred Craddock writes that a student may report that his professor lectured for forty minutes and then preached the last ten minutes of the

---

16. Ibid., 43.
17. Ibid., 51, n. 22.

period. What was the difference? Was the delivery more lively, the content more personal, or the implications more hortatory?[18]

People normally think of teaching as a dispassionate transmission of facts. However, this is the Hellenistic notion rather than the Hebraic or New Testament understanding. Karl Heinrich Rengstorf writes that in Hellenistic usage, *didasko* is used for the impartation of practical or theoretical knowledge. This is included in the Hebrew concept of teaching (*limmed*), as can be seen for example in 2 Samuel 22:35, "He trains my hands for war." However, the predominant usage of *limmed* in the Old Testament is the teaching of God's statutes and ordinances for the sake of doing them. This is how *limmed* is used in Deuteronomy (4:1, 5, 10, 14, etc.) and the Psalms. "The term is always marked by the fact that it has a volitional as well as an intellectual reference."[19]

Thus it is not the prophets but the priests who do the work of teaching. The Levites are the ones who "taught in Judah, having the book of the law of the LORD with them; they went around through all the cities of Judah and taught among the people" (2 Chr 17:9). While the prophets heralded (*qara'*) God's judgments or salvation, the priests taught the revealed will of God so that the people can live in right relationship with God and neighbors.

This biblical concept of teaching is something that traditional Chinese martial artists understand very well. In an essay about the decline of traditional kung fu, Patrick Daly records an interview with an aging master in the city of Sibu, in the state of Sarawak, East Malaysia. He had asked the master why was he not more active in teaching kung fu, and the old man replied:

> In my opinion, the world has changed. I never teach my son and my grandson. People asked me to teach, but people's minds nowadays are wicked. You know them in appearance but not their inner character. If I accept him as my disciple, I must know his character! If he has a quick temper, after learning, he may create problem and will bring disgrace to the school and even your name. People will look for his master. They will come to find me.
>
> A real master can only teach real kung fu to his disciple who learns under him for at least 10 years in order to know his character well or he will create problems. We'll not teach the

---

18. Craddock, *Preaching*, 16–17. Craddock does not answer the question but simply makes the point that it is hard to define preaching.

19. Rengstorf, "διδάσκω," *TDNT* 2:135, 137.

practical use of kung fu to those who learn for only 2 to 3 years. This is the traditional culture. That's why a lot becomes extinct. Chinese traditional kung fu is like this.[20]

Training in kung fu is not just a matter of passing on information and skills, but it is training in a way of life and the inculcation of values. This belief is something that no *shi fu* (master) worth his salt will compromise because too much potential for good as well as for evil is at stake. So also, the preacher cannot be satisfied with just imparting knowledge alone because people's lives and God's glory are at stake. Now then, how does teaching compare against the four qualities of preaching?

a. Teaching is authoritative

God vindicated Jesus's teaching with power and healing (Matt 13:54; Mark 6:2; Luke 5:17); John presents Jesus's teaching as originating from the Father (John 8:28) and the disciples' teaching as coming from the Spirit sent by the Father (John 14:26). This same Spirit continues to teach the believers in the church (1 John 2:27), and the church is to teach one another through the Word (Col 3:16; 2 Tim 3:16). Teaching is authoritative because it is enabled by God and based on his inspired Word.

b. Teaching is transformative

While teaching does not announce the saving event as heralding does, it brings the reality of that saving event into every sphere of life. As in the Old Testament, teaching in the New Testament is not for the sake of storing knowledge but for building up lives. Preachers are to address not only the mind but also the will. It is not only the herald who calls for a decision but also the teacher. Matthew first used *didasko* when Jesus taught his disciples on the Mount (Matt 5:2). The entire sermon ends with the parable of the wise and foolish builders, challenging hearers to act on Jesus's words (Matt 7:24). Matthew's last use of *didasko* is in the Great Commission where the disciples are instructed to make disciples, baptizing and teaching them to obey everything that Jesus has commanded. Note that it is teaching to obey rather than teaching to know.

---

20. Patrick Daly, "Traditional Chinese Martial Arts and the Transmission of Intangible Cultural Heritage," in *Routledge Handbook of Heritage in Asia*, eds. Daly and Winter (London: Routledge, 2012), 361.

Jesus's teaching amazed the people precisely because he challenged the hearers ethically. Rengstorf explains that scribal learning had become exegetical and theoretical as a reaction by conservative Judaism to the philosophical challenges of Hellenism, but Jesus insists on the practical component of teaching.[21] Paul teaches in order to present everyone mature in Christ (Col 1:28), laying down the Household Code to guide believers in their marital, parental, and vocational relationships. Paul expounds on Christology, soteriology, and eschatology, but he always ends with down-to-earth praxis. The challenge of teaching is to confront the will of men and women with the will of God. Where the herald ushers one into kingdom life, the teacher leads one into kingdom living.

c. Teaching is authentic

More than the herald, the educator must set the example, for as the adage goes, more is caught than taught. Ezra embodies this ideal, for he "set his heart to study the law of the LORD, and to do it, and to teach the statutes and ordinances in Israel" (Ezra 7:10). Similarly, Paul says his conduct is observed by all (2 Tim 3:10) and enjoins Timothy to pay close attention to his own life and teaching (1 Tim 4:16).

In a fascinating study, the psychologist J. Philippe Rushton gave 140 elementary- and middle-school-aged children tokens for winning a game. They could keep the tokens or donate some to a child who had less. A teacher in the group would either preach about generosity or selfishness, while also modeling either acts of generosity or selfishness. The results showed that when the teacher acted selfishly but talked about sharing, the children behaved selfishly. Conversely, when the teacher taught and modeled generosity, the children were more willing to give away their tokens (85 percent more than the norm). What was surprising was that even when the teacher promoted selfishness but acted generously, the students still gave 49 percent more than the norm. Clearly, actions speak louder than words, though a congruent combination of both is best.[22] When God's word shapes our lives, then our teaching will shape the lives of others.

---

21. Rengstorf, *TDNT* 2:142.

22. J. Philippe Rushton, "Generosity in Children: Immediate and Long-Term Effects of Modeling, Preaching, and Moral Judgment," *JPSP* 31, no. 3 (1975): 459–466.

d. Teaching is relevant

People learn best according to their needs and interests. When the church was first formed, the disciples taught about Jesus as the Messiah (Acts 5:42) because new believers needed to understand the person and work of Christ. In Luke 11:1, the disciples asked Jesus to teach them how to pray, and he responded to their interest. In the early church, Timothy focused on sound doctrines in the face of heresies (2 Tim 4:2). Against a hedonistic environment in Crete, Paul charged Titus to teach self-control (Titus 2). Preaching as teaching requires preachers to know their congregations, their afflictions and aspirations, so that they can teach relevantly. Teaching addresses not just the mind but also the will. The next model will focus even more on appealing to the heart and will.

3. Preaching as Exhorting (parakaleo)

Parakaleo generally means "to appeal" and has various nuances including exhorting others to act in a difficult situation or consoling someone in grief. It is usually used in the Septuagint to translate the Hebrew *niham*, which means to comfort in times of grief.[23] Exhorting also reflects the four qualities of preaching.

a. Exhorting is authoritative

God himself is the chief comforter. Otto Schmitz and Gustav Stählin point out that for all the Greek attempts at consolation, there was a profound lack of hope and comfort – one is simply admonished to stop weeping. However in the Old Testament, "comforting is God's proper work."[24] He is the Shepherd who comforts in the valley of the shadow of death (Ps 23:4) and in the exile – "Comfort, O comfort my people, says your God" (Isa 40:1). The prophets who brought God's message of comfort were speaking with the authority of God. In the New Testament, Paul says that God himself comforts the hearts of the people (2 Thess 2:16–17), while preachers are "ambassadors for Christ, since God is appealing (*parakaleo*) through us" (2 Cor 5:20). Exhortation is not just stirring up emotions but persuading people as God himself would.

Preachers from charismatic traditions are usually more adept at appealing to the emotions. Though their sermons may be more experiential than

---

23. Otto Schmitz and Gustav Stählin, "παρακαλέω," *TDNT* 5:775–777.
24. Schmitz and Stählin, *TDNT* 5:786, 789.

expositional, people feel comforted and uplifted. Judging by the numerical growth of their churches, such preachers are meeting a need. Traditional churches tend to prize the cognitive and fear the emotional, whether by choice, ignorance, or inability. The congregation may be well-fed in biblical knowledge and may even be serving committedly, but something may be missing in their passion and personal relationship with God. Preaching needs to be holistic. God made human beings with a mind to understand, a will to act, and a heart to feel. We honor the image of God when we address all the different aspects of a human being.

In fact, several studies have shown the link between emotions and decision making. For instance, participants in a study who had been induced to feel sad were likely to set a lower selling price for an item they were asked to sell. In another study, people were engaged in a card-drawing task. When drawing from risky decks and experiencing losses and negative emotions, they subsequently made safe choices for long-term gain. However, people with damaged amygdalae (two organs deep in the brain associated with emotions, memory, and decision making) did not change their behavior in the card game because they were unable to experience the emotional effects of winning and losing. Psychologists explain that emotions affect decision making in four ways: Emotions provide information, improve the speed of decision making, assess relevance (especially associated with regret and disappointment), and enhance commitment (with emotions such as guilt and love). Little wonder that *parakaleo* occurs very frequently in the book of Acts and the Pastoral Epistles.[25]

Paul speaks to the emotions of the hearers in order to galvanize them to act. He appeals to the people's sense of gratitude to God: "I appeal to you therefore, brothers and sisters, by the mercies of God, to present your bodies as a living sacrifice, . . ." (Rom 12:1). He also entreats readers based on his own relationship with them. He urges the Corinthians (1 Cor 4:15-16) and Thessalonians (1 Thess 2:11-12) to be imitators of him as their father through the gospel; to the Ephesians, he appeals on the basis of his suffering for them (Eph 4:1-2). In other places, Paul reminds people of their personal

---

25. Jennifer S. Lerner, Deborah A. Small, and George Loewenstein, "Heart Strings and Purse Strings Carry over Effects of Emotions on Economic Decisions," *Psychological Science* 15, no. 5 (2004): 337–341; Antoine Bechara, Hanna Damasio, Antonio R. Damasio, and Gregory P. Lee, "Different Contributions of the Human Amygdala and Ventromedial Prefrontal Cortex to Decision-Making," *Journal of Neuroscience* 19, no. 13 (1999): 5473–5481; Hans-Rüdiger Pfister and Gisela Böhm, "The Multiplicity of Emotions: A Framework of Emotional Functions in Decision Making," *Judgment and Decision Making* 3, no. 1 (2008): 5–17.

relationship with one another (1 Tim 5:1–2). It is this personal relationship with God and others that gives a preacher the authority to exhort.

b. Exhorting is transformative
While heralding presents the reality of God's kingdom, exhortation persuades hearers to step into it through repentance. This was what John the Baptist did (Luke 3:18). Barnabas, known for his gift of exhortation, encouraged believers to remain faithful, especially in a time of persecution (Acts 11:23; 14:22). Exhortation thus has a transformative function.

c. Exhorting is authentic
Paul says in 2 Corinthians 1:3–4 that the God of all consolation "consoles us in all our affliction, so that we may be able to console those who are in any affliction with the consolation with which we ourselves are consoled by God." When you prepare a sermon, you need to first hear God speaking to you about your own struggles, discouragement, fears, and hurts. When you allow God to minister to you, then you will be able to minister to your flock.

d. Exhorting is relevant
Of all the keywords on preaching, *parakaleo* takes the needs and context of the listeners most seriously. To have their desired effect, words of exhortation must address the situation that the listeners are facing, whether individually or corporately. To the divided Corinthian church, Paul appeals to them to be in agreement (1 Cor 1:10); to the Thessalonians who were anxious about the death of their loved ones, Paul taught them about eschatology and then told them to comfort one another in their grief and to exhort one another to be ready for Christ's coming (1 Thess 4:18). Do you know the issues that your congregation are grappling with? If you are speaking to youth, do you know the stress they are facing in school? If you are preaching at a time of economic downturn, are you aware of the listeners' anxieties?

Preaching as exhorting parallels the pastor imagery that Long critiques. While the herald focused on the biblical word, the pastor focuses on the listener.[26] Long notes that with the rise of psychology and therapy in the mid-twentieth century, the preacher became a counselor. Sermons are seen as healing words addressed to human needs, and pastoral preachers strive to help listeners feel better. Long warns that this approach focuses too much

---

26. Long, *Witness of Preaching*, 28.

on the individual rather than the community and stresses needs rather than strengths; it seeks for solutions now rather than struggle with the not-yet of the kingdom and "runs the risk of reducing theology to anthropology by presenting the gospel merely as a resource of human emotional growth."[27]

Long's critique rightfully warns against a lop-sided preoccupation with individual needs. Biblical exhortations are often addressed to believers in the context of a community (1 Thess 2:11), comforting them in times of need and grief but also challenging them to lead lives worthy of God (Eph 4:13; 1 Thess 2:12), and to do so while waiting for the coming of the Lord (1 Thess 5:11). However, if exhorting is linked to heralding and teaching, then it keeps its theocentric roots. Long prefers the model of the witness, and to this we now turn.

4. Preaching as Witnessing (martyreo)

Long points out that in this model, the authority of the preacher lies not in his status but in what he has seen and heard from the text. Further, a witness does not merely disseminate facts but testifies to an encounter with God through Scripture. Although a private encounter, it is one that is relevant to the people because he comes on behalf of his community of faith, bringing their struggles and issues with him as he listens to the Word.[28]

It is this divine encounter that gives a preacher the confidence and conviction to deliver his message. Nervous seminary students often ask me how they can be sure that their message is biblically correct, especially when they have to preach in front of their peers and professors. I ask them first of all, "Have you done your exegesis?" Then second, "Has God spoken to your heart?" If they say yes to both questions, then I assure them they have a message worth delivering. Their professors may know more than them in terms of Greek, Hebrew, and theology, but all of us need to hear a life-giving word from the Lord, a word that the preacher has heard for himself and for us. How can we understand *martyreo* in terms of the four qualities of preaching?

a. Witnessing is authoritative

Long explains that a witness is authorized by his community, through ordination, to listen to God through the Word on their behalf. His authority

---

27. Ibid., 35–36.
28. Ibid., 47–48.

lies not in himself but in God's call to the ministry that the church has recognized.[29] However, in a pluralistic society, witnessing is not an adequate basis for authority by itself, since witnesses of other faiths are also able to give their testimonies. Rather, we need to hold all the other models together: Authority lies with God whose kingdom is heralded through Christ; it lies in God's Word that teaches us how to live in that kingdom; in the Spirit as the comforter who exhorts believers; and in the church that testifies of God's work. Undeniably, witnessing is one crucial aspect of authority, for preachers' experiences corroborate and challenge hearers to at least consider their claims. A preacher is the hearers' first though not ultimate encounter. A preacher is like the Samaritan woman who told others about meeting with Jesus at the well until they themselves say, "It is no longer because of what you said that we believe, for we have heard for ourselves, and we know that this is truly the Savior of the world" (John 4:42).

b. Witnessing is transformative

The point of giving a testimony is not just to relay information but to invite listeners to encounter Christ. The Greek usage of *martyreo* has two possible meanings: One, as a witness to facts in the legal sphere and, second, as a witness to truths or views that cannot be empirically verified but of which the speaker is convinced.[30] Testifying to a fact may make a difference in the passing of a court sentence, but it does not change the lives of everyone. Testifying to a truth, especially the universal claims of God, is world changing. The faithful Israelites in Babylon are called God's witnesses in Isaiah 43:10:

> You are my witnesses, says the LORD,
>   and my servant whom I have chosen,
> so that you may know and believe me
>   and understand that I am he.
> Before me no god was formed,
>   nor shall there be any after me.

These Israelites testified of God's supremacy in a world where foreign idols appeared to be in control. In the New Testament, John is fond of the word *martyreo*, testifying that Jesus is the Messiah in his Gospel so that people may be transformed by believing (John 20:31; 21:24).

---

29. Ibid., 48.
30. H. Strathmann, "μάρτυς," *TDNT* 4:476–478.

c. Witnessing is authentic

A witness is one who tells of one's own encounter with the risen Word through the written Word. While only the twelve apostles were eye witnesses of Jesus's life, death, and resurrection (Luke 24:48; John 15:27; 1 John 1:1–2), Paul and Stephen were also called witnesses since they had encountered Christ and testified to his truth (Acts 22:15, 20). John explains that subsequent believers who accept the testimony of the apostles also have fellowship with God (1 John 1:3; 5:6, 10), that is, they know God in a personal way. "Hence new witnesses can arise," says Strathmann,[31] and all are called to be Christ's witnesses to the ends of the earth (Acts 1:8).

d. Witnessing is relevant

A witness adapts his message so that it will be relevant to the hearers. For the Jewish exiles, the testimony in Isaiah 43 was a polemic against the competing worldview of idolatry. In his Gospel, John said that while Jesus did many things, he selected those he thought most relevant for his readers (John 20:30; 21:25). In the book of Revelation, John's apocalyptic visions were addressed to a church travailing under persecution. Thus, a witness listens to the Word as a representative of his community and brings a message appropriate for their hopes and struggles. In the rest of this chapter, I integrate these four models into an overall framework to help us get a fuller understanding of preaching.

5. A Framework for Preaching

It is useful to compare the biblical model for preaching with classical rhetoric. In his treatise, Aristotle distilled three components in the art of persuasion: *ethos*, *pathos*, and *logos*. *Ethos*, as the personal character of the speaker, is the weightiest: "We believe good men more fully and more readily than others." *Pathos*, stirring the emotions of the hearers, is of second importance: "Our judgements when we are pleased and friendly are not the same as when we are pained and hostile." Third, *logos* is persuasion through the speech itself by means of suitable arguments.[32] Homiletics shares several areas of similarities with classical rhetoric, but there is one critical difference: God (Gk. *Theos*) as the source of authority in preaching. My framework is represented by the

---

31. Strathmann, *TDNT* 4:499.
32. Aristotle, *Rhetorics*, book 1, ch. 2, 1356.

diagram below, and I will discuss this in terms of the four qualities of preaching.

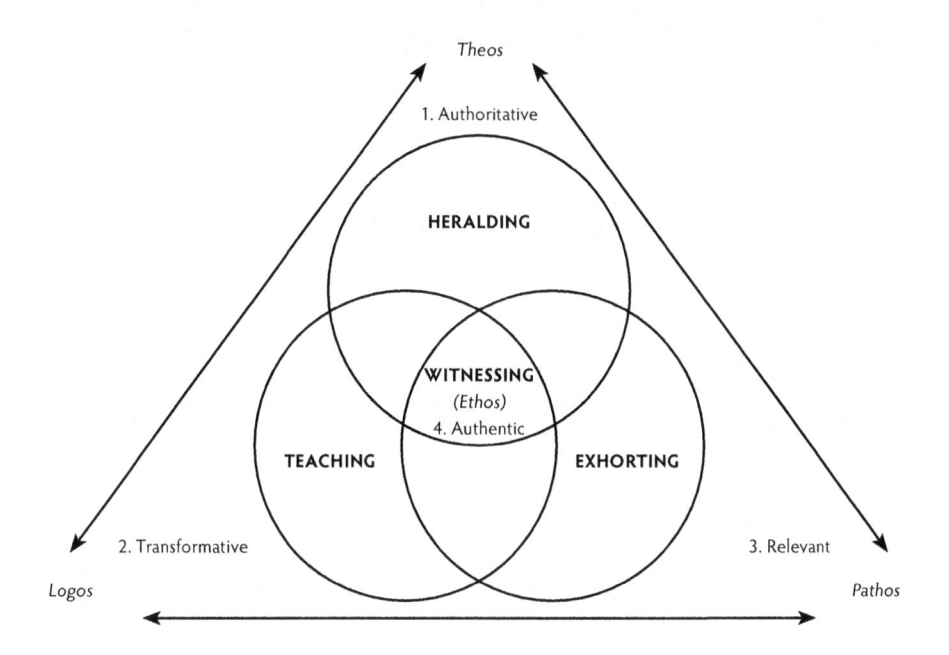

```
                        Theos
                    1. Authoritative

                        HERALDING

                        WITNESSING
                         (Ethos)
                        4. Authentic
             TEACHING              EXHORTING

       2. Transformative              3. Relevant
   Logos                                     Pathos
```

a. Preaching is authoritative

Authority is most clearly represented by heralding, since it brings with it the reality of God's kingdom. But all other aspects of preaching also proceed from God's authority. In teaching, the preacher teaches about life in the kingdom based on God's word. In exhorting, it is God himself who appeals through the preacher. Witnessing is the central overlap of the three spheres, and while authority does not lie intrinsically with preachers, their calling is authorized by God through the church, and their personal encounter with the Lord through the Scripture demonstrates the truth. Preachers can stand unapologetically to deliver the sermon, trusting that God will speak through the Word to the hearts of the hearers. This implies, of course, that they need to pay careful attention to the text, and we will come to the matter of exegesis in chapter 3.

b. Preaching is transformative

All models of preaching work together in calling for a response to God, but teaching may best represent the ongoing work of transforming lives through the teaching of the Word. The herald calls people to enter the kingdom, but the preacher is also to make disciples through teaching (comparable to using *logos*), to move hearts and wills to obey through exhortation (*pathos*), and to demonstrate the truth in his own life (*ethos*). Conversely, people are challenged and comforted not merely through emotional speech and stories but through sound teaching and reasoning. The church father Augustine understood this when he described preaching as an appeal to mind, heart, and will.[33]

In his review of preaching in eighteenth-century England, John Stott observes that preachers valued reasonableness and shunned emotional display. He attributes this to the Anglican value of scholarship and the ideal of the educated minister.[34] We see this malaise in our modern church as well: When rationalistic sermons sedate the faithful, one cannot tell whether eyes are closed in meditation or in slumber and whether heads are nodding in affirmation or in stupor. Stott calls for a synthesis of reason and emotion, exposition and exhortation.[35]

If *logos* and *pathos* are to work together towards a transformative end, then the preacher needs to keep that end clearly in mind, and this will be the subject of chapter 2 on the crux of preaching.

c. Preaching is authentic

There is no discrete circle for witnessing in the framework because all other models must contain this component of authenticity at its heart. Aristotle says that a speaker's character "may almost be called the most effective means of persuasion he possesses." When a preacher is convicted by Word and Spirit, then the sermon will ignite like fire in his bones (Jer 20:9). Or as Martyn Lloyd-Jones puts it, preaching is "theology on fire. And a theology which does not take fire, I maintain, is a defective theology."[36] Such fire does not necessarily mean that the preacher speaks in a fiery tone, thundering voice, or dramatic gestures. It can come across differently in different personalities.

Jonathan Edwards sparked the Great Awakening in North America, yet he was a preacher who regularly read out his sermons. It was said of him that "he had no studied varieties of voice, and no strong emphasis. He scarcely

---

33. Augustine, *On Christian Doctrine*, cited in Craddock, *Preaching*, 37.
34. John R. W. Stott, *I Believe in Preaching* (London: Hodder & Stoughton, 1982), 280.
35. Ibid., 283.
36. Martyn Lloyd-Jones, *Preaching and Preachers* (Grand Rapids, MI: Zondervan, 1971), 97.

gestured, or even moved." But Edwards was so gripped by the truth he was presenting that he spoke "with such intenseness of feeling, that the whole soul of the speaker is thrown into every part of the conception and delivery so that the solemn attention of the whole audience is riveted, from beginning to the close, and impressions are left that cannot be effaced."[37] Would that we preach like Edwards, without gimmicks or dramatics, but with the glow in our hearts of having met God!

How can we encounter God and hear what he has to say to us and to our congregations? In chapter 4 I will show one way to do this through the ancient spiritual discipline of *lectio divina*.

d. Preaching is relevant

Christianity is not just a set of timeless beliefs but a relationship with the person of God as revealed in Scripture. As in any relationship, God communicates in a way that makes sense to us in our context. The herald may bring a message of judgment or comfort, the teacher may teach about right behavior or refute heresies, and the exhorter may comfort the suffering or rebuke the lazy. The preacher comes as a witness to hear God speak so that he or she can be a witness to Jews, Samaritans, and to those at the ends of the world: Asians, Singaporeans, migrants, youth, young adults, seniors, blue-collar workers, professionals, stay-home moms, domestic helpers, etc. Exhorting best represents this aspect of preaching as bringing a relevant message. Besides studying the Word, the pastor also needs to study the condition of his flock. And because the church doesn't exist in a vacuum, the preacher also has to understand the world in which the church lives. This will be further developed in chapter 11 on applications.

Conclusion

It is apparent that different preachers have different gifts and strengths. There are fiery fundamentalist heralds, scholarly mainline teachers, and lively charismatic exhorters. No doubt these are caricatures, but there is a kernel of truth in these stereotypes, and they all have their part in the body of Christ. The point is that we need to be aware of our own gifts and tendencies so that we can preach appropriately and give our congregations a balanced

---

37. Sereno Dwight, "A Memoir of Jonathan Edwards," in *The Works of Jonathan Edwards*, vol. 1 (Edinburgh: Banner of Truth, 1974), cxc.

diet. While the four qualities of preaching (authoritative, transformative, authentic, and relevant) are constants in any preaching, the four models (heralding, teaching, exhorting, and witnessing) may vary in terms of how much weight is given to each.

Different texts may require different emphases, and different situations also call for different styles. This may mean inviting other speakers to share the pulpit from time to time. However, be prepared for the reactions. If the congregation appreciates someone new, don't feel threatened because your strength may lie elsewhere. If the people react adversely to a novel approach, don't feel discouraged because it takes time to learn something new. Which model(s) of preaching do you gravitate towards? Rejoice in your gift and use it unabashedly to minister to the flock God has entrusted to you. Which model(s) do you least identify with? Then take steps to grow or work with others in the body of Christ.

We have heard the call to preach, so how are we to preach? Homileticians have offered different theories and approaches, so we turn next to the crux of preaching.

2

The Crux of Preaching: Homiletical Foundation

The chef serving the buffet is overenthusiastic. He zealously scoops food from every tray and piles it all onto your plate: roast beef, fish curry, *assam* prawn, fried rice, *mee siam*, dim sum, *popiah*, sushi, chicken wings, broccoli, scallops, mushroom. He won't take no for an answer and slaps the desserts on top too: pastries, cakes, macaroons, *nonya kueh* (cakes), mango pudding, durian *pengat* (paste). I'm not sure what that does to your appetite. If asked what you are eating with each spoon, you would probably say, "I don't know." That is what a worshipper might also say after hearing a sermon packed with many different points. The result would be indigestion and an over-fed person who may know a lot but is not necessarily healthy.

Some pastors are resistant to having just one main idea in a sermon. In their earnestness, they want to teach as much as they can. This is commendable, but the teaching ministry should not be confined to the Sunday sermon. That would be like having one meal for the entire week. Homileticians agree with the need to have one clear thesis in a sermon. One can teach many things, but they should all be related to the one main idea that the preacher wants to bring across. Different authors use different terms: Haddon Robinson is well known for "the big idea"; Thomas Long has his "focus statement," and Bryan Chapell emphasizes the "fallen condition focus." They are all useful and legitimate, but words like "thesis," "theme," "idea," "statement," "focus," and "point," tend to convey cognitive knowledge. If preaching comes with the authority of God for a transformative purpose, then there should be something more than just information.

The Old Testament prophets preached judgment or salvation from God, a word that makes a difference between death and life. Long quotes from a telling passage by Marvin A. McMickle:

> During my first pastorate . . . one of the deacons would ask me the same question every Sunday morning . . . "Reverend, is there any word from the Lord?" . . . The voice that they want to hear is not really the voice of the preacher . . . The message that people have assembled to receive is not whatever wit or wisdom may be on our mind on any given Sunday. After all the intervening years, I can still hear the voice of that deacon haunting me as I write my sermons and then stand to deliver them: "Reverend, is there any word from the Lord?"[1]

The crux of the sermon is hearing and delivering "a word from the Lord." *A* word, not *the* Word, because the preacher's word is not equivalent to Scripture. It is a word "from the Lord" that causes preaching to come alive. In the rest of this chapter, I explore the importance of having such a word based on the purpose and rhetoric of preaching. However, the phrase "a word from the Lord" is quite a mouthful, so I will also use "central word" as an alternative term.

A. Why Have "A Word from the Lord"?

1. Purpose of Preaching

Since preaching is authoritative, transformative, authentic, and relevant, the herald should be clear about what is announced, and the teacher should be unmistakable about the obedience required. Supposing the herald of Isaiah 61:1 had said:

> He has sent me to bring good news to the oppressed, to bind the brokenhearted, to proclaim liberty to the captives. Isn't that good news? You should thank God. Count your blessings every day because that will keep you happy. Give thanks even when things aren't going well. And though you have liberty, that doesn't mean you can live any way you like. You still have to observe the Ten Commandments because they are still our guide even in an age

---

1. Marvin A. McMickle, *Living Water for Thirsty Souls: Unleashing the Power of Exegetical Preaching* (Valley Forge, PA: Judson, 2001), cited in Long, *Witness of Preaching*, 52.

of liberty. But liberty means that you are free from sin and anger. So God wants you to forgive those who have hurt you, even your worst enemies . . .

By the end of the sermon, we would have heard about giving thanks, following the Ten Commandments, and forgiveness, but what was the word from the Lord? In Isaiah 61, the Jews had returned from the Babylonian exile but were despondent that they were still under Persian dominance. Nonetheless, the herald announces that God will restore liberty to the people in the coming messianic age. Did you catch the revolutionary hope of that word in the rambling example above?

Jonah had a word from the Lord: "Forty days more, and Nineveh shall be no more!" Did he repeat that one-liner for three days? We don't know. He might have exalted the sovereignty of God or recounted his own testimony about running away, and certainly he would have confronted the Ninevites with their sins. Whatever it was, his audience had no doubt about the message: "Forty days more, and Nineveh shall be no more!" It was so clear that everyone repented. The preaching of the early church, too, had a clear thrust. In Acts 2, the point of Peter's sermon was not to explain speaking in tongues but to turn people to Jesus, the Messiah whom they have crucified. At the end of his sermon, 3,000 persons repented and were baptized (Acts 2:41). If we agree that preachers need to be clear about the purpose of their sermons, what exactly then is that purpose?

Andy Stanley and Lane Jones write that a preacher can have three possible goals: First, teach the *Bible* to the people. This is about transmitting biblical information. A second possible goal is to teach *people* the Bible. Here the preacher focuses on getting the message across in creative ways, but it is still mainly about knowledge transferal. In Singapore, congregations appreciate informational sermons because we value education as the way to success. But as Paul says, "If I understand all mysteries and all knowledge . . . but do not have love, I am nothing" (1 Cor 13:2). Stanley and Jones argue that the third and proper goal of preaching is "to teach people how to live a life that reflects the values, principles, and truths of the Bible." They want people to know what to do with what they have heard so that they will be able to trust God with every arena of their lives – family, finances, career, relationships, everything.[2] I largely agree with them, although I would put the purpose of preaching in a more relational way, which I will come to.

---

2. Andy Stanley and Lane Jones, *Communicating for a Change* (Colorado Springs, CO: Multnomah Books, 2006), 93–98.

Brian Chapell, in *Christ-Centered Preaching*, argues that it is the "fallen condition focus" (FCF) that reveals a text's and sermon's purpose. He explains that the FCF "is the mutual human condition that contemporary believers share with those to or about whom the text was written that requires the grace of the passage for God's people to glorify and enjoy him . . . Ultimately, a sermon is about how a text says we are to respond biblically to the FCF as it is experienced in our lives." The FCF includes not only specific sins but also physical, emotional, or social needs due to our fallen condition.[3] However, not every text deals with a fallen condition, though many do. A praise or thanksgiving psalm may simply focus on praising God. What is the FCF of the Priestly text of Genesis 1, unless it is merely taken as a prelude to the non-priestly account of the fall in Genesis 3?[4] Even though Chapell says that God's grace is the ultimate answer to the fallen condition, the FCF tends to have an anthropocentric focus on human sin or need.

Even the goal to transform lives is too anthropocentric. I realized this when I was telling a student that preaching is transformative. "So preaching is about changing lives?" she reflected. It then struck me how result-oriented that sounded. What if we do not see transformation despite all our persuasion? I have often held up the prophet Jeremiah as a prophet who never got to see the fruits of his labor. Was he a failure? Did his agony and tears serve any purpose at all? His words only sank in when the people were in exile, but they were the words that eventually turned a rebellious people back to God. So, is preaching about transformation? "That sounds too task-oriented, doesn't it?" I replied to my student. "I would rather say that preaching is about helping people hear God." "Yes!" she responded, "That's what we need – to hear God speaking to our spirits."

What do people hunger for every Sunday morning when they sacrifice sleep and drag their children out of bed to make their way to church? More Bible knowledge? More check lists of Christian duties and behavior? I doubt it; rather they hope to meet with God and to hear God speak to them. It is about a relationship with God. When they have been touched by God, they will be transformed. The change will be from within, not because the preacher has led them on a guilt trip, or cajoled them, or rebuked them, but because they have heard God's voice. Does God seek a change? Yes, but first

---

3. Bryan Chapell, *Christ-Centered Preaching: Redeeming the Expository Sermon*, 2nd ed. (Grand Rapids, MI: Baker Academic, 2005), 50–51.

4. This is based on developments from the Documentary Hypothesis Theory (see ch. 3, n. 24).

God seeks us, just as we are, to be God's child and God's people. In the new covenant, "They shall all know me, from the least of them to the greatest" (Jer 33:34).

This is why I prefer the word "transformative" rather than "transformational." Both are regarded as synonyms in *The American Heritage Dictionary of the English Language* (5th ed.), but the *Oxford English Dictionary* (8th ed.) and *Merriam-Webster's Collegiate Dictionary* (11th ed.) recognize a difference. "Transformative" describes something that has the power to transform, while "transformational" is simply concerned with or characterized by transformation. "Transformational preaching" is concerned with changes in the listeners, leading to a performance-oriented goal, but "transformative preaching" focuses on God's power to transform, by the Scripture and the Spirit.

Stephen Farris, in *Preaching That Matters*, shares a similar view. He writes that preaching is an encounter with God: "I believe that the true 'word of God' *for us* is the word that *happens* between God and the congregation as a result of this encounter between the biblical text and the people."[5] While a lecture seeks to create understanding about God, a preacher prays that the sermon may become an encounter between the congregation and the living God (although lecturing may at times segue into preaching). Paul Scott Wilson writes insightfully in *Preaching and Homiletical Theory*:

> Preaching is transformational because this is what it means to have a relationship with the Divine who is for us: Individuals are restored to what God intended, and communities are shaped and empowered for discipleship. Transformation may be something preachers can assist, but it is God's activity that is transformative.[6]

Note that preaching is transformative not just for the individual but also for the community; we are preaching to the individual-in-community. The transformation is mutual – the individual's transformation infuses the community, and the community also forms the individual. Wilson traces the idea of the word of God as an event of God's encounter to Martin Luther and to Barth, both believing that Christ meets us through the spoken word of

---

5. Stephen Farris, *Preaching That Matters: The Bible and Our Lives* (Louisville, KY: Westminster John Knox, 1998), 10–11. Original emphasis.

6. Paul Scott Wilson, *Preaching and Homiletical Theory* (St Louis, MO: Chalice, 2004), 43.

the gospel.[7] Therefore, the preacher needs to be clear what is the word that God would have him deliver, lest he obfuscates it. Rhetoric also demands a singular clarity for communication.

2. Rhetoric of Preaching

Stanley and Jones write about a mentor advising an anxious preacher:

> "Let's try something," the mentor said. "Ready? Forty-two, seventeen, eleven, thirty-nine, seventy-six, twenty-four, nine, twelve, eight-four. Now, repeat those numbers back to me."
>
> "Well . . . I can't do that," sputtered the preacher. "I can't remember all that."
>
> "Good. Now let's try again. Forty-four, forty-four, forty-four, FORTY-FOUR. Now repeat back the number."
>
> The preacher answered sheepishly: "Forty-four."
>
> "Very good. Look, I know it's a silly illustration. But it's an important point. You give people too much to remember, they won't remember anything . . . Everything you say can be life-changing; but if they can't remember it then it won't change a thing . . . You've got to narrow the focus of your message to one point. Then everything else in the message supports, illustrates, and helps to make it memorable."[8]

Research also shows that our brain works better by association. James Cattell, the founder of psycholinguistics, showed that people remember words by their shapes. He flashed words and individual letters at test subjects for fractions of a second, and surprisingly, they remembered words better than letters. Cattell surmised that our brains pick out letters in the context of a word better than in isolation.[9] This implies that people do not learn by being told random pieces of facts but that they need connections in order to understand and retain information. Therefore, a communicator ought to relate everything to one idea rather than to pack his message with many useful but unrelated points.

---

7. Wilson, *Homiletical Theory*, 59–60.

8. Stanley and Jones, *Communicating*, 39–50.

9. "Your Brain: A User's Guide," *National Geographic* (Washington, DC: National Geographic Society, 2012): 23–25.

This is something that effective communicators have known since the time of Aristotle. In his *Rhetoric*, Aristotle put forward the strategy of a single propositional line of argument. Wilson writes that the standard rule for devising a thesis statement is that it be a complete and declarative single sentence. Duane Litfin notes that there has been a remarkable consensus in the last twenty-five hundred years that "a speech, to be maximally effective, ought to attempt to develop more or less fully only one major proposition."[10] J. H. Jowett, in his Yale lecture on preaching, puts it across even more stringently:

> I have a conviction that no sermon is ready for preaching, not ready for writing out, until we can express its theme in a short, pregnant sentence as clear as crystal. I find the getting of that sentence is the hardest, the most exact, and the most fruitful labour in my study. . . . I do not think any sermon ought to be preached or even written, until that sentence has emerged, clear and lucid as a cloudless noon.[11]

Robinson's well-known analogy is that a sermon should be a bullet, not buckshot: "Ideally each sermon is the explanation, interpretation, or application of a single dominant idea supported by other ideas, all drawn from one passage or several passages of Scripture."[12] In a country where weapons are banned, I would prefer the analogy of the laser beam. Science tells us that a laser differs from other sources of light by emitting light "coherently." Normally, photons are diffused, but in a laser, each photon moves in step with the others. This is what makes a laser beam so powerful that it can cut metal. A simpler comparison would be the childhood experiment of focusing the sun rays through a magnifying glass onto a piece of paper. Soon enough, one would see a brown singe on the paper, and then it would burst into flames. So also, a sermon needs a focal point that will pierce through the fog of confusion, boredom, and distraction, a focus that will organize every other thought into a penetrating delivery.

---

10. Aristotle, *Rhetoric*, Bk 1, Ch. 2, 1359a; Wilson, *Homiletical Theory*, 9; Duane Litfin, *Public Speaking: A Handbook for Christians*, 2nd ed. (Grand Rapids, MI: Baker, 1992), 80.

11. J. H. Jowett, *The Preacher: His Life and Work* (New York: Hodder & Stoughton, 1912), 133, cited in Haddon W. Robinson, *Biblical Preaching: The Development and Delivery of Expository Messages* (Grand Rapids, MI: Baker, 1980), 18.

12. Robinson, *Biblical Preaching*, 17.

Below is an outline of a sermon that I heard based on 2 Timothy 3, entitled "Radically Rooted in God's Word." The Singaporean lay preacher shared his outline below with me after the sermon:

1. Introduction: Illustration of getting lost with a map
2. Benefits of reading the Bible:
   a. Overcome distractions, deceptions, and temptations
   b. Know God better
   c. Know God's will
   d. Learning to be salt and light
3. Practical applications for reading the Bible
4. Conclusion: The secret to be radically rooted in the Bible is to be in love with God, for example, courtship, parental relationship, knowing God in heaven.

One congregant had said to me after listening to the sermon: "He said a lot of good things, but I wasn't sure what he was talking about." Little wonder because the speaker packed too much into his sermon. Each benefit of reading the Bible was already a sermon in itself. In the point about overcoming distractions, he gave many good examples of worldly temptations, consumerism, family discord, and faulty doctrines. This could have already constituted a sermon entitled: "Radically Rooted in God's Word in the World."

After the service, I asked my friend the speaker what he would say if he were to sum up the message in one sentence. He admitted that he had not thought that through, but on hindsight, he said it would be "Read the Bible and draw closer to God." Indeed, that was what came across most fervently in his conclusion when he illustrated the point by talking about courting his wife, playing with children, and enjoying the presence of God. It should have been his central word around which all the other points could flow. For example, if we knew the love of God, we would not be lovers or self or money, a point that Paul made in 2 Timothy 3. As Jowett said, never begin a sermon till you can say what the theme is in a short, pregnant statement.

Many writers have suggested various ways of formulating this one sentence. We will review their work and then draw a conclusion at the end of this chapter.

B. How to Formulate "A Word from the Lord"

1. Haddon Robinson

For Robinson, the "big idea" is made up of a subject and complement. The subject answers the question "What am I talking about?" The complement "completes" the subject by answering the question "What am I saying about what I'm talking about?" For example, the subject may be "the importance of faith," and the complement may be "in times of trials" or "for Christian growth." The exegetical idea elicited from the text is then turned into the homiletical idea for the sermon by making it more up-to-date or personal. He advises that the idea should be stated in a simple, memorable way, focusing on the response. So, instead of saying, "You can rejoice in trials because they lead to maturity," it is better as, "Rejoice when hard times come." Besides the big idea, Robinson also argues for the need to have a purpose by asking, "Why did the author write this?" A purpose statement should state the change of behavior expected.[13] However for Robinson, the big idea takes precedence over the purpose statement, and he does not adapt the purpose to the congregation's context.

2. Paul Scott Wilson

Wilson provides a more structured approach by advocating a movement from law to gospel, or in more contemporary terms, from trouble to grace. The law is God's judgment on sin as well as the consequences of sin suffered by humanity. The gospel is God's salvation and the experience of God's grace in our lives. Wilson presents the image of "the four pages of the sermon":

> Page One – Trouble in the biblical text
>
> Page Two – Trouble in our world
>
> Page Three – Grace in the biblical text
>
> Page Four – Grace in our world

---

13. Robinson, *Biblical Preaching*, 21–22, 69–71, 72–73. Wilson, *Homiletical Theory*, 10, traces Robinson's approach to H. Grady Davis in *Design for Preaching* (Philadelphia, PA: Muhlenberg, 1958).

These four pages may be shuffled around to vary the sermon structure, although grace is usually the end note.[14]

However before writing the sermon, Wilson instructs students to break a passage down into its possible concerns and then select one as their "major concern of the text" (MCT). They then reword it to form the "major concern of the sermon" (MCS), which should contain a complete thought in a short and memorable way. By inverting the major concern, a preacher may then determine the trouble to focus on. What is most important to Wilson is that the theme sentence (the MCS) should focus on God (in one of the persons of the Trinity) and that it should be about an action of God's grace in or behind the text. This is because he believes God should be the focus of the sermon.[15]

Wilson's proposal is helpful, but I think the trouble-to-grace approach faces three shortcomings. First, it is too narrow to embrace the breadth of biblical theology. While covenant theology and salvation history is fundamental to Christian beliefs, the canon contains more than this. Long rightly points out that the larger narrative of the Bible does not move from trouble to grace but begins with creation, which God says is "very good."[16] Besides the doctrine of redemption, there are also creation theology, wisdom tradition, and the apocalyptic writings. Even redemption is not an end in itself but results in the process of sanctification until the coming of Christ and the restoration of all creation. In this framework, "law" is not always trouble but is also "grace" in guiding people to live in the kingdom. The Ten Commandments are not a legal burden but God's gracious revelation of how a freed people are to continue in the freedom of loving God and neighbors. The Sermon on the Mount is Jesus's exposition of the law that can only be lived by grace. One, then, can also move from "grace" to "law."

The second problem with the trouble-to-grace school is that even Wilson himself admits that his God-centered approach may force texts into a predetermined mold, but he contends that "we are called to preach the gospel, not a text or what one defines as a text."[17] As a biblical scholar, I find this statement troubling. For one, all Scripture is inspired by God and is profitable for teaching (2 Tim 3:16). For another, we should let the text speak for itself lest we read our own pre-conceived notions into it. In terms of the

---

14. Paul Scott Wilson, *The Four Pages of the Sermon: A Guide of Biblical Preaching* (Nashville, TN: Abingdon, 1999).

15. Wilson, *Homiletical Theory*, 12–14, 95.

16. Long, *Witness of Preaching*, 130–131.

17. Wilson, *Homiletical Theory*, 95.

homiletical framework, Wilson seems to have elevated *kerysso* (heralding) and *euangelizo* (bringing good news) at the expense of *didasko* (teaching).

The gospel is indeed at the heart of proclaiming, but teaching requires attention to all of Scripture in its applications to human life. The book of Ecclesiastes, for one, is very anthropocentric in calling people to enjoy life in the here and now. This is not about hedonism or a way of coping with a meaningless life. Properly understood in its context, the preacher is calling people to live humbly and fully under God's sovereignty. I could phrase the major concern as "Live life under God's sovereignty," but to be faithful to the message of Ecclesiastes, I would prefer to say "Enjoy your life before it is too late." It is in enjoying what we have that we honor God. Would people be drawn to God through a miserable, stressed-out Christian? As part of wisdom tradition, Ecclesiastes has a this-worldly focus. The Christian faith calls us to live a paradoxically balanced life – to be fully aware of eschatology and also to be fully alive in this world here and now. Therefore, in response to Wilson, a theocentric thesis need not be one that is always written around God and God's grace. Rather, a theocentric pulse is listening for a word from the Lord: "What is God saying to me and to God's people?"

The third problem with Wilson's method is highlighted by Long: A congregation treated week after week only to a problem-solving design learns that the gospel only works when problems are solved.[18] But sometimes the gospel does not solve our troubles but creates more trouble because we go against the grain of the world and because we still await the coming reality. Despite the focus on grace, Wilson's approach may end with an anthropocentric side-effect.

3. Bryan Chapell

Chapell's "fallen condition focus" (FCF) shares a redemptive goal similar to Wilson's trouble-to-grace scheme and therefore suffers from the same weaknesses. Wilson himself critiques Chapell for concentrating more on God's redemptive work than on an encounter with the person of God.[19] In fact, the danger is that Chapell focuses so much on the FCF that grace is simply presented as a solution for the FCF. But do you speak to your spouse just to solve his or her problems? That would make it a pragmatic rather than

---

18. Long, *Witness of Preaching*, 129–130.
19. Wilson, *Homiletical Theory*, 103, 98.

a personal relationship. We may go to the text because we have problems, but even if we don't have problems, are we not to go to the text just to meet God?

The second problem has to do with Chapell's claim that "the FCF is present in every text."[20] As already pointed out above, the Bible is not solely about salvation history; it also celebrates God and God's creation. While humanity may be central in Psalm 9, human beings in Psalm 104 are only one small part of God's creation that he cares for. What is the FCF in Psalm 104? It is possible to create an FCF, such as human hubris or anxiety, but in reality, the psalm does not address human concerns because it is simply caught up with wonderment about God. Like Wilson, the preacher should not overemphasize *kerysso* at the expense of *didasko* but should respect the purpose of the text. It is not necessary to hunt for an FCF under every stone.

4. Fred Craddock, Thomas Long, and Stephen Farris

Craddock simply advises the preacher to ask at the end of the exegetical process, "In one sentence, what is the text saying?" Long applies this to the sermon as its "focus statement." Second, Craddock also has the preachers ask, "What is the text doing?" Long calls this the "function statement" that derives from the rhetorical intent of the text to correct, celebrate, admonish, or encourage.[21] However, the text's function needs to be adapted to the needs of the congregation as the *sermon's* function. Using Romans 8:28–29 as an example, Long writes that for a troubled congregation, the preacher may make the following statements:

> Focus: Because we have seen in Jesus Christ that God is for us, we can be confident that God loves and cares for us even when our experience seems to deny it.
>
> Function: To reassure and give hope to troubled hearers in the midst of their distress.

Alternatively, if the same text is used in another congregation that wants to be triumphant, then the statements may be different:

> Focus: True faith does not mean pretending that life is always cheerful and positive, but trusting that God's love in Christ will be with us even in the midst of peril and distress.

---

20. Chapell, *Christ-Centered Preaching*, 50.
21. Craddock, *Preaching*, 122; Long, *Witness of Preaching*, 108, 106.

> Function: To help the hearers be less afraid of life's dark valleys and to help them move from a superficial "sunshine and success" understanding of the faith towards a willingness to trust God in the fullness of their experience.[22]

Taking two distinct steps may be helpful for the preacher's thinking process, but it seems rather complicated. I doubt that a preacher will be able to articulate these sentences by heart, much less expect his hearers to do so.

Farris prefers a combination of both statements: While agreeing with the distinction between focus and function, he believes that the focus statement should be expressed functionally. Thus, a summary statement for Mary's Magnificat (Luke 1:46–55) may be: "In Jesus Christ, God acts on the side of the poor and downtrodden." Farris then rewrites it functionally: "Mary rejoices that in Jesus Christ, God acts on the side of the poor and downtrodden." Farris prescribes that the sentence "should be grammatically complete, verb and all, but it should not bloat into a pseudo paragraph."[23] A single, pithy sentence combining focus and function sticks in the minds of both preacher and hearers. However, Farris's single statement is a summary of the exegesis and needs to be rephrased for the sermon, for example: "Rejoice that in Jesus Christ, God acts on the side of the poor and downtrodden."

Conclusion

In the above review, all the homileticians are agreed on having a crux or one main idea for the sermon. Robinson's "big idea" is based on the content of the text but may overlook the purpose of the text and the sermon. Wilson structures his "major concern" of the text and of the sermon to provide God's grace for a problem. Likewise, Chapell looks for the FCF and the text's provision of grace for that fallen condition. However, I have pointed out that not every text has a redemptive focus and that we ought to let the text speak for itself.

This brings us to Craddock's and Long's focus statement coupled with a function statement that is derived from the text and adapted to the congregation. Since preaching is to be transformative and relevant in calling for a response according to the context of the hearers, then being clear about the function of the sermon is indispensable. Applying a quote attributed to

---

22. Long, *Witness of Preaching*, 110–112.
23. Farris, *Preaching That Matters*, 71–72.

Dietrich Bonhoeffer, the preacher needs to "comfort the troubled and trouble the comfortable." Farris then helpfully combines these two statements into one, that is, as a focus statement that is written functionally. I added further that it should be a statement that addresses the hearers.

This then is what the crux of a sermon should look like: A word from the Lord encapsulated as a focus statement that is expressed functionally and addressed to the congregation. But how do we hear this word? First, we need to listen to the text exegetically and second, to listen to God devotionally. These will be covered in the next two chapters.

3

Seeing the Bones: Exegetical Foundation

It feels like creation *ex nihilo* (out of nothing). You're staring at a blank screen with a blinking cursor, wondering if you have anything worthwhile to say to your congregation or anything to say at all. Will your words bring forth life or be formless and void? But you can't cancel the service or run away. So you cut and paste from commentaries, books, Internet sermons, and half-forgotten illustrations. You survived the Sunday, and your congregation? Are they just as relieved as you that the sermon is over?

Creating a sermon *ex nihilo* is too overwhelming a comparison. I prefer the concept of creation *ex materia*, that is, out of pre-existing material. This is not an unorthodox idea but one that is familiar to Old Testament scholars. (Yes, even conservative ones!) Genesis 1 in its ancient Near Eastern context is understood as God establishing order out of pre-existing chaos.[1] There is good evidence for this from the Hebrew syntax of Genesis 1:1–2. I won't go into the technicalities here, but the Tanakh version (published by the Jewish Publication Society) has a more sensitive rendering of the text:

> When God began to create heaven and earth –
>> the earth being unformed and void,
>> with darkness over the surface of the deep
>> and a wind from God sweeping over the water –
> God said, "Let there be light"; and there was light.

---

1. Bruce Waltke, *Creation and Chaos: An Exegetical and Theological Study of Biblical Cosmogony* (Portland, OR: Western Conservative Baptist Seminary, 1974); Bernhard W. Anderson, *From Creation to New Creation: Old Testament Perspectives* (Minneapolis, MN: Fortress, 1994); W. Sibley Towner, *Genesis*, Westminster Bible Companion (Louisville, KY: Westminster John Knox, 2001), 18–21.

This idea of God establishing order over formless chaos is also echoed in other parts of the Old Testament, especially in the Zion psalms (46, 48) and the enthronement psalms (24, 29, 47, 93). Admittedly, there are other places in the Old and New Testaments (e.g. Isa 45:7; Rom 4:17) that hint of creation *ex nihilo*, possibly as a response to Hellenistic philosophy.[2] The important point is that God the Creator reveals his truth in a way that is relevant to the recipients.

If sermon preparation is like creation *ex materia*, then we start by staring at the text instead of the blank screen. Instead of going straight to the commentaries, preachers should put their exegetical training to good work and not simply regurgitate other people's thoughts. A personal study gives you insights that may not be in the books – you could raise issues relevant to your own context, or you could conclude with a different perspective. Use the references mainly for extra-biblical information. It may seem chaotic at first, but the Spirit is brooding over the process, waiting to birth a sermon.

Jesus commissioned pastors to feed his sheep (John 21:27), and exegesis is a labor of love in preparing a nutritious meal. It starts with gathering fresh ingredients, marinating, chopping, boiling, baking, grilling, or frying so that hearers can dine on the goodness of the Word. If you just feed the flock with scraps thrown together from your leftover time, you will have a malnourished congregation. The pastor's study time is non-negotiable. It should be scheduled in his planner so that visiting, counseling, or meetings will not distract him from his call. Ministry never ends, but only the pastor has been trained to preach. One is ordained to the ministry of the *Word* and Sacrament, and the pastor's priority should be prayer and serving the Word (Acts 6:4). In fact, as you build your congregation up with a proper diet, they will be equipped to do the other ministries of the church.

There are, of course, times when the minister must attend to an emergency or a crisis, and his time for preparation is cut short. At such times, the grace of God will be sufficient. There is no need to preface the sermon with apologies if the preacher has done his best in the limited time because the effectiveness of the sermon does not depend on him but on the Spirit.

---

2. Gerhard May, *Creatio Ex Nihilo: The Doctrine of 'Creation out of Nothing' in Early Christian Thought* (Edinburgh: T&T Clark, 1994); and Frances Young, "'*Creatio Ex Nihilo*': A Context for the Emergence of the Christian Doctrine of Creation," *SJT* 44 (1991): 139–152, suggest that this was a response to Gnostic teaching; but Markus Bockmuehl, "*Creatio ex nihilo* in Palestinian Judaism and Early Christianity," *SJT* 65, no. 3 (2012): 253–270, argues that it is found in Palestinian Judaism in both the Second Temple and rabbinic periods.

Other than that, there is no excuse for not applying oneself to exegesis. I have seen too many pastors start well but become distracted by programs and fads. Their messages become shallow, the congregation languishes, and the pastor grows discouraged. Either the members or the pastor move on to greener pastures, but they may find that the grass is the same on both sides of the fence. A key ingredient for church growth is simply solid preaching that comes from a conscientious study of Scripture.

There are several books dedicated to exegesis. For those with Greek and Hebrew, the standard textbooks are written by Douglas K. Stuart and Gordon D. Fee.[3] I propose seven exegetical steps below and show how each step can contribute towards a sermon. Just as Ezekiel was led back and forth to observe the dry bones (Ezek 37:2), so we also look for the bones with which to construct the sermon. Then the Lord began the prophetic process by asking Ezekiel a question (37:3), "Can these bones live?" The question forced the prophet to look beyond the surface to the sovereignty of God. Similarly, the preacher can begin the exegetical task by asking questions about the text, for example, why did this happen, what does this word mean, how are these passages connected, etc. Such questions direct the exegete to look beyond the surface of the text to theological truths. The student should go through each step systematically, but depending on the text, some steps may be more relevant than others.

1. Determine the Limits of the Text

Knowing where the pericope begins and ends may make a difference to its interpretation. Sometimes, one may be assigned a text from a lectionary, but the limits may not be appropriate. Examine the preceding and following passages to see whether they relate to the text you are working on.

For example, the parable of the Good Samaritan is often told on its own and has been used to propound a religion of love and good works. However, the parable was actually Jesus's response to a lawyer who first asked about the way to inherit eternal life (Luke 10:25–29). The lawyer knew that the answer was by loving God and one's neighbor, but he was hoping for a narrow definition of neighbor. So in the larger context, the exhortation to love one's neighbor is given to people who are already in a covenant relationship with

---

3. Douglas K. Stuart, *Old Testament Exegesis: A Handbook for Students and Pastors* (Louisville, KY: Westminster John Knox, 2009); Gordon D. Fee, *New Testament Exegesis: A Handbook for Students and Pastors* (Louisville, KY, Westminster John Knox, 2002).

God. That is, practical acts of love are not a means but a manifestation of salvation.

A Singaporean student was assigned to preach on Daniel 10:2–19 according to the lectionary. This is Daniel's vision of a divine being that appeared to him in response to his fasting. But why was Daniel fasting in the first place? The student decided that the text should begin from Daniel 10:1 and not 10:2. Verse 1 says, "In the third year of King Cyrus of Persia a word was revealed to Daniel, who was named Belteshazzar. The word was true, and it concerned a great conflict. He understood the word, having received understanding in the vision."

The student noted that the Hebrew for "conflict" (*tsava'*) refers both to warfare and hardship. So, the word refers both to a vision of warfare and Daniel's hardship in understanding the vision. The student incorporated this word study into his sermon:

> There is a play on the word "conflict," which is the Hebrew word *tsava'*. It could mean there will be a great war after the Babylonian exile, one that will destroy or enslave the Jewish people. It could also mean that Daniel is greatly disturbed by his vision. No matter how you translate it, the news is grave. It is apocalyptic. It could be the end of the Jews. No wonder Daniel immediately starts fasting, never mind the New Year festival. He does not bathe for three whole weeks. He weeps. He mourns over the desperate situation.

Getting the limits right enabled the preacher to explain the text with greater depth and feeling. Listeners could identify with Daniel's despair.

2. Dig Up the Historical Context of the Text

Because God speaks to a specific people at a specific time, the message must be understood in its historical context. For instance, when Jesus told a man who wanted to bury his father, "Let the dead bury their own dead" (Luke 9:60), is Jesus disregarding filial piety? This would contradict the fifth commandment to honor one's parents!

When something sounds strange to us, we should check the historical background. It turns out that Jewish burial practice in Jesus's time was a two-stage process. The corpse is placed in a sealed tomb and allowed to decompose over a year; this is followed by a secondary burial when family members collect the bones into an ossuary (bone box) for reburial. Jesus was referring to this period between the first and second burial when the physically dead in the tomb "bury" the one who has just died with them.[4] He was not negating duty to parents; rather he was compelling a sense of urgency to proclaim the kingdom of God.

Returning to the Daniel 10 sermon, the student initially failed to do sufficient historical study on the "great conflict" that had troubled Daniel. I directed him to study the persecution of the Jews under the Greek Empire, particularly the massacre by Antiochus Epiphanes. (This is where seminary courses on Old Testament Survey come in useful. It's time to blow the dust off your old textbooks.) He then rewrote part of his sermon:

> But now, despite the end of the exile, God is telling Daniel that things will get worse. If the Jews thought the Babylonian exile was bad, the Greek persecution by Antiochus Epiphanes is going to be hell. The book of Maccabees described the sacking of Jerusalem in 167 BCE in this way:
>
> Antiochus "ordered his soldiers to cut down without mercy those whom they met and to slay those who took refuge in their houses. There was a massacre of young and old, a killing of women and children, a slaughter of virgins and infants. In the space of three days, 80,000 were lost, 40,000 meeting a violent death, and the same number being sold into slavery."

When delivering his sermon at this point, the speaker became visibly moved. Later, he shared with me that it was only after he had done his research that the full anguish of the persecution gripped him. He then preached more fervently about God's sovereignty:

> Despite the horror to come, God is telling Daniel that just as he is on top of things in the Babylonian and Persian Empires, he is also on top of things in the Greek Empire.
>
> Then came the Roman Empire: Babies massacred in Bethlehem; God's son crucified on the cross; disciples burned at the stake. Still, God was on top of it all.
>
> Today, we face the threat of terrorism, the martyrdom of 21 Coptic Egyptians in Libya, the shooting of 147 Kenyan Christians

---

4. Joel B. Green, *The Gospel of Luke,* New International Commentary on the New Testament Series (Grand Rapids, MI: Eerdmans, 1997), 408.

in their university. Empires rise and empires fall. There is still one who is on top of it all.

The sermon draws parallels between the Greek persecutions and the wonton acts of terrorism in our world today. This sermon was written before more killings had taken place in Europe, Africa, and Asia. The issue then is still the same today: Is God really in control when evil runs amok?

Being aware of the historical context enables us to link the analogous situations between then and now. Farris gives helpful steps in finding these analogies. For instance, he says that the most important task of the interpreter is to ask, "What is God doing in the text?" Then the more challenging question is, "Is God doing anything similar in our world?"[5]

3. Delineate the Literary Context of the Text

Believing that all Scripture is inspired by God means appreciating that even its literary arrangement is purposeful. To study passages in isolation from its literary context might lead us to overlook their larger intent or, worse, to misinterpret them.

I was preaching on Luke 9:57–62 about Jesus's three would-be followers. If I look at the passage on its own, Jesus's demands to abandon home, duty, and family seem draconian. To preach the text without its context would make it legalistic and guilt-inducing. But if we look at the Lucan chapter carefully, we see that this passage occurs between two parallel incidents that function as book ends: the Mission of the Twelve (Luke 9:1–6) and the Mission of the Seventy (Luke 10:1–12). Jesus's challenge to the three followers comes after various significant events between these books ends, such as the feeding of the 5,000, the revelation of his death, the transfiguration, and the healing of the demon-possessed boy. How are all these events related to the call of discipleship? We see that it is made in the light of the transfiguration and also in the shadow of the cross. Those who follow him will find that he is the one who provides, the one who has all authority, and the one who made the ultimate sacrifice for us. With this understanding, the demands of discipleship can be preached unapologetically and joyfully.

---

5. Farris, *Preaching That Matters*, 122. Farris also points out that we should compare how we are similar or different from the individuals or groups in the text. Further, the message needs to be assessed as to whether it should be a confirmation or challenge for the hearers now.

When preaching from the Gospels, one should be particularly careful not to conflate all the parallel versions of a pericope because each Gospel was written in a particular way for its specific purpose. For instance, in the Matthean parallel of the would-be followers (Matt 8:18–22), there are only two men instead of three (the last one who wanted to say goodbye to his family is omitted). Further, Matthew presents both men as seeking to follow Jesus, albeit on their own terms. On the other hand, Luke has Jesus seeking out one of them. In terms of literary context, Matthew's record of this encounter comes after three episodes of Jesus's healing that attracted a large crowd. Matthew was thus dissuading people from following the Lord merely for rewards and blessings. In contrast, Luke was calling disciples to endure hardships for the sake of the gospel. We need to hear both Matthew's and Luke's teachings and give the relevant emphasis to our own congregation.

4. Discern Genre, Form, and Structure

Different genres require different rules of interpretation: how Old Testament prophecies are fulfilled, whether Old Testament laws still apply, whether narratives set up precedents for faith and practice, or how apocalyptic literature are to be understood. For these, the preacher must have an understanding of hermeneutics or equip himself with the relevant books.[6]

It is also helpful to know that each genre and its subgenres may follow a certain form or structure. The psalms, for example, contain many subtypes such as thanksgiving, lament, trust, royal psalms. Recognizing the form will help us to interpret it more meaningfully. Again, the preacher may refer to specialized books on the genre he is preaching on.[7] Discerning the form of the text will provide preachers with a ready-made outline for their sermon (to be discussed in ch. 7 on Textual Forms).

Alexander McLaren, a nineteenth-century Baptist preacher was said to have an extraordinary gift for analyzing a text. "He touched it with a silver hammer, and it immediately broke up into natural and memorable

---

6. Gordon D. Fee and Douglas Stuart, *How to Read the Bible for All Its Worth*, 4th ed., (Grand Rapids, MI: Zondervan, 2014); Sidney Greidanus, *The Modern Preacher and the Ancient Text: Interpreting and Preaching Biblical Literature* (Grand Rapids, MI: Eerdmans, 1988).

7. For the Psalms, see Tremper Longman III, *How to Read the Psalms* (Downers Grove; Leicester, England: IVP, 1988); C. Hassel Bullock, *Encountering the Book of Psalms: A Literary and Theological Introduction* (Grand Rapids, MI: Baker, 2001).

divisions."[8] Stott remarks that we need to pray that the Lord will distribute a few more silver hammers among us today. Actually, silver hammers can be acquired by studying the forms of a genre, and where a text does not fall into a set form, one then needs to analyze its key words, narrative movement, or logical connections. For a Hebrew text, one should also look out for chiastic arrangements, that is, where ideas are repeated in a reversed structure (ABB'A' or ABCB'A'). The most important idea is usually in the center, with the surrounding matters seen as contributory causes or effects. A chiastic outline may be too complex to follow in a deductive sermon outline, but now that the preacher knows where the emphasis lay, he or she can decide whether to stress it at the beginning or at the end of a sermon.

In a sermon on Psalm 1, I presented a chiastic structure where verses 1–2 (A) parallel verses 5–6 (A') based on repetition of various words such as "wicked," "stand," "sinners," "way," "Lord." Verse 3 (B) parallels verse 4 (B') with their agricultural similes of "tree" and "chaff." Right at the end of verse 3 is the climax (C): "In all that he does, he prospers." This structure is represented diagrammatically below:

A 1. Blessed is the man who does not walk in the counsel
of the <u>wicked</u>
or <u>stand</u> in the <u>way</u> of <u>sinners</u>
or sit in the seat of mockers.

2. But his delight is in the law of the <u>LORD</u>,
and on his law he meditates day and night.

 B 3. He is like a *tree* planted by streams of water,
which yields its fruit in season
and whose leaf does not wither.

 C Whatever he does prospers.

 B' 4. Not so the wicked!
They are like *chaff* that the wind blows away.

A' 5. Therefore the <u>wicked</u> will not <u>stand</u> in the judgment,
nor <u>sinners</u> in the assembly of the righteous.

6. For the <u>LORD</u> watches over the <u>way</u> of the righteous,
but the <u>way</u> of the wicked will perish.

---

8. William Robertson Nicoll, *Princes of the Church* (London: Hodder & Stoughton, 1921), 245, 239, cited by Stott, *I Believe in Preaching*, 229–230.

Because prosperity is such an appealing idea to today's congregation, I used it in the introduction by asking, "How can one live a prosperous life?" Knowing that Psalm 1 belongs to the genre of a wisdom psalm, I employed its inherent comparison between the blessed man and the sinner. My answer to the introductory question consisted of two points: (1) what the blessed man does not do, and (2) what the blessed man does do (which is to meditate on the Word of God).

Apart from chiasms, key words are signposts in locating the natural seams of a text. For instance, in Genesis 12:1–9 on the call of Abraham, the verb "go" is repeated several times in its different Hebrew aspects or "tenses." It occurs in 12:1 "*Go* from your country"; 12:3 "And Abram *went*"; 12:5 "they set forth to *go*"; 12:9 "And Abram journeyed on, still *going* . . ." It is best to study the passage in the original language if possible because the English translation may omit the key word or translate it differently. If that is not possible, then paying attention to similar words repeated in English can still help. Using this key word as the "silver hammer," the exegete can tap the text and break it up into the following outline:

1. God's call to Abram (12:1–3)
    a. Go with God's promises
    b. Go be a blessing
2. Abram went in obedience to God (12:4–5)
    a. Abram went despite weakness (of age)
    b. Abram went despite wealth (of Haran)
3. Abram kept going with God (12:6–9)
    a. He kept going with God's presence
    b. He kept going by worship

The above is an outline of the text, and it can translate easily into a sermon outline with some appropriate rephrasing (see ch. 5 on Deductive Forms).

5. Dissect the Syntax and Grammar

This is again best done with the Hebrew or Greek text, but careful attention to the English version will also yield insights. Speakers are often warned not to show off their seminary training by using theological jargon and technical analysis. On the other hand, we should not underestimate the congregation.

We can't presume on what they know, but neither should we suppose that they aren't interested or able to learn. Perhaps the Asian audience, with our age-old esteem for education, plays a part in hearers wanting to be schooled in the biblical text. Of course, hearers also want to learn what is relevant for their own lives and not just listen to an academic lecture. The preacher should do two things: (1) only explain what is significant to support your main point(s), and (2) explain the concept as simply as possible. I have explained Greek and Hebrew words in my preaching, and after the sermon, some members of the congregation have enthusiastically repeated back to me their newly acquired vocabulary.

When explaining grammar, focus on the function rather than the form of the word. There is no need to explain how an aorist is to be identified; rather, depending on its context, highlight its "once and for all" meaning, especially in comparison to a Greek present tense that has a continuing sense. For instance, Ephesians 5:18 reads, "Do not get drunk with wine, for that is debauchery; but be filled with the Spirit." The two imperatives in this verse ("do not get drunk" and "be filled") are in the present not aorist tense, and therefore, the injunction is better understood as, "Do not keep on getting drunk with wine, for that is debauchery; but keep on being filled with the Spirit." The present tense tells us that being filled with the Spirit is to be a regular and not a once-and-for-all experience.

Syntax (sentence structure) is particularly important in the Hebrew text – a disrupted syntax indicates what is emphasized, for instance, what appears first in a sentence (other than a verb) is the main focus. A Singaporean student was preaching on Joshua 10 in which Joshua fought against five Amorite kings. What was it that gave Joshua the confidence to do battle? God promised, "Do not fear them for I have handed them over to you; not one of them shall stand before you" (Josh 10:8). The clause "for I have handed them over to you" is literally in Hebrew, "for into your hands I gave them." The stress is on Joshua himself being the victor, assuring him that he is appointed by God to go and fight. Further, the student notes that the Hebrew verb "give" or "handed over" has a perfect aspect, meaning that it conveys a completed sense and should be translated in the past tense. In other words, God says that the enemies are already defeated. The student explained this in her sermon:

> It is already accomplished, completed, a done deal. Thus Joshua takes God at his word. He goes into a battle that has already been won. He simply had to go claim the prize that God promised to him.

6. Define Key Words

Word studies can be deeply enlightening. If trained to do so, the exegete should use the Greek and Hebrew lexicons. If not, then looking at commentaries that explain the original text, such as Anchor and Word Bible Commentaries, will provide some help.

My favorite example is one based on an oft-overlooked Hebrew particle: *Hinneh*, usually translated as "behold," if it is translated at all. According to the Brown-Driver-Briggs Hebrew-English Lexicon, *hinneh* has three possible functions, one of which is to enable the reader to enter into the surprise or satisfaction of the narrator or actor. With this insight, a Vietnamese student expounded on Genesis 1:31, "And God saw every thing that he had made, and, behold, it was very good" (KJV), in her sermon:

> God felt satisfied. God was pleased. God was happy with the goodness of everything that he had made. Are we working for the goodness of God's world? Do we enjoy our work like God?
>
> One day last year, when I was stressed out with assignment deadlines, a first-year student asked me, "How are you?" "Tired," I replied immediately. Later while we were having lunch, he commented, "I wonder why students here are always complaining. I seldom see people enjoying what they are called to do here."
>
> I was taken aback by what he said. Yes, I get worried when I can't complete my work in time. I pressurize myself to get good results and raise my GPA. I get stressed, and I fall sick. I realized I was working for myself, and I could not enjoy my work. I hope you are not like me.
>
> Do you enjoy your work? Can you say *hinneh* – I am satisfied with my work; I am pleased with my reading; I am happy with my writing? We can, if we know we are working for God and for the good of God's world. Let's ask God to help us work like him.

The listeners appreciated her candor and learned to enter into the satisfaction of *hinneh*.

A note of warning here that a little knowledge can be a dangerous thing, and one should not over-exegete and build an entire doctrine on flimsy analysis. For example, some have claimed that the Greek word *rhema* refers to a word of knowledge or revelation inspired by the Spirit. But it simply means a spoken word and can also refer to the gospel (1 Pet 1:25) or words of the Old Testament prophets and commandment of the Lord through the apostles (2 Pet 3:2). Context is always mandatory in interpreting a word.

7. Discuss Biblical Theology

Biblical theology sets a truth within a larger context so that one can avoid extremist misinterpretations and also consider how the Old and New Testaments inform each other. I will consider these two issues separately.

a. A holistic framework

One passage gives only one aspect of the truth, and though it is not possible to cover the whole gamut of biblical theology in one sermon, the preacher can indicate that this is but one aspect of a larger framework. For example, God's promise of blessing to Abraham in Genesis 12:1–3 in its context would include material wealth. But this is not a justification for the health-and-wealth gospel. Within the larger Old Testament teachings, the laws legislate the redistribution of wealth to the poor, the prophets declare judgment against materialism, and the wisdom literature warns against greed. In the New Testament, riches are but a prototype of spiritual blessings (1 Tim 6:17–19; Eph 1:3), for we look not to an earthly kingdom but an eternal one (Heb 12:22; 13:14).

However, some preachers may be so concerned about being balanced that they fail to be convincing about anything. For example, if we only emphasize spiritual blessings, then we fail to assure that God provides for present needs. Jesus promised God's sufficiency for our physical needs while urging followers to seek first the kingdom of God (Matt 6:25–34). To be holistic in our preaching does not mean watering down God's promises. A particular text should be expounded in all its glorious fullness, while keeping the larger perspective in mind. A church should have a comprehensive teaching syllabus over a period of time to teach the whole counsel of God (Acts 20:27 ESV).

b. A Christian framework

"If you preach a sermon that would be acceptable to the member of a Jewish synagogue or to a Unitarian congregation, there is something radically wrong with it," says Jay E. Adams. He advocates that "the import of Christ's death and resurrection – His substitutionary, penal death and bodily resurrection –

on the subject under consideration" should be in every sermon.[9] I agree with Adams's concern that the preacher should not merely preach a moralistic sermon and that obedience should be a response to the saving work of Christ. However, does this necessitate mentioning Christ in every sermon? I think we need to look at the broader contexts of preaching in terms of biblical theology and also in terms of the church.

i. The context of biblical theology

Scholars have warned that the christocentric approaches to the unity of the Testaments are akin to Christomonism, which disregards the Trinity and reads Christ into every text without regards to the context. "They suffer from a reductionism of the multiplicity of OT thought, which merely becomes a pale reflection of the Messiah to come."[10] To understand these multifarious relationships between the Old and New Testaments, I will have to refer the preacher to other books.[11]

Augustine's maxim that "the new is in the old concealed; the old is in the new revealed" should not be simplistically followed. Rather, as Brevard S. Childs notes, "Both testaments make a discrete witness of Jesus Christ which must be heard, both separate and in concert."[12] In fact, to read the Old Testament exclusively through the lens of the New is to impoverish both. Chris Wright argues that it is a two-way process: "On the one hand, we are able to see the full significance of the Old Testament story in the light of where it leads – the climatic achievement of Christ; and on the other hand, we are able to appreciate the full dimensions of what God did through Christ in the light of his historical declarations and demonstrations of intent in the Old Testament."[13] The implication is that we need to study each text in its own historical context to appreciate the fullness of God's work. Using the Exodus as an example, Wright points out that the New Testament indicates a fuller spiritual liberation, but the Old Testament informs the New that God's

---

9. Jay E. Adams, *Preaching with Purpose: A Comprehensive Textbook on Biblical Preaching* (Grand Rapids, MI: Baker, 1982), 147.

10. Gerhard Hasel, *Old Testament Theology: Basic Issues in the Current Debate*, 4th ed. (Grand Rapids, MI: Eerdmans, 1991), 177–178.

11. Hasel, *Old Testament Theology*; Bernhard W. Anderson, *Contours of Old Testament Theology* (Minneapolis, MN: Fortress, 1999); Christopher Wright, *Knowing Jesus through the Old Testament: Rediscovering the Roots of our Faith* (London: Marshall Pickering, 1992).

12. Brevard S. Childs, *Biblical Theology of the Old and New Testaments: Theological Reflection in the Christian Bible* (Minneapolis, MN: Fortress, 1993), 78.

13. Wright, *Knowing Jesus*, 33.

deliverance is not merely spiritual but also entails freedom from political-economic oppression.[14]

Even Chapell, author of *Christ-Centered Preaching*, writes in his preface to the second edition that it is not required to mention Christ in every sermon. In fact, he says that his preaching has increasingly focused on the grace evident in the passages: "The more I have become aware that God's redemptive character occurs at the micro- as well as the macro-level of Scripture, the more I have delighted to preach his redeeming character from virtually every page of the Bible." Thus, "exposition is Christ-centered when it discloses God's essential nature as our Provider, Deliverer, and Sustainer whether or not Jesus is mentioned by name."[15]

Chapell gives two examples of expounding on this theocentric, redemptive grace on a micro-level: from a doctrinal statement in the text, or from relational interaction between God and characters in the text. Using the doctrinal statement in Genesis 15:16 ("Abram believed God, and he credited it to him as righteousness") as an example, Chapell says that a preacher could relate the text to Paul's usage of it in the New Testament, or he could just focus on God's grace within the immediate passage. For relational interaction, Chapell uses God's forgiveness of King David as an example: "This grace on a micro level may prove equally (or more) meaningful as demonstrating on a macro level how the preservation of David's lineage resulted in the birth of the Messiah."[16] That is, a sermon on the mercy of God without mentioning Jesus can be just as effective.

However, not every text focuses on grace – it may be a response to grace or the consequence of spurning grace. Holiness, the law, or the Sermon on the Mount, are about sanctification, and Chapell recognizes this as preaching about the resultant work of Christ. Perhaps his transition to preach redemptive grace at a micro-level has to do with a better appreciation of letting each text speak for itself. This avoids "the error of making imaginative rather than expository references to Christ or tacking on a mention of Calvary."[17] Such interpretation errors set a bad example of hermeneutics for the congregation to follow and weaken the sermon because a tacked-on mention of grace can only be a cursory one.

---

14. Wright, *Knowing Jesus*.
15. Chapell, *Christ-Centered Preaching*, 16, 301.
16. Ibid., 307, 308.
17. Ibid., 287, 310.

ii. *The context of the church*

In response to Adams's fear that a sermon might be equally acceptable to a Jew or Unitarian, or in our Asian context, to a Muslim or Buddhist, we need to consider the ecclesiastical and liturgical contexts of preaching. The sermon is preached in a Christian faith community, based on the Christian Scripture, in the midst of worship to a Trinitarian God, with prayers to a personal God, and sacraments conducted commemorating Christ and the cross. Not least, the preacher is a Christian, and his life is a witness of his sermon. Even if the sermon does not mention Christ, even if parts of it are acceptable to a Jew or Muslim, a sermon that is based on the Christian canon in the context of a Christian church or liturgy signifies its distinctiveness.[18]

In fact, God is not mentioned at all in the books of Esther and Song of Solomon. The hiddenness of God better conveys the books' emphases on God's providence and his creational gifts. So also, whether Christ is mentioned or not depends on the function and occasion of the sermon. For instance, if the occasion is evangelistic, or the Holy Communion is being celebrated, then it would be appropriate to relate the sermon to Christ and the gospel. For my sermon on Psalm 23, I did not mention Christ because what the congregation needed to know at that time was the assurance of God's sovereignty over the obstacles that they were facing. If the occasion required it, I could have juxtaposed Psalm 23 with the shepherd metaphor in John 10, though there is no direct intertextual connection between these two texts.[19] One could make a comparison between the protection of the kingly shepherd in Psalm 23 and the self-sacrifice of the good shepherd in John 10.

Therefore, it helps to be aware of the complexity of biblical theology and the context in which we preach. Then in deciding whether to mention Christ, listen for a word from the Lord for the congregation. It may be an occasion for heralding, or perhaps it is teaching or exhorting that is more needed. This leads us to the next topic: Is there only one main idea from the text?

Conclusion

This subheading is a misnomer, for I am not concluding this chapter but discussing the conclusion of the exegesis. Some homileticians think that the

---

18. Craddock, *Preaching*, 42, points out that the liturgy is also vital lest the preacher becomes self-centered, thinking that people come to hear him.

19. John 10 has more intertextual connections with Ezekiel 34.

exegesis of a text should conclude with its one main point, which is usually understood as the author's intention.[20] Others believe that a text can have multiple points, and as a biblical scholar, I think it is too superficial to say that a text has only a single point because that would assume a simplistic understanding of the author, the Spirit, the Scripture, and the reader.

It is a simplistic assumption that a book has only one author. Sometimes it is not clear who the author is, or there may be multiple authors, so it is more accurate to refer to the text's rather than to the author's intention. I agree with Johnson T. K. Lim that textual intention does not eliminate the author, but the author's (or authors') historical and linguistic contexts act as a control for interpretation, lest one could make a text say anything. Even if it is clear who the author is, he may have more than one intention. Duane Litfin points out that Luke may have multiple purposes for writing Acts (ecclesiastical, missionary, pneumatic, christological, legal-political) that are not mutually exclusive. Thus a pericope may have more than one thrust. Using an Old Testament example, Genesis 1 is a foundational text written by the priestly writers that teaches many things about God as Creator and King, the *imago Dei*, and Sabbath. Which of these is the main idea? Or are they all important as part of a multi-pronged polemic against the prevalent polytheistic worldview at that time?[21]

One should also not have a simplistic understanding of the Spirit. Under the inspiration of the Spirit, an author may say more than he intended. This is especially true of Old Testament prophecies. For example, the prophecy of "Immanuel" in Isaiah 7 was originally delivered as a promise and warning to King Ahaz in his historical context 700 years before the birth of Christ. Isaiah would probably be surprised albeit delighted to know that he had unknowingly prophesized about Christ's birth. This fuller meaning, intended by God but beyond the author's original intention, is called the *sensus plenior*. Greidanus warns, however, that the fuller sense should be established only as an extension of the original sense and as guided by subsequent biblical revelations.[22]

---

20. Johnson, *Glory of Preaching*, 113; Robinson, *Biblical Preaching*, 23, 43; Chapell, *Christ-Centered Preaching*, 46.

21. Johnson T. K. Lim, *Power in Preaching*, rev. ed., (Singapore: Word N Works, 2005), 50–52; Duane Litfin, "New Testament Challenges to Big Idea Preaching," in *The Big Idea of Biblical Preaching: Connecting the Bible to People*, ed. Keith Willhite and Scott M. Gibson (Grand Rapids, MI: Baker, 1998), 61–63. Litfin also points out that the Epistle of James does not have a clear central idea.

22. Greidanus, *Modern Preacher*, 111–112. Also see Wright, *Knowing Jesus*, 57.

Source- and redaction- criticisms also tell us that we cannot have a simplistic view of Scripture. A book may have been put together by more than one author, and Greidanus suggests that the purpose of the last major redactor is determinative.[23] However, there may be several layers of meaning in the final form that enriches the interpretation. For example, Old Testament scholars understand Genesis 1 as a priestly chapter, while Genesis 2 is traditionally considered a "J" (Yahwist) writing.[24] Both present different views of creation, especially in the creation of human beings. Genesis 1 speaks of male and female as equals, and Genesis 2 describes them in differentiated and complementary ways. There is no certainty about the final redactor of the Primeval History, so it is best to hold the two views of creation together, meaning that God created male and female equal but complementary. There is no idea of hierarchy that readers tend to impose from supposed New Testament perspectives onto Genesis 2. Rather, the Old Testament should inform the interpretation of the New Testament texts in Ephesians 5 and 1 Timothy 2, while noting that the pre-fall relationship can only be recovered through Christ.

Even if there is a single author, he might have used an original story for a different purpose. Taking the parable of the Prodigal Son in Luke 15 as a case in point, Chapell takes it that the story of the older brother is the major theme because Jesus directed the parable at the Pharisees and scribes (Luke 15:1–2, 28–32).[25] However, if we consider the recipients of Luke's gospel, then he was writing to Theophilus (Luke 1:3), probably representing Gentiles around AD 85. In such a context, the story of the younger brother would be the major theme, representing God's outreach to sinners. Greidanus believes that the preacher should do justice to these two levels of reading, but Craddock argues that "one cannot sustain two sermons at one time" and that the preacher should choose one or the other.[26] On the other hand, Farris allows the preacher to decide whether to preach the text at single or multiple levels. The bottom line is that the preacher should be aware of different possibilities so that he can make a choice. A consideration is the hearer's situation: Are

---

23. Greidanus, *Modern Preacher*, 108.

24. The state of Old Testament studies is much more complex now. There is no longer any consensus on the "J" source, and it is best to refer to it as a non-priestly text. See Gordon Wenham, *Exploring the Old Testament, vol. 1 The Pentateuch* (London: SPCK, 2003), 159ff.

25. Chapell, *Christ-Centered Preaching*, 46.

26. Greidanus, *Modern Preacher*, 301; Craddock, *Preaching*, 119.

they like the prodigal son or the elder brother? Or perhaps there are both in the church.[27]

Finally, different kinds of literary criticisms today offer different lenses for reading, so one cannot be simplistic about the reader. There are feminist, socio-economic, cultural, post-colonial, and ecological readers, to name a few.[28] While these methods may be insightful, they ought not become reductionistic but should be employed within the authority and historical context of the text. I, for one, do not employ feminist criticism merely to promote women over men or to undermine biblical authority. Rather the feminist lens helps readers to be more aware of cultural or sexist blinkers, lest we read the Bible from a purely androcentric or elitist point of view. By removing the blinkers, we are better able to see the truths in the text. For instance, it is usually thought that Eve is subject to Adam because he named her. But is naming really an act of authority? After all, Hagar was the first person to name God (Gen 16:13), and she was a woman and a foreigner to boot.[29]

In view of the richness of the inspired Word, there can be more than one main idea in a text, so a preacher need not tie himself up in knots over whether he has got the one right point. He simply needs to listen to a word from the Lord. Long points out that the claim of a text is very occasion specific: "It is what we hear on *this day*, from *this text*, for *these people*, in *these circumstances*, at *this junction* in their lives."[30] So, how do we hear? We will turn our attention to this in the next chapter.

---

27. Farris, *Preaching That Matters*, 128–134.

28. Wilson, *Homiletical Theory*, 32. Lim, *Power in Preaching*, 50, puts it in another helpful way by maintaining "a distinction between meaning and significance whereby the context of the text remains the same but context of the readers changes. . . . A work's significance can change depending on the context, the person's social location, from generation to generation . . . ," but the meaning of the text does not. Hence, there is textual stability, while there may be several significances.

29. George W. Ramsey, "Is Name-Giving an Act of Domination in Genesis 2:23 and Elsewhere," *Catholic Biblical Quarterly* 50 (1988): 24–35; Phyllis Trible, *Texts of Terror: Literary-Feminist Readings of Biblical Narratives* (Philadelphia, PA: Fortress, 1984), 28.

30. Long, *Witness of Preaching*, 100.

4

The Heart of Preaching: *Lectio Divina*

Her eyes were welling with tears. An attractive young lady in her thirties had come up for prayer after I preached one Sunday, stating simply that she wanted to come back to the Lord. As I talked with her, I said, "I'm not sure if this makes sense to you. If it doesn't, it's perfectly alright, but I have this impression about the Samaritan woman in the Bible, and I don't know whether that makes sense to you."

Her tears brimmed and overflowed. "Yes," she whispered. I assured her that Jesus did not rebuke the Samaritan woman but even commended her for her honesty. After a while she recounted how a bitter childhood drove her to look for love in one relationship after another. When she shared about her family, I pulled out a note in which I had written, "Someone who feels rejected by her mother." She looked a little startled when she saw the note. "God knows what you are going through," I assured her. After our time that Sunday, I met up with the young lady a few more times to pray through various issues, and she has begun to find healing and restoration. If the Spirit had not prompted me, we would still be groping in the dark. I believe that the Spirit still speaks today and that is why I urge preachers to listen for a word from the Lord.

Those who have been confused by charismatic extremes may wonder, though, whether this is indeed true or whether God spoke in this directly personal way only in biblical times. After all, don't we already have the canon and all that we need for faith and salvation? In this chapter, I will lay the biblical foundation for hearing God, and then explore the spiritual discipline of *lectio divina* as a means of hearing a word from the Lord through the text. Finally, I will give three guidelines for crafting that word for your sermon.

A. The God Who Speaks

1. Through the Old and New Testaments

"The entire Bible is a record of God's speaking in human history," says Klaus Bockmuehl, former professor of theology and ethics in his book, *Listening to the God Who Speaks*.[1] In the Old Testament, there are already hints that the Spirit who directed the prophets will be shared among all God's people in the messianic age. In Jeremiah's new covenant, God promised that his people will not need to be taught, for all shall know him (Jer 31:33-34). This does not do away with the teaching ministry, but rather, Jeremiah is referring to an innate ability to keep God's law. In a similar promise, Ezekiel speaks of a new heart and the dwelling of God's Spirit within God's people so that they will follow God's way (Ezek 36:25-27). "These passages present, then, the prospect of some kind of 'democratization' of anointment. Originally available only to the king and the prophet, the prophetic experience appears to have been decisively expanded to include all God's people."[2]

The anointing of the Spirit is also for prophecy, and this goes back to Moses's time. In Numbers 11:25-29, when the Lord took some of the spirit that was on Moses and imparted it to the seventy elders, they prophesized. Two elders, Eldad and Medad, had remained in the camp, but they also prophesized. When Joshua told Moses to stop these two, he said, "Would that all the LORD's people were prophets, and that the LORD would put his spirit on them!" These elders did not prophesy again, but in the post-exilic era, Joel prophesized that God will pour out his spirit on all flesh such that "your sons and your daughters shall prophesy, your old men shall dream dreams, and your young men shall see visions" (Joel 2:28). This promise was fulfilled in the New Testament at Pentecost (Acts 2:17-18), and because all Christians are now endowed with the Sprit, all can prophesy. John in his Gospel also discusses the ministry of the Holy Spirit: "But the Advocate, the Holy Spirit, whom the Father will send in my name, will teach you everything, and remind you of all that I have said to you" (John 14:26). Further, "When the Spirit of truth comes, he will guide you into all the truth; for he will not speak on his own, but will speak whatever he hears, and he will declare to you the things that are to come" (John 16:13-14). Some interpreters take this

---

1. Klaus Bockmuehl, *Listening to the God Who Speaks: Reflections on God's Guidance from Scripture and the Lives of God's People* (Colorado Springs, CO: Helmers & Howard, 1990).
2. Bockmuehl, *Listening*, 28.

as merely meaning that the Spirit gives us understanding of Jesus's earthly teaching, which is now recorded in the Gospels. Note, however, that the Spirit will declare "the things that are to come," that is, he will guide the church in facing every new situation in accordance to Jesus's revealed will.[3]

This is what we find in the Acts of the Apostles, where the Spirit's guidance is not just about teaching but is also about ministry direction for a particular time, place, and people. In Acts 8:29, it was the Spirit who prompted Philip to go over and join the chariot of the Ethiopian eunuch, thus realizing an opportunity to share Christ. When Peter hesitated about going to the Gentiles, the Spirit commanded him to go with Cornelius's three messengers (Acts 10:19; 11:12). Agabus predicted by the Spirit that there would be a famine, enabling the church to prepare for it (Acts 11:28). It was the Spirit who told the church in Antioch to set apart Barnabas and Saul to be missionaries (Acts 13:2–4), and he guided them at critical junctures of their journey, forbidding them to go to Asia and Mysia but directing them to Macedonia instead (Acts 16:6–9). It was under the compulsion of the Spirit that Paul resolved to go to Jerusalem, even though the same Spirit warned him that imprisonment and persecutions awaited him (Acts 20:21–22).

To those who believe that the Holy Spirit guides solely through the Scriptures and the community of the church (cf. Acts 15:28: "It has seemed good to the Holy Spirit *and to us* . . ."), Bockmuehl points out from the above accounts in Acts that there is also the personal conviction of the Spirit.[4] He lists some characteristics of the Spirit's leading: the instructions came to individuals who were called by name,[5] and they were immediate and personal, given not to guide or change someone else's action but to guide or change the one who receives it. To this, we could add from Paul's writing that the Spirit may also reveal something that is for another's rebuke or encouragement. "But if all prophesy, an unbeliever or outsider who enters is reproved by all and called to account by all. After the secrets of the unbeliever's heart are disclosed, that person will bow down before God and worship him, declaring, 'God is really among you.' . . . you can all prophesy one by one, so that all may learn and all be encouraged" (1 Cor 14:24–25, 31). However, these prophecies are to be carefully considered, not indiscriminately accepted (1 Cor 14:29).

---

3. Ibid., 64.
4. Bockmuehl, *Listening*, 77–78.
5. The Spirit can also address a community, like the church in Antioch.

How are we to test the word of the Spirit? The first test would be Scripture, since the Spirit guides in accordance to Christ's teaching; the second test is the community's discernment, and third, wisdom is needed. As 1 Thessalonians 5:19-21 says, "Do not quench the Spirit. Do not despise the words of prophets, but test everything; hold fast to what is good; abstain from every form of evil." We need wisdom to decide what is good, guided by love for others (1 Cor 13).

2. Through Church History

What has happened to this gift of prophecy in the church today? Do the Pentecostal and charismatic churches have a monopoly on this gift that traditional churches have lost or are wary of? Bockmuehl traces the Spirit's work through church history. Augustine, Bishop of Hippo in North Africa (AD 354-430), was an intellectual trapped in a hedonistic lifestyle before his conversion. Struggling with himself one day, he heard a child's voice calling out, "Take it and read, take it and read!" There was no child to be seen nor any children's game with that refrain, but moved by that voice, he opened a volume of the New Testament lying on a table and read, ". . . not in revelry and drunkenness, not in licentiousness and lewdness, not in strife and envy. But put on the Lord Jesus Christ, and make no provision for the flesh to fulfill its lusts" (Rom 13:13-14 NKJV). His heart was pierced by these words.[6]

In the Middle Ages, Bernard of Clairvaux (AD 1090-1153), the reformer of the Cistercian monks, believed in the necessity of the "inward testimony of the Holy Spirit." His biographer relates numerous stories of his supernatural insight, summing up, "Much is revealed to him in prayer." Bernard also called on others in the monastic movement to listen to what God would reveal to them in their intercessory prayers.[7] Bockmuehl lists the examples of Francis of Assisi, Patrick the first missionary to Ireland, Ansgar the evangelist to Scandinavia, and others from the late Middle Ages.[8] But as we turn to the Reformers, we will begin to understand why the mainline Protestant churches became uncomfortable with the inner speaking of the Spirit.

Martin Luther was well versed in the concept of the "inner witness of the Holy Spirit," but in his conflict with the militant and quietist Anabaptists, he

---

6. Augustine, *Confessions*, Book VIII, ch. 12.

7. P. Sinz, ed., *Len des heiligen Bernhard von Vlairvaux (vita prima)* (Düsseldorf, 1962), 92, cited in Bockmuehl, *Listening*, 109.

8. Bockmuehl, *Listening*, 109-117.

was alarmed by their sole reliance on the inner voice of God to the exclusion of Scripture. This led them to reject all forms of authority and to assert their own autonomy. Luther therefore concludes in *Against the Heavenly Prophets* (AD 1524/25) that the Spirit works only through the written and preached Word. "This position became effective historically in the mainline Protestant churches. The concept of God speaking 'immediately' – without mediation – to a person is frowned upon, as is listening to God."[9]

John Calvin expounded on the witness and experience of the Spirit in Book III of his *Institutes*. He cites many verses (e.g. Rom 8:9, 11, 14, 16) to show that the Spirit gives one the assurance of salvation and continuing relationship with God. In fact, immersion in Word and Spirit nurtures a deep familiarity with God that enables one to discern God's guidance.[10] However, in his contention against the spiritualist Anabaptists, Calvin was appalled by their disregard for God's law, based on their claim of being guided by the Spirit alone. This led the reformer to insist that the right interpretation of Scripture is given through the teaching office of the church.[11]

Bockmuehl points out that this brought the laity under the tutelage of the church, so much so that in the Enlightenment period, thinking lay people began to chaff against the church's control over their freedom of thought. "Rousseau and Kant replace orthodox Christian objectivism with their own secular subjectivism . . . The watchword merely changes from 'listen to God yourself' (which Reformational orthodoxy had ruled out) to 'listen to yourself.'"[12]

Into this milieu, John Wesley recovered the inner witness of the Spirit in the revival of the eighteenth century. He sees the Spirit as giving the assurance, first, that one is forgiven and second, that one is sanctified.[13] Thus the Spirit takes truth that is known rationally and makes it personal. It is not just an emotional experience but an assuring sense of a personal relationship with God. However, Wesley subjected personal experience to the authority of

---

9. Ibid., 127.

10. Jimmy Boon-Chai Tan, "Retaining the Tri-Perspective of History, Theology and Method in Spiritual Direction: A Comparative Study of Ignatius of Loyola and John Calvin," PhD diss., (Fuller Theological Seminary, 2014), 266.

11. Bockmuehl, *Listening*, 127–130, citing Calvin's *Treatises against the Anabaptists and against the Libertines* (1545) and a letter to Edward Seymour, Duke of Somerset and Lord Protector (1548).

12. Bockmuehl, *Listening*, 132.

13. John Wesley, "A Plain Account of Christian Perfection," in *The Works of John Wesley* vol. 11 (Oxford: Clarendon; Nashville, TN: Abingdon, 1984–2013).

the Scripture. This is a life-giving balance that the church must recover today: Pentecostals and charismatics must ground their teaching in the Scripture, while the traditional churches need to make room for the experience of the Spirit. Moving knowledge from head to heart is something that only the Spirit can do, and if we do not attend to this, then we will fail to encounter God.

By the way, if you are wondering about the story at the beginning of this chapter and the note that I had written about someone being rejected by her mother, this stems from my personal practice. I usually invite people to come forward for prayer at the end of the service, and I ask God ahead of time to show me what specific needs to pray for. I then write down what the Spirit impresses upon my heart, partly for the sake of my own memory and partly as an assurance to the potential recipient that God knows their situation. As people come forward for prayer, I share with them my notes as appropriate. Different people have different ways of doing ministry, but this is what I am comfortable with. Sometimes what I have written is spot on and sometimes less so. This is why the gift of the Spirit needs to be discerned by others, but sometimes the notes make a real difference.

Now, how are we to listen to God in preparation for a sermon? I recommend the *lectio divina*.

B. *Lectio Divina*: Hearing a Word from the Lord

The *lectio divina* (or *lectio* for short) has a prominent place in St Benedict's Rule (AD 525) for his monasteries. For several hours each day, a monk would go to a private place and meditate on a text. In the twelfth century, Guigo II, a French Carthusian monk, established the four steps of the *lectio* in his *Scala Claustralium* (*The Ladder of Monks*). The four steps are:

1. *Lectio* (Reading): Read the passage of Scripture aloud and listen for a word or phrase from the text that speaks to you. What is the Spirit drawing your attention to?

2. *Meditatio* (Meditation): Repeat aloud the chosen word or phrase. What is God saying to you through this word or phrase for your life?

3. *Oratio* (Praying): Respond to God in prayer as you hear the Spirit speaking to your life. What is God leading you to pray? It may be a thanksgiving, repentance, or a petition.

4. *Contemplatio* (Contemplating): Rest prayerfully in God's presence and be open to God. It is a time of peaceful stillness, of simply being with God. How is God revealing himself to you?[14]

Michael Casey, a Cistercian monk, writes that these four steps need not be implemented mechanically in one session. Some may combine reading, reflection, and prayer in a single exercise, while others may separate them in time and space. There can be a lot of flexibility.[15] Usually I would take 30 minutes to an hour on the *lectio*, but sometimes when nothing seems to speak or there are too many questions crowding my mind, I take a break and come back to the text at another time. The Spirit speaks at his own timing. I will first discuss the attitudes needed for doing the *lectio* and then show how we can use the *lectio* to hear a word from the Lord.

1. Attitudes for the Lectio Divina

I want to highlight three attitudes needed for practicing the *lectio*. The first is patience.[16] We are so caught up with busy work for our own sense of achievement and self-worth that we fear being still. Stillness niggles at us like a waste of time, so to cope with our restlessness or perceived meaninglessness, we turn to our mobile devices to occupy ourselves with social updates or mobile games. Perhaps we are trying to avoid a workaholic God that we have created in our own image, one who expects us to be productive all the time. But God is inviting us to stop running in our hamster wheels. Just be still and enjoy God's love, not as a reward for hard work or a prelude to more responsibilities, but simply because God loves us.

Second, we need to come to the *lectio* with reverence. It is because of reverence for God that we carve out space and time to listen. It is saying to God, "Speak, LORD, for your servant is listening" (1 Sam 3:9). Reverently, we come to the *lectio* to seek God and not just to get a word for the homily, for our anxiety to get the sermon ready will drown out the Spirit's voice. Worse, we are reducing God to a means for our own end. And what we will meet at that end is not God but our human ideas, probably along the line of pray

---

14. Richard Peace, *Contemplative Bible Reading: Experiencing God through Scripture* (Colorado Springs, CO: Navpress, 1998), 12–13.
15. Michael Casey, *Sacred Reading: The Ancient Art of Lectio Divina* (Ligouri, MO: Ligouri/Triumph, 1995), 59.
16. Casey, *Sacred Reading*, 8.

more, serve more, give more, run more in your little Christian hamster wheel. M. Basil Pennington, a Trappist monk, reminds us:

> We come to *lectio* not so much seeking ideas, concepts, insights, or even motivating graces; we come to *lectio* seeking God himself and nothing less than God. We come seeking the experience of the presence of the living God, to be with him and to allow him to be with us in whatever way he wishes.[17]

The attitude of reverence also applies to the Scripture. We do not come to read our own interpretations into the text but to respect that God spoke to a certain people in a certain historical, cultural, and linguistic context. This is why the preacher should do his exegesis first so that he can hear from the text correctly. The *lectio* is a vital practice but not a substitute for rigorous exegesis.

Prayerfulness will help us maintain reverence. Prayer takes place not only at *oratio*. We begin with prayer when we ask God to open our hearts and speak to us. During the *lectio*, we ask God for a word. "That is why the exercise of sacred reading is sometimes said to be a technique of prayer." Such a prayerful attitude keeps us from slipping into a study mode that "can be insulation from challenges inherent in the text."[18] Casey warns against turning an incipient insight into a marketable commodity just so that we can have nuggets of wisdom to share or worse, something to apply to someone else. Rather, we ask God what he wants to say to our lives. For this reason, I like to do my *lectio* away from my office lest I listen only to preach to others. Sometimes, I get a table in a quiet café or go on a walk.

The third attitude is to slow down. Read the text slowly to savor every word and detail. We are used to scanning an article quickly to extract its useful points. In our busyness, we also eat quickly, leading to indigestion, reflux, heartburn, and obesity. If we do the same with *lectio*, we will have spiritual indigestion. The Word does us no good if we only want to tick it off our to-do list. If prayer is a conversation, then reading slowly gives room for God to speak to us, otherwise we are only absorbed in a soliloquy. To slow down, it helps to revert to the ancient practice of reading aloud to ourselves.[19] This is what the Hebrew word for meditation *hagah* means: a low, growling sound, reflecting the sound that one makes when reading to oneself (Ps 1:2:

---

17. M. Basil Pennington, *Lectio Divina: Renewing the Ancient Practice of Praying the Scriptures* (New York: Crossroad, 1998), 27.

18. Casey, *Sacred Reading*, 61.

19. Ibid., 83.

"But their delight is in the law of the LORD, and on his law they meditate [*hagah*] day and night"). By vocalizing, we activate our physical senses to help us focus on the text. Hearing the words is also a reminder that the *lectio* is a conversation in which God is not an object of study but a subject who speaks to us.

There will always be times when God seems silent. Casey deals with some possible causes, such as ill-health, for which one needs rest. It could be a lack of training, and practice will sharpen our acuity. There might be relational conflict, and one should seek resolution. If one is preoccupied with projects, then we need to either re-examine our priorities or simply jot down the concerns to attend to them later.[20] However, sometimes there is no discernable cause except for the mystery of God's transcendence. But if a preacher hears nothing, he might panic that he has nothing to preach. What is he to do?

Pennington shares his experience when God "just didn't seem to show up." At the end of the time, he would just choose a word to carry with him. He shares that after one such *lectio*, he encountered a troubled young man later in the day and was wondering what to say to the lad when "the Lord sort of poked me in the ribs." He then realized that his earlier word from the *lectio* was something appropriate for the young man. Later that day, when faced with an exhausting task, Pennington said that the Lord gave him another little poke. He was reminded again of the Lord's word that encouraged him to finish his task.[21] Following Pennington's example, one may simply have to choose a word or phrase as a word from the Lord and work with that. It may speak to the congregation in ways that we do not know. Ultimately, the Lord speaks not at our bidding but according to his own sovereignty, and we trust that he will feed his hungry flock.

2. Acting on the Lectio Divina

The steps for the *lectio* below are adapted from Norvene Vest's method for a group exercise.[22] I incorporate two other steps that are variations to the traditional four rungs of Guigo's Ladder. These two steps, *Operatio* (Operation/

---

20. Ibid., 87–100.
21. Pennington, *Lectio Divina*, 75–76.
22. Norvene Vest, *Bible Reading for Spiritual Growth* (San Francisco, CA: HarperCollins, 1993).

Action) and *Compassio* (Compassion) are attributed to a twelfth-century Augustinian priest, Richard of St Victor. Adding these two steps directs one in a movement from hearing God for oneself to going forth to serve in God's world. They will also help one to arrive at the function of the focus statement. Step-by-step guidelines are laid out below, and I use my own reflections on Psalm 23 as an example.

Preparation:	Quieten ourselves to listen. One can simply pray, "Speak, Lord, for your servant is listening" or sing a short chorus. Speak or sing each word slowly, growing in awareness of God's presence.
1. *Lectio*:	Read the passage slowly for the first time, listening for a word or phrase from the text that stays with you.
2. *Meditatio*:	Read the passage for a second time. One could read a different version for fresh insights. Chew on your word or phrase by repeating it and asking, "What is God saying to me in my life through this word?"

        God is a personal and relational God. He is concerned about all that you are concerned about: your needs, struggles, anxieties, work, family, past, present, and future. We listen with an awareness of our whole lives being present before God.

        Sometimes, an inner thought arises immediately, and you may be convicted that God is addressing a certain need, attitude, or behavior. Sometimes you may need to be patient and engage in a dialogue with God as part of your meditation. Voice your doubts, feelings, or questions till you arrive at some conviction.

        When I was meditating on Psalm 23, verse 4 caught my attention: "I fear no evil, for you are with me." I heard God say to me, "Do not be afraid, for I am with you." It was an encouragement to me as I was facing obstacles in work and ministry that were beyond my control, and I felt like I was walking off a cliff. So I told God my fears, "You say you are with me, but what if this or that happens? What if no one understands or defends me?" The Lord assured me that his authority is far greater than any human authority.

3. *Operatio*: Having heard a word from the Lord, ask, "What is God calling me to do?" It may be a call to some specific actions for others or for oneself. Or, it may be a call to rest and trust.

 In my meditation on Psalm 23, I was emboldened to continue in a specific direction. Painful though it may be to knock my head against a wall, God will make my forehead harder than flint (Ezek 3:9). I heard God say, do this for the sake of his people.

 In *Meditatio*, one arrives at what Long would call a "focus" statement. *Operatio* then leads one to the "function" statement. It is good for a beginner to keep the two questions distinct so that one will not only hear but also do the Word. However, there can also be times when the function and focus statements merge (i.e. when what God is saying to me is also what God is calling me to do). *Lectio* is an aid to help us listen to God, so we do not need to be enslaved to the steps but respond as the Spirit leads.

4. *Oratio*: This is our response to God's word and will. We can respond with thanksgiving, repentance, petition, or intercession till we have laid everything before God.

 In my response to Psalm 23, I forgave those who hurt me, and I ask forgiveness for my fear and anger. I pray for strength and for unity so that God's will can be done. I lay the burden down from my shoulder and leave it in God's authoritative hands.

5. *Contemplatio*: Having entrusted everything to God in prayer, we can now rest in God's presence and enjoy being with our Lord. You may find that you are in a hurry to skip this step so that you can get to your waiting sermon. Pennington warns that ignoring contemplation can be a sign of idolatry.[23] It signifies that we are seeking our own satisfaction, pride, learning, or ministry more than God. If we do not know the depth of a relationship with God or the breadth of God's love, how can we speak of it to others? We will only be imparting mere knowledge about God or more duties to do for God.

From Psalm 23, I spent a few minutes basking in the presence of a God who is greater than my obstacles, and I am infused with courage and hope.

6. *Compassio*: Read the passage for the third time, and think of the congregation that you are going to preach to. If it is a familiar church, let different people come to mind. If you are an invited speaker, think about what you may have gleaned from general enquiries or from the church's website. Consider the people with compassion, for they are people whom God loves. Ask God, "What is your word for your people at this time?"

In all likelihood, it would be a word similar to what God spoke to you. As Long said, you come as a witness on behalf of the people, and so God will send you back as his mouthpiece. This is the heart of the sermon that will pump blood through the whole body, bringing the sermon to life.

Write this word in a sentence and express the focus functionally so that hearers are prompted to respond rather than just to learn facts. For example, my word from Psalm 23 for the congregation was exactly the same: "Do not be afraid, for I am with you." This is not surprising, since I was going to preach to a group of seminary students, and they would be facing the same challenges as me. In fact, after delivering that sermon, a graduating student sent me an email asking whether I was preaching to her in particular, since she had shared some of her apprehensions with me. "Not particularly," I said because I thought she had already resolved the issue. "But I guess the Spirit was."

---

23. Pennington, *Lectio Divina*, 80.

When I was preaching Psalm 23 on another occasion, this time to a church congregation, the *lectio* took me in a different direction. The word that spoke to me was, "The LORD is my shepherd," with the emphasis on "my." When it came to *Compassio*, I knew that some in the church had gone through difficult times and were deeply hurt. I felt that God wanted to reassure them that he cares for them personally. Functionally, I believed that God is calling them to come to him, and so, the word for the sermon was: "Come to the Lord because he cares for you personally." At the end of that sermon, more people than I had anticipated responded to my invitation for prayer. God spoke, and the people came.

At the end of *Compassio*, end with prayer for the congregation, and thank God for the word you have received.

C. Writing Out a Word from the Lord

After hearing a word from the Lord in your *lectio*, express it as a sentence described in chapter 2 on the Crux of Preaching. State the focus (the truth to be conveyed from the text) in a functional way (the response called for from the hearers). For beginning preachers, this can be easier said than done, but arriving at this statement gets the sermon halfway done and saves one from writing a confused homily. To help you write the word from the Lord cogently, I offer three guidelines: Be clear, be coherent, and be concise.

1. Be Clear

Don't assume that you know what the sermon should be about, but be able to articulate the word that the Lord has given you even before you start writing your sermon. The absence of a word results in the absence of a message, no matter what you may cut and paste together. A Nepali student was assigned to preach from Hebrews 12:4–13. The Hebrews passage is a powerful text on suffering, but his sermon was just a patchwork of dry, intellectual comments from various commentaries.

I sat the student down and asked him what his central idea was. He confessed he did not have one. So I changed the question and asked whether the text had spoken to him personally. He said "yes" and recounted an experience when he was imprisoned and severely beaten for converting to Christianity. I asked what kept his faith going in the prison. He said that he was singing a song in his cell when the presence of the Lord came upon him, and he was filled with peace and joy even in his agony. A few days later, he was inexplicably released. After he had recovered from his injuries, he started to encourage other Nepali Christians who were facing similar persecutions.

His account sounded like the New Testament experience of persecution taking place today. I then asked what message he wanted to share with others in the light of the text and his experience. "Endure suffering because God wants to train you," he replied almost without hesitation, a point that came from Hebrew 12:11. I was surprised because I thought he might have highlighted God's presence or God's love. Later, I realized that this young man was descended from the warrior tribe of his people, which explains his understanding of being trained by pain.

With this word from the Lord, I sent him back to rewrite his sermon. It was a simple message because of the language barrier, but it was powerful. He knew what it meant to suffer and to be trained by it. For the rest of us who have never known persecution, his witness made God more real and our troubles smaller by comparison. God is now using him as an evangelist in Nepal, sharing the gospel to many in his country.

A clear word from the Lord also means that it should not be so broad that it raises more questions than it answers. For example, an Indonesian student was preparing a sermon on Philippians 3:17–20, which calls on the Philippians to follow Paul's example. His word from the Lord was, "Be an example." It was correct but vague. It could be an example of rejoicing, suffering, serving, and so on. If the word is not clear, it lacks impact, and there is the danger that the preacher may veer off in many other directions. The student tried again with "Be an example in all your ups and downs." It was as if he hit the light switch because we could now see how we, a seminary audience, could set an example for others as Paul did in his trials and victories. A clear word, sharpened like an arrow, is more likely to penetrate the minds and hearts of the hearers.

Rather than untangle incoherent sermons, I now have students practice the *lectio* before submitting their sermons, and I am relieved by the improved clarity. One such example comes from a Mongolian student who had a hard time keeping up with her studies in English. She was assigned to preach from Jonah 3:1–10 in her last semester before graduating. She was apprehensive about returning to serve because of the political, economic, and social barriers in her homeland. During her *lectio* on Jonah, she heard God say to her, "Arise and go in the power of God." In Jonah 3, she saw how we can arise and go in God's power by keeping our focus on God and knowing that God is the one at work among the pagan enemies. In her sermon, she talked about visiting a church member in prison and being unexpectedly given the opportunity to share the gospel to the inmates. Two hundred prisoners showed up, and though trembling on the inside, she testified boldly of the gospel. By the grace of God, a few accepted Christ. She ended her chapel sermon on Jonah by saying, "Even though you preach a strange message, it is not your message, it is God's message. So arise and go in the power of God." That day we saw one of our weakest students become one of our best preachers. It begins with having a clear word from the Lord.

2. Be Coherent

Coherence means that one has *a* word from the Lord, that is, there should be only one idea, not several. (See ch. 2 on the Crux of the Sermon.) Just as too many cooks spoil the broth, so also too many ideas spoil the sermon. A thoughtful, mature Singaporean student was assigned to preach from 1 Samuel 2:22–26. The text is about God warning Eli that his family will be judged because he failed to discipline his sons when they abused their priestly status. 1 Samuel 2:30 is a familiar verse: ". . . those who honor me, I will honor, and those who despise me shall be treated with contempt." The student wrote out her word as "Honor God for he is righteous. Be responsible for our roles. It is a privilege to serve God."

I told her that is three points not one! I could follow her written sermon, but it lacked challenge. Trying to do justice to everything left a message without a clarion call to any. I asked her to write her word from the Lord in one sentence, one that she was most convicted about. She came back with "Honor God because of the privileges he has given us." It was now one idea with just one conjunction "because" connecting two clauses – "Honor God" as the function of the statement and "the privileges he has given us" as the reason for that function. Having a centripetal center pulled all her points together in a compelling way.

In fact, her eventual sermon structure can be compared to Wilson's four pages: She talked about the privileges that Eli enjoyed and the privileges of grace that we enjoy; then she described how Eli failed to honor God, and how we should be honoring God in our life and service. However, unlike Wilson, it was not a law-to-grace movement but a grace-to-law direction. Her sermon soared with God's grace that carried her through past trials, but such grace was forgotten under the stress of ministry. She wanted to run away from people's expectations, just as Eli wanted to avoid conflicts with his son. But upon recalling God's grace, she overcame her fears and honored God by doing what God has called her to do. The congregation also heard God's call, based on one coherent word from the Lord.

3. Be Concise

To be concise means to state the word from the Lord in a succinct way. After an exegetical study of Isaiah 30:15–18, another Singaporean student came up with "God is calling his struggling saints to rest and trust in him in their journey to wholeness and service because he is their peace and victory." This summarized the text well, for God was calling Israel to return to him for deliverance from their enemies. But the sentence was too cluttered with adjectives (struggling), hendiadys (wholeness and service, peace and victory), and there were three clauses in that one sentence: (1) "God is calling his struggling saints to rest and trust in him," (2) (while they go) "in their journey to wholeness and service," and (3) "because he is their peace and victory."

I advised the writer to make his statement shorter, something that he can repeat easily from memory and that hearers can also repeat to themselves when they walk out of the chapel. His second effort was an improvement: "Our gracious God calls us to surrender our lives to him, for he is our salvation and strength." This was now two clauses joined by one conjunction "for." However, adjectives (like "gracious") are usually superfluous, unless it is one of the main points in the sermon. More importantly, the sentence needs a sharper function so that hearers know how they are to respond.

He rewrote it for the third time: "Return and wait upon the Lord, for he is your salvation and strength." His sermon used "return" and "wait," and "salvation" and "strength" with different nuances, so they were not merely repetition. His final statement had cut away all extraneous words, and his sermon resounded with an unmistakable call to repent from self-reliance. A sharp sermon requires a concise word from the Lord.

We now have the heart of the sermon: a word from the Lord heard through the *lectio,* with the focus written functionally as a clear, coherent, and concise statement. In Part II, we will begin to build the body of the sermon around the heart, beginning with the skeleton – the outline.

Part II

Shaping the Skeleton

5

Shaping the Skeleton I: Deductive Forms

Form matters. Just as a skeleton holds the body together, so a good form or structure holds a sermon together. A captivating sermon structure keeps boredom at bay. Not only that, they also form the faith of the congregation. For example, ministers who set up their sermons as arguments against other beliefs convey that being a Christian means proving you are right. Those who constantly use the "before/after" testimonies imply that Christians should always live victorious lives. Craddock reiterates, "Regardless of the subjects being treated, a preacher can [by his choice of forms] nourish rigidity or openness, legalism or graciousness, inclusiveness or exclusiveness, adversarial or conciliating mentality, willingness to discuss or demand immediate answers."[1]

In this and the next two chapters, we will look at three basic types of sermon outlines: deductive, inductive, and textual. To keep the meanings between deductive and inductive straight in our head, let me define them using alliterations:

> A **d**eductive sermon begins by **d**eclaring the word from the Lord and then **d**evelops the **d**etails.

> An **i**nductive sermon begins with **i**nformation or **i**nquiry and then **i**nfers the word from the Lord.

Textual forms are based on the literary form of the text. Each of these forms will affect the congregation in different ways: A congregation fed a diet of the three-point deductive sermons may tend to be well-informed,

---

1. Craddock, *Preaching*, 174.

intellectual Christians; those on a course of inductive narrative sermons may have more enthusiasm but be less knowledgeable; while textual forms are excellent for appreciating the biblical passage but may lack the breadth of biblical theology. All three forms, therefore, have their strengths and weaknesses, and should be employed according to the subject matter, the occasion, and the context of the congregation.

Long also points out that hearers have different learning styles and so "forming sermons is an act of pastoral care."[2] The preacher should therefore use a variety of forms, even those he or she may be uncomfortable with, for the benefit of different hearers. Lenny Luchetti observes that there are four kinds of listeners. Some listen with the mind for exegetical information. Such people typically want a logical sermon outline with clear points drawn from a deep study of the text. This would call for a deductive or textual form. A second group wants their hearts touched and inspired to live for Christ, especially with the difficulties that they face. An inductive narrative form would speak to their struggles. A third kind are those who listen with the soul for theological reflection. The difference between them and the exegetical listeners is that the theologically reflective people want to focus on the forest and not the trees; they want to grasp the nature and purposes of God. An inductive format leading to a deductive explanation will be useful for teaching doctrines. The inductive half allows one to explore different perspectives, while the deductive half integrates or holds the truths in paradoxical tension. The fourth kind are those who listen with their hands for application. They desire practical wisdom that they can apply immediately to their lives, such as in the areas of dating, marriage, parenting, finances, vocation, etc. They will appreciate the straightforward deductive sermons that enumerate a list of exhortations, for example, "Five Ways to Deepen Your Marriage," "Six Biblical Principles for Managing Your Finances," etc.[3]

Luchetti reminds us that the needs of a particular listener may change, sometimes from week to week, as they face different challenges. The preacher can vary the forms of his sermon to accommodate the diverse and shifting needs of his listeners. One could possibly try to meet all four needs for exegesis, inspiration, reflection, and application in a sermon, but the more

---

2. Long, *Witness of Preaching*, 171.

3. Lenny Luchetti, "Connecting with More Listeners: Preaching That Connects to the Diverse Needs of Your Listeners," accessed 9 Sept 2015.

realistic approach will be to use different forms for different types of topics so that the range of needs are met over time.

On the other hand, Long proposes that listeners can be trained to appreciate different kinds of sermons and so develop greater spiritual capacities. Nevertheless, there are basic preferences, and the preacher needs to adapt for the sake of his hearers. After all, as Long says, "The gospel comes to us in a wide variety of forms, and the preacher who faithfully bears witness to the gospel will allow the fullness of the gospel to summon forth a rich diversity of sermon forms as well."[4]

In this chapter, I focus on the basic three-point deductive sermon that preachers and congregations are most familiar with. It is a reliable way of feeding the flock regularly. It behooves preachers, therefore to learn this basic form and to do it well. With experience, they can go on to experiment with other forms to enhance the learning experience of the congregation.

A. Why Deductive Forms?

The main advantage of the deductive sermon is clarity. The word from the Lord is stated at the beginning and then reinforced throughout the sermon. For expository preaching where the central word and its supporting main points are derived from the text, listeners acquire a deeper understanding of the text.[5] Although the three-point sermon may be so tried and true that it may seem tired and overused, Chapell shares a fresh perspective:

> When I hear discussions about some sermon form being outmoded, I recall something musician Richard Wagner was reportedly reminded upon hearing Johannes Brahms play his scintillating *Variations and Fugue on a Theme by Handel*. Although Wagner was not especially fond of Brahms, he was so moved by the composer's genius that he declared, "That shows what still may be done with the old forms provided someone appears who knows how to use them."[6]

---

4. Long, *Witness of Preaching*, 171.

5. A topical sermon may have points taken from several different texts to present a more comprehensive teaching of a particular topic.

6. James Earl Massey, *Designing the Sermon: Order and Movement in Preaching*, ed. William Thompson (Nashville, TN: Abingdon, 1980), 24, cited by Chapell, *Christ-Centered Preaching*, 133, fn. 11.

Here then are four guidelines to help the preacher use the old deductive form effectively: Write the main points in complete sentences, connect them to the word from the Lord, connect them to one another, and connect them to the hearers.

B. How to Shape Deductive Forms

1. Write the Main Points in Complete Sentences

Let me use my sermon on Psalm 23 as an example. I had discerned a word from the Lord for the congregation: "Come to God because he cares for you personally." Supposing my outline was as follows:

1. Provision (23:1–3)
2. Protection (23:4–5)
3. Pursuit (23:6)

Does the outline convey the word from the Lord? The points are so broad and vague that it is open to misinterpretations. Does "provision" cover needs or wants? What is "protection" from: enemies or accidents? Now compare it to the one below:

1. Come to God because he provides for your needs (23:1–3).
2. Come to God because he protects you from enemies (23:4–5).
3. Come to God because he pursues you with goodness and love (23:6).

Writing in complete sentences not only clarifies the points but also reinforces the central call.

Because preachers are calling people to respond in some way, they should write the main points using active rather than passive verbs. As Chapell explains, clauses with passive verbs do not exhort people to do anything; they simply state what happens to people.[7] See what the outline of Psalm 23 would be like if I use passive sentences:

1. You are provided for by God.
2. You are protected by God.
3. You are pursued by God.

---

7. Chapell, *Christ-Centered Preaching*, 151.

The invitational call to come to God is lost; the listeners have become mere consumers of information. Comforting information, no doubt, but passive words tend to produce passive people.

It so happens that my outline above has an alliteration of three "P's" (provide, protect, pursue). Is this a helpful mnemonic or an awkward artifice? Steve Mathewson, advises preachers not to intentionally create outlines that people will remember because it is not a natural form of communication.[8] I agree with Mathewson if an alliterated word does not fit the text or obscures the point. A preacher should not force a text into a clever outline. Nonetheless, some alliteration may work naturally and would provide an effective memory aid, besides enabling hearers to enjoy a poetic outline. After all, as Chapell notes, the psalmist was not beyond teaching truth through an acrostic (alphabetical) pattern.[9] In fact, Psalm 119 takes this to the extreme, for it is not just each line that begins with a letter of the Hebrew alphabet, but each of the eight verses that make up one stanza begins with the same letter, and this goes on for twenty-two stanzas, based on the twenty-two letters of the alphabet.

2. Connect the Main Points to the Word from the Lord

Supposing my sermon was outlined this way:

1. Come to God who provides for your needs.
2. Don't be afraid of enemies.
3. You will dwell in the house of God forever.

How does it come across? Would you know what the central focus is? Without a clear connection to the central word, the outline sounds like three independent ideas that could be three distinct sermons. Only the first point is connected to the main word. The second switches the focus from God to enemies and could get sidetracked into dealing with temptations or all kinds of fears. The third point switches the focus yet again, this time to the hearers, and might spin off into the hope of eternal life (which is not in the context of this psalm). An incoherent outline usually indicates that the preacher did not

---

8. Steve Mathewson, "Outlines That Work for You, Not against You," accessed 7 September 2015.

9. Chapell, *Christ-Centered Preaching*, 138.

have a clear word from the Lord in the first place. If he can state that word clearly, the main points usually follow.[10]

3. Connect the Main Points to Each Other

Each main point needs to advance the sermon by making a distinctive contribution and not be merely repetitive, otherwise the listeners will either be bored or confused. For example, the outline below would be problematic:

1. Come to God because he provides for your needs (23:1–3).
2. Come to God because he protects you from evil (23:4).
3. Come to God because he protects you from enemies (23:5–6).

The problem is that the second and third points overlap – there is no clear distinction between "evil" and "enemies." This is due to a failure to understand Hebrew poetic parallelism. Psalm 23:4 and 5 are parallel verses having to do with the same subject matter of the psalmist's foes. The fact that God is addressed in the second person "you" ties these two verses together, while the other verses address God using the third person "he" (vv. 1–3) and "the LORD" (v. 6).

I heard a Singaporean pastor preach a sermon based on Genesis 23:1–20 about Abraham purchasing a burial site from the Hittites to bury his wife Sarah. The central word was clearly presented and repeated – God's delay is not his denial (it would be better if it were functionally expressed though). The outline, however, was somewhat problematic. He listed three important lessons to learn:

1. The death of a vision.
2. God's promise never fails.
3. Walk by faith and not by sight.

The problem begins with the first point because it is not connected to the central word or to the other points. While points 2 and 3 are lessons to learn, point 1 merely states a problem. The first point would serve better as

---

10. Chapell, *Christ-Centered Preaching*, 147–150. Chapell proposes two ways of writing the outline, based on God's response to the FCF: "Because God . . . , we must/should . . ." However, "should/must/ought" sounds legalistic. It is better to use the functional exhortation, such as "come/trust/etc." The response is not something that one has "got" to do but what one "gets" to do.

an inductive introduction posing the problem of God's delay. The next two points could then respond to the problem in the following way:

1. God's delay is not his denial because God's promise never fails.
2. God's delay is not his denial, so walk by faith and not by sight.

It can be seen that the logical connection between these two points is not in terms of a list as in the Psalm 23 outline. Rather, the first point gives the *reason* for the central word, while the second point is the *response* to that word. Long calls this the "indicative-imperative" form: It starts by announcing the claim of the text and then explores its ethical implication(s).[11] Unfortunately, because of the inconsistent outline, some listeners found the sermon hard to follow as a whole, although they remembered the central idea because the speaker repeated it clearly. This shows the importance of having a word from the Lord above all else – at least that got across!

It may seem that main points that are consistently connected to the central word and logically connected to each other are rather monotonous. However, a sermon is heard not seen, therefore unless a preacher repeats the important points, listeners may not follow, especially if they were momentarily distracted or stopped to reflect on a certain point. Even if the outline is printed in the sermon bulletin or flashed on PowerPoint, hearers may still not realize that the preacher has transitioned to another point unless it was repeated to signal its importance. Repetition is redundant for a reader but a relief for a listener.

Since your outline is advancing the sermon, your strongest point should be your last point because that is what the congregation will leave with. It should provide the climactic motivation for hearers. Usually in an expository message, the strongest point is already the last point because the author of the biblical text also has a natural sense of rhetoric. Psalm 23, for example, already ends with a strong assurance: "Surely goodness and love shall [pursue] me all the days of my life, and I shall dwell in the house of the LORD my whole life long." The verse reinforces the assurance with "surely," while "goodness and mercy" is a comprehensive coverage of God's care, and the verb "pursue" (which is what the Hebrew word means rather than the usual English translation of "follow") underscores God's desire to bless. It turns the focus back on God's grace and impels hearers to respond to their Shepherd-King.

---

11. Long, *Witness of Preaching*, 166.

At other times, I re-arrange my expositional outline in order to end with the point that is most relevant to the congregation. For example, when preaching on the *Shema* in Deuteronomy 6:4–5, the outline based on the text would be:

1. Hear: The LORD our God, the LORD is one (Deut 6:4).
   a. The LORD our God
   b. The LORD is one
2. Love the LORD your God with all your (Deut 6:5).
   a. Heart
   b. Soul
   c. Might

(In the above outline, I have indicated the subpoints to my main points, which are explanations of the text.) For a complacent church, the above outline calls for an active response to love God. But in another church that was feeling weary, I reversed the outline and ended with God's love and sovereignty so they might be comforted and encouraged.

4. Connect the Main Points to the Hearers

The outline below is based on the story of David and Goliath in 1 Samuel 17:

1. Goliath challenges God's people.
2. Saul cowers with God's people.
3. David conquers for God's people.

Mathewson writes that after his fellow seminarian had presented this outline in their homiletics class, their professor Haddon Robinson remarked, "Nobody talks like this anymore, except in the pulpit."[12] What is wrong with this outline? It has complete sentences, clever alliteration, and a chronological connection between the main points.

Besides the central word being indistinct, the outline is an *exegetical* rather than a *homiletical* outline. This is a sermon that explains the text but has no relevance to the congregation. If there is no relevance to their lives, listeners will quickly lose interest in a history lesson that occurred almost

---

12. Mathewson, "Outlines That Works."

3,000 years ago in a land far, far away. The main points need to be addressed towards the hearers in the first- or second-person pronouns (we/you). They should also be expressed as truth principles that apply to the lives of your congregation.[13] If you have heard a word from the Lord for the congregation, this would be easy to do. Supposing the word from the Lord for the 1 Samuel 17 sermon were, "Look to God when you face problems," then the outline could be:[14]

1. Look to God, not your problems.
2. Look to God, not other people.
3. Look to God, not yourself.

We preach the text, but ultimately, preaching is delivering God's word to God's people. Below are a couple of examples of my students' deductive outlines. How would you critique and rewrite their first drafts? Then compare it to their final versions.

C. Examples

This sermon by a Singaporean student is based on Judges 2:6–15 regarding the Israelites who had just arrived in the promised land. The first generation was faithful to God during the lifetime of Joshua, but the next generation went astray after idols. As a consequence, God used their enemies to discipline them.

Word from the Lord: Serve God with undivided faithfulness.

1. Undivided faithfulness of God's servants
2. Beware of idols

The second sermon by another Singaporean student is based on Amos 8:1–7. God shows a vision of "summer fruits" to the prophet Amos, which in Hebrew is a pun for "end," that is, God was going to bring an end to Israel for their oppression of the poor.

---

13. Also Chapell, *Christ-Centered Preaching*, 153.
14. Actually, as a sermon based on a narrative text, it would be more interesting to use an inductive outline for the sermon, which will be explored in the next chapter.

Word from the Lord: Uphold justice and build people up because this is true worship.

1. Israel subverted human dignity

2. Israel subverted true worship

3. God calls you to uphold justice and build people up

Analyze the above outlines, and rewrite them according to the four guidelines above. Then compare your outlines to their improved versions on the following page.

For the first sermon based on Judges 2, the first point is not a complete sentence and does not connect to the hearers. Further, the two main points need to be more clearly connected to the word from the Lord and to each other. This is his revision:

1. An undivided faithfulness to God requires you to know God.

2. An undivided faithfulness to God requires you to repent from idols.

How would you improve on this further? Rewrite the main points based on the functional aspect of the central word so that the call to respond is inescapable:

1. Serve God with undivided faithfulness by knowing God.

2. Serve God with undivided faithfulness by repenting from idols.

In the second sermon on Amos 8, the main points are complete sentences, but they are not clearly connected to the word from the Lord and to each other, and neither do they connect to the hearers. The student revised the outline to:

1. God calls us to true worship that builds people up (Amos 8:4–5).

2. God calls us to true worship that upholds justice (Amos 8:5–6).

Can you improve on them further? You could rewrite them functionally:

1. Build people up because that is true worship (Amos 8:4–5).

2. Uphold justice because that is true worship (Amos 8:5–6).

There was no need for the third point, since it is an application that can be worked into the two main points.

Conclusion

Various criticisms have been levelled against the deductive form. The most common one is that it lacks the element of surprise and discovery and thus reduces the audience's interest and engagement. Further, Don M. Wardlaw points out that the dissecting and rearranging of the Word into a logical, cognitive format "make the word of God subservient to one particular, technical kind of reason."[15] This kind of cognitive preaching conditions the

---

15. Don M. Wardlaw, "Need for New Shapes," in *Preaching Biblically: Creating Sermons in the Shape of Scripture*, ed. Don M. Wardlaw (Philadelphia, PA: Westminster, 1983), 11–12, cited by Greidanus, *Modern Preacher*, 146.

congregation into an intellectual faith, possibly one that slides into a nominal Christian life. Finally, not every text fits into a three-point sermon and to force it into a prefabricated mold may distort the biblical message. Greidanus points out, "For passages whose aim is specifically to teach doctrine, the didactic form may work well, but for passages whose aim is to proclaim, to surprise, to encourage, to seek praise, etc., the didactic form is not very appropriate because the message becomes transformed into an intellectual topic."[16] As a response to these criticisms, homileticians have turned to the inductive form, which we will explore in the next chapter.

---

16. Greidanus, *Modern Preacher*, 147.

6

Shaping the Skeleton II: Inductive Forms

A. Why Inductive Forms?

It's hard to change people's minds. We all suffer from confirmation bias or its more telling name, "myside bias." In Singapore, we run up against the NIMBY (Not In My Back Yard) syndrome. Residents protest against the building of nursing homes or columbariums in their neighborhood because it will affect their property value, forgetting that they themselves may have need of such services one day. We instinctively defend our own territory, values, and beliefs. In an American study, participants were asked whether they would allow a dangerous German car on American streets, and conversely, whether they would allow a dangerous American car on German streets. The participants were more likely to ban a dangerous German car on American streets than an American car on German streets.[1] Many other psychological tests also show that we tend to support our own familiar beliefs. How then can we persuade people through our preaching, especially those who are skeptical or even hostile?

In Acts 17, Paul found himself in such a situation in Athens when he was asked to explain the gospel to Greek philosophers. He started off by saying:

"I see you are a religious people."

Yes, we are (the audience's possible mental response).

"The Creator God made us all, as your poets said."

---

1. K. E. Stanovich, R. F. West, and M. E. Toplak, "Myside Bias, Rational Thinking, and Intelligence," *Current Directions in Psychological Science* 22, no. 4 (2013): 259–264, accessed 22 December 2015.

Yes, that's true.
"Since we are made by God, we should not think God is an idol."
Well, you have a point.
"So he commands people to repent."
Maybe we should.
"He will judge the world by a man he has appointed."
Really, who's that?
"A man he raised from the dead."
Really? What nonsense!
Hmm, explain more.

Paul, the master rhetorician, started by getting people to agree with him, then he challenged them to think, and finally presented his claim. Even if some disagreed with his final point, they would have heard enough to give them something to mull over. Though some rejected his message, others wanted to hear more, and some were eventually convinced. This is an example of the inductive approach.

Inductive sermons engage both receptive and hostile listeners because they start from where the hearers are and then take them on a process of discovery towards new insights. In a pluralistic society like Singapore, it is good to address people of other faiths like Paul did. This is how I would engage with the Taoist or Buddhist idea of reincarnation:

"All religions want to help us be better people."
That's true.
"But we know that we can't be good enough in one lifetime."
Yes, we know that.
"That is why some believe in reincarnation so that a person can learn to be better in the next life. One hopes to get better and better until one reaches enlightenment."
That's what we believe.
"In that case, the world should be getting better and better."
I suppose.
"If you look at the daily newspaper, the world doesn't seem to be getting better."
Well, you have a point.
"That is why God wants to give us a totally new heart and life because he knows that the old one is not good enough."
Really? I believe I can get better on my own.
Hmm, tell me more.

Taoist and Buddhist hearers will respond much like Paul's Greek audience – some with rejection and skepticism because changing a mindset takes time, but some may be open for new ideas to take root.

For those in the church, the inductive form conveys old truths in a fresh way that challenges the usual assumptions. It is not just a matter of garnering interest but more fundamentally, an experiential way of learning. The listener is led to think, analyze, evaluate, and conclude for himself. One can think of it as a monologue model of the dialogical Socratic method of reasoning. The Socratic question-and-answer process between the teacher and student is a dialogue, but in preaching, the preacher voices the questions that listeners may have and proceeds to deal with them. As Robinson says, "The inductive sermon is closer to a conversation than to a lecture. To make it work, we have to know how people actually think and act."[2] When listeners feel that the preacher understands them, then they are more likely to pay attention and lower their defenses.

Jesus also challenged people to think for themselves by asking them questions. At the end of the parable of the Good Samaritan, Jesus asked, "Who was the neighbor?" (Luke 10:36) The lawyer had asked Jesus the same question earlier, hoping for a narrow definition, but was now forced to admit that he himself must be a neighbor to all, even to those he despised. On another occasion, at a crucial juncture in the Gospels, Jesus asked his disciples, "Who do you say that I am?" (Matt 16:15; Mark 8:27–29; Luke 9:18–20). Peter declared, "You are the Messiah." Why did Jesus pose that question instead of merely declaring the truth to them? At that point in time, they had been with Jesus long enough to draw their own conclusion from their observations and interactions with the Lord. They needed to take personal ownership of the truth and its implications for their lives. Thereafter, Jesus began to teach them about his coming suffering, and to withstand the imminent adversities, the disciples must be deeply convinced about who they were following.

In the modern homiletical movement, Craddock's monograph, *As One without Authority*,[3] turned the tide towards inductive preaching. He proposed that just as preachers discover the meaning of the text through exegesis, so they should help listeners enjoy that same process of discovery. At the end of an inductive sermon, says Long, hearers should "ideally have become so

---

2. Robinson, *Biblical Preaching*, 89.
3. Fred B. Craddock, *As One without Authority* (Nashville, TN: Abingdon, 1971).

engaged in this discovery process that they, and not the preacher, complete the sermon by naming its resolution in their own minds and lives."[4]

Don Sunukjian gives some helpful guidelines in deciding whether to shape a sermon inductively or deductively. He writes that a deductive structure is most effective when the central word catches the listener's attention and causes them to have some questions about it. They will want to know one or all of three things: What does it mean? Is it true? What difference does it make? These questions provide the tension, suspense, or interest to keep listening. On the other hand, if the main idea does not provoke any of these questions in the listeners' minds, then an inductive structure would be a better choice.[5]

There are two kinds of central idea that would call for an inductive approach – a truth that is too well accepted and a truth that is too hard to accept. A truth that is too well accepted is usually one based on a familiar text. The command to love our neighbor based on the parable of the Good Samaritan is one such example. We all identify with the Samaritan protagonist of the story, but Jesus's listeners would have been revolted at that thought. The preacher needs to re-create the same effect in today's hearers, and an inductive form works towards turning the tables on the audience.

Conversely, a word from the Lord that is too hard to accept also requires an inductive approach. Paul's preaching to the Greeks in Acts 17 about Jesus's resurrection was hard for his Greek audience to swallow. For Christians, it could be a practical truth that is hard to follow, for example, giving up an addiction, forgiving, sexual purity, or practicing the Christian disciplines. It's always easier to direct a rebuke to someone else (especially one's spouse or enemy) than to oneself. Thus, a familiar or a tough truth is best served through an inductive sermon, starting with the listeners own questions and struggles. There are a variety of inductive outlines and I will discuss them according to two broad categories: the propositional and the narrative types of inductive forms.

---

4. Long, *Witness of Preaching*, 125.

5. Don Sunukjian, "Sticking to the Plot: The Developmental Flow of the Big Idea Sermon," in *The Big Idea of Biblical Preaching*, eds. Keith Willhite, Scott Gibson and Haddon Robinson (Grand Rapids, MI: Baker, 1999), 116–117.

B. How to Shape Inductive Forms

1. Inductive Propositional Forms

An inductive propositional sermon is one where the preacher takes the hearers through a series of propositions to convince them of his central idea. Robinson also has a semi-inductive outline that consists of an "induction-deduction" format. This involves an extended inductive introduction, presents the biblical solution in the middle of the sermon, and then expounds that idea deductively in the rest of the message. Robinson describes the introduction portion as where the preacher "identif[ies] a personal or ethical problem, explore[s] its roots, and perhaps discuss[es] inadequate solutions."[6] Wilson's trouble-to-grace movement, built around the four pages of the sermon (discussed in ch. 2), is an example of an inductive-deductive outline – it begins with trouble either in the biblical text or in our contemporary world and then shows how grace overcomes that trouble in the biblical text and in our world.

An inductive propositional outline is generally structured as follows:

> **Question**: Identify some personal, ethical, social, expository, or doctrinal problems that arise from the text or the central word.
>
> **Proposition #1**
> Problem with Proposition #1
>
> **Proposition #2, etc.**
> Problem with Proposition #2, etc.
>
> **Biblical Answer/Central word**
> Explanation (this may come before or after the biblical answer)
> Application

In a semi-inductive sermon, less time may be spent on the second and third proposals so that more time is given to explaining the biblical answer/word from the Lord deductively. Below I give some examples of the fully inductive and the semi-inductive propositional forms.

---

6. Robinson, *Biblical Preaching*, 87.

a. Fully inductive propositional form

Here is an example of an inductive sermon based on Mark 10:17–22 where Jesus challenges a rich young ruler to sell his possessions, give the money to the poor, and follow the Lord in order to receive eternal life. This is both a familiar and hard truth. David Day suggests the following inductive outline that I adapt:[7]

> **Question**: Must a Christian sell everything to follow Christ?
> **Proposition #1**: You need to sell everything *in order to* get eternal life.
> Problem: Even the last six commandments of the Decalogue is not the way to eternal life (Mark 10:19). So, did Jesus get his theology wrong? Let's try another proposition.
> **Proposition #2**: You need to sell everything, *since* you have eternal life.
> Problem: Jesus did not tell every Christian to sell everything. So, did Jesus get his ethics wrong? Let try another proposition.
> Explanation: The man failed to keep the first four commandments because he loved his possessions more than God.
> **Central word**: Put God first in order to have eternal life.
> Application: What idol is Jesus calling you to give up in order to follow him?

You can almost hear a sigh of relief sweeping over the crowd after the preacher deals with the first two propositions. But the final step then unmasks the real god that held the ruler and the hearers in bondage. It was not just about money, or theology, or ethics, but it was really about idolatry and one's fundamental relationship with God. The congregation, too, are confronted with the same challenge to break their own idols lest they miss out on God and the way to eternal life.

The above example begins with a question from the text, which is whether one needs to sell everything to follow Christ. Alternatively, one can formulate a question from the central word, for example, "How can you have eternal life?" This then provides a red thread for listeners to follow the intricacies of an inductive sermon, especially when the passage may be more complex.

---
7. David Day, *Preaching Workbook* (London: SPCK, 1998), 78.

b. Semi-inductive propositional form

Robinson actually lists two kinds of semi-inductive outlines – the inductive-deductive form and the subject-to-be completed form.

i. Inductive-deductive form. Below is an example of an inductive-deductive sermon based on an earlier outline of Amos 8:1–7 in chapter 4 on *lectio divina*. The word from the Lord was: "Uphold justice and build people up because this is true worship." This is not a familiar text and so will require a deductive explanation, but it is a hard truth warning against selfishness and apathy. In Amos 8:1–3, God warns that he will put an end to Israel. Listeners think that Israel deserves it for their numerous sins, but we are usually blind to our own culpability, so this sermon began inductively as outlined below:

Question: Is God really going to punish God's own people including us?
Proposition #1: Surely not. Look at how he has blessed them and us.
Problem: But they kept the blessings for themselves.
Proposition #2: Surely not. Look at how religious they are and we are.
Problem: But they neglected the poor and needy. So, God is justified in punishing God's own people. What are we to do?
Central word: Uphold justice and build people up because this is true worship.
Explanation: 1. Build people up because this is true worship (Amos 8:5)
2. Uphold justice because this is true worship (Amos 8:6)[8]

ii. Subject-to-be-completed form. Here, the introduction presents only the subject but not the main points. The major points are basically a list that completes or describes the subject and are revealed one at a time.[9] Examples are sermons entitled "Five Ways to a Healthy Marriage," "Four Reasons to

---

8. My colleague, Jeffrey Truscott, is so attuned to the Singapore culture that he suggests making the above outline more memorable in the following local way of speaking:
Question . . .
Is it this? No, lah!
Is it that? No, lah!
Central word: Actually, it's like this . . .
Explanation: This is because . . .
9. Robinson, *Biblical Preaching*, 85.

Praise God," etc. In my sermon on Psalm 23 for example, my word from the Lord was, "Come to God who cares for you personally." I could begin by saying, "How does God care for you? Psalm 23 tells us three ways." The three main points are then disclosed one at a time so as to maintain the congregation's interest throughout the sermon. (This means that the entire sermon outline should not be revealed beforehand in the bulletin or on PowerPoint.) However, even Robinson admits that this form can be boring when over used.

We now move on to the second major category of inductive sermons that uses stories rather than propositions.

2. Inductive Narrative Forms

Lowry proposed in his groundbreaking 1980 book, *The Homiletical Plot*, that "a sermon is not a doctrinal lecture. . . . We begin by regarding the sermon as a homiletical plot, a narrative art form, a sacred story."[10] He considers the narrative form as *the* form that all sermons should take. Others, like Richard Jensen, are less doctrinaire and see the narrative form as one of many possibilities, but one that is especially relevant when the biblical text is itself a narrative. "Why should we de-story these stories in our sermons and simply pass on the point of the story to our listeners? Why should we rip the content out of the form as our normal homiletical process?"[11]

The narrative form is particularly suited to experiential learning. Listeners are immersed in the story such that they identify with the characters and their emotions. This utilizes the right brain hemisphere that controls our "intuition, holistic, imagistic thought processes" as opposed to our left hemisphere that controls our "rational, logical, sequential thought processes."[12] Scripture actually appeals to both sides of the brain through narrative and didactic texts. The Old Testament prophets delivered their oracles in poetic form because it appeals to the right brain that evokes emotions and action.

---

10. Eugene L. Lowry, *The Homiletical Plot: The Sermon as Narrative Art Form*, expanded ed. (Louisville, KY: Westminster John Knox, 2001), 6. Wilson, *Homiletical Theory*, 88, suggests that Lowry was dependent on Milton Crum Jr., *Manual on Preaching: A New Process of Sermon Development* (Valley Forge, PA: Judson, 1977).

11. Richard A. Jensen, *Telling the Story: Variety and Imagination in Preaching* (Minneapolis, MN: Augsburg, 1980), 128, cited by Greidanus, *Modern Preacher*, 148.

12. Jensen, *Telling the Story*, 123, 125.

Chapell adds that sharing a story not only forms the individual but also the community through a common experience. "Through a story, listeners are introduced to an experience, vicariously live through the events or impressions described, and take away shared impressions of its implications so that meaning is formed and held in community." However, he rightly cautions that the modern narrative theory is based on the post-modern philosophy that propositional truth is not transcendent or transferable and that the shared experience of a narrative provides some basis for the acceptance of an idea.[13] Rather, based on the biblical models of preaching, the preacher can rest on the authority of Scripture, which contains both propositional and narrative truth, and on the work of the Spirit to convict the hearers of what is true.

A unique advantage of the narrative form is the effectiveness of overheard communication. A study done by two psychologists, Elaine Walster and Leon Festinger, in 1962 showed that people are more convinced by an overheard conversation than by direct communication. In their experiment, they had participants listen in to a supposed conversation between graduate students about the "misconception" that smoking causes lung cancer. The students even cited (non-existent) data to claim that smoking might be beneficial since it releases tension. Some of the participants were told that the graduate students were aware of them listening in, while others were told that the speakers were unaware of their presence. A week later, the participants were asked to fill in a medical survey purportedly administered by a health organization. It was found that participants who overhead the conversation believing that the speakers were unaware of them had significantly changed their attitude about smoking.[14] Craddock explains that a narrative is a form of overhearing: "A narrative is told with distance and sustains it in that the story unfolds on its own, seemingly only casually aware of the hearer, and yet all the while the narrative is inviting and beckoning the listener to participation in its anticipation, struggle and resolution."[15]

A story may also be told as a first-person narrative where the preacher speaks as if he or she were one of the characters in the story. This allows the preacher to express the inner thoughts and feelings of the character that

---

13. Chapell, *Christ-Centered Preaching*, 164, 166–167.
14. Elaine Walster and Leon Festinger, "The Effectiveness of 'Overheard' Persuasive Communications," *Journal of Abnormal and Social Psychology* 65, no. 6 (1962): 395–402.
15. Craddock, *Overhearing the Gospel*, 135.

would reflect the listeners' own questions and struggles. In this format, the conversation is not overheard as the speaker is directly addressing the hearers, but there is a greater sense of immediacy, engagement, and identification. This is a useful approach when a fresh perspective is needed for a familiar text and when the congregation is receptive to the message. In contrast, a story told in the third person makes a hard truth more palatable, since it is not directly addressing or challenging the listeners.

The indirection of a narrative, however, is both its strength and its weakness. A story, obliquely told, could totally miss the mark and leave the audience scratching their heads wondering what the point was about. Greidanus emphasizes that a story is not told merely for aesthetic enjoyment but is primarily a proclamation of God's word. "It will not do, then, simply to tell a story and leave the interpretation to the hearers."[16] As he pointed out, King David did not realize the point of Nathan's poignant story until the prophet announced, "You are the man!" (2 Sam 12:7). The king only repented at that point, but he repented deeply and genuinely. Therefore, it is absolutely necessary to make the word from the Lord clear by the end of the story. Like Nathan, the preacher needs to point out how the story applies to the listeners and what difference it will make to their lives. This is especially true in contexts like Singapore, where congregations are more used to deductive sermons, given our didactic form of education.

Greidanus points out another problem with the story form: It may be isolated from its historical and literary contexts.[17] Re-telling a story without its context will lead to, at best, a fragmentary understanding of Scripture or, at worst, a story that is completely misinterpreted. The story of the woman who poured the alabaster jar of expensive ointment on Jesus in the contexts of Matthew and Mark (Matt 26:6-13; Mark 14:3-9), for example, is more about Christ's sacrificial death than about our sacrificial service. The preacher can incorporate historical and literary details into his sermon as part of the storytelling such that they come alive for the contemporary audience. Below I suggest four approaches to narrative preaching.[18]

---

16. Greidanus, *Modern Preacher*, 149.
17. Ibid., 153, 151.
18. These four models are adapted from Eugene Lowry, *How to Preach a Parable* (Nashville, TN: Abingdon, 1989); Long, *Witness of Preaching*, 168; Day, *Preaching Workbook*, 80-83.

a. The moral of the story

This is the most straightforward approach where the preacher tells a biblical story or retells it in a contemporary way and then expounds on the moral or application of the narrative. I once encouraged a Singaporean student to craft an inductive sermon based on 1 Kings 19:19–21 because it is a narrative about the call of Elisha. After Elijah throws his mantle on Elisha, the young man rushes back to bid farewell to his family. He slaughters his oxen and burns his plough and throws a barbeque for the people. His word from the Lord was: "Sacrifice all to serve the God of all."

The sermon starts as a dialogue between Elisha and his father. The bewildered patriarch cannot understand why his son is giving up his home and livelihood. Elisha's reply weaves in the historical, theological, and literary contexts of 1 Kings. Despite Elisha's internal apprehensions, the prophet-to-be is apprehended by the awesome reality of Elijah's God: the Lord who routed Baal at Mt Carmel. Having delivered the biblical story, the preacher then shares his own struggle between seeking material satisfaction and serving God. He urges the listeners to focus on the sovereignty of God lest they be tempted by worldly desires. It was an affective story with a provocative challenge.

b. A series of stories

A series of short stories can provide the experiential proofs to support the central idea. Below is an outline of one such sermon that I preached based on Revelation 21:1–5. My word from the Lord was: "Rest in God's relationship with you." I chose an inductive form because it was a familiar idea that needed to be presented in a fresh way and also because it would mirror the chiastic outline of Revelation 21:1–5.[19]

> **A** Then I saw a *new* heaven and earth
>   **B** for the *first* heaven and earth had passed away
>   **C** and the sea was *no more*
>   **D** the holy city . . . coming down out of heaven from *God*
>   **D'** *God* himself will be with them
>   **C'** Death shall be *no more*
>   **B'** the *first* things have passed away
> **A'** "See, I am making all things *new*."

---

19. David E. Aune, *Revelation 17–22*, Word Biblical Commentary (Nashville, TN: Thomas Nelson, 1998), 1114.

The parallel lines of the chiastic structure are indicated by the repeated words in italics. The text tells us that the goal (D, D') is the relationship between God and his people. I built my sermon on an inductive-deductive arrangement around the idea of relationships:

   A A story about my childhood relationship with my father:
   We enjoyed simple pleasures like *chendol*, a local dessert
      B A story about a friend's childhood relationship with her late father:
      She remembered her father's anxiety when she was stung by a jellyfish
         Problem: Relationships are important but people are imperfect
         Central word: Rest in God's relationship with you
         Deductive Explanations:
            1. Rest in God's relationship with us in salvation history
            2. Rest in God's relationship with us in work and ministry
      B' A story about a life set free from fear, based on a relationship with God:
      With God's love, an Indian student overcame parents' expectations and relatives' criticisms that had debilitated her confidence.
   A' A story about myself set free from striving, based on my relationship with God:
   By learning to accept myself before God, I learned to preach what I hear from God rather than strive to be the most knowledgeable and popular preacher.
Conclusion: Are you resting in God's relationship in all that you do?

c. An integrated story

Lowry suggests the outline below for a narrative sermon in *The Homiletical Plot*. He outlines five stages that he later streamlines into four:

1. Conflict: Upsetting the equilibrium (Oops!)

    In the beginning, the preacher presents an "itch," that is, a problem that is felt by the hearers, whether personal, social, expository or doctrinal.[20]

2. Complication: Analyzing the discrepancy (Ugh!)

    In this stage, the preacher asks why there is this problem. Depth of analysis is needed to understand the human condition and motives. This prepares the listener for the next stage of resolution.[21]

3. Sudden Shift: Disclosing the clue to the resolution (Aha!)

4. Good News: Experiencing the Gospel (Whee!)

    Lowry has now combined these two stages. The sudden shift, based on biblical truth, is where the reversal of the plot takes place. Because there is a radical discontinuity between the gospel and worldly wisdom, Lowry suggests that reversal may occur in a variety of ways: a reversal of cause and effect, a reversal of assumption, or a reversal of logic.[22]

5. Unfolding: Anticipating the future (Yeah!)

    In this conclusion, the preacher asks about what can be expected, should be done, or is now possible. Lowry cautions that this is not the climax of the sermon; the climax is the resolution provided by the gospel in the previous step. Human response is not a work of righteousness but "a consequence of the grace of God."[23]

The word from the Lord would be delivered and explained at the Aha! stage, and its application can be unfolded at the Yeah! section. When using

---

20. Lowry, *Homiletical Plot*, 35.

21. Eugene Lowry, *The Sermon: Dancing the Edge of Mystery* (Nashville, TN: Abingdon, 1997), 107; Lowry, *Homiletical Plot*, 44–45.

22. Lowry, *Homiletical Plot*, 70, 72.

23. Ibid., 80, 83. In the 2001 rev. ed., 120, Lowry changed "Anticipating the consequences" to "Anticipating the future" for a more positive connotation. For Lowry, this outline applies to all sermons, but I use it as an especially appropriate guide for narrative texts.

the above structure to retell a biblical narrative, the preacher can integrate some reflections after each stage. This will make the narrative relevant to the contemporary audience. Below is an example of a first-person narrative preaching that integrates reflection and application at various stages of the account. The Indonesian student's sermon is based on Deuteronomy 3:23–28 where God refused Moses' request to enter the promised land because God was angry with Moses on the people's account (a reference to the incident of Moses striking the rock for water in Numbers 20:1–13). His word from the Lord was: "Let go of your ministry because God is God." I reproduced some parts of the sermon that were well written:

Oops! Moses could not enter the promised land.
Reflection: "Sometimes you don't get what you earnestly pray for."

Ugh! Moses sinned, but it was actually the people's fault. God is unfair in disregarding all that Moses has done.
Reflection: "Haven't you ever cried out, 'God, you called me to this. I went out of my way to start this ministry. I started it with sweat and tears. Nobody knew about my sacrifices then, and now, nobody's going to know what I've done because someone else will take the credit. God, this is unfair!'"

Aha! Moses realized who he is speaking to: A God who is gracious and merciful, but also a holy God. (In Lowry's term, this is a reversal of assumption because the ministry does not belong to us but to God.)
Reflection: "Who do you think God is? A God who submits to what we want or a God to whom we must submit?"
Central word: "Let go of your ministry because God is God."

Yeah! In obedience, Moses lets go of his ministry.
Reflection: "I realized these are not my people but his. That land across Jordan is not my land but his. This is not about my glory and legacy. This is about his glory and his grand purpose. He is the one leading the people into the promised land, not me."

> Application: "What is God telling you to let go of?
> A cell group that you've been nurturing for years?
> The baton in the music ministry that you have to pass to someone you think is not good enough?
> The ministry you've built up and to move on to God-knows-where?
> Maybe it doesn't seem fair.
> Maybe it doesn't even seem to make sense.
> But God is God, isn't he?
> He knows what he is doing even if you don't. Let it go when God says so."

The preacher had everyone's attention all the way to the end. This was despite his initial doubts about his ability to carry it off.

d. A suspended story

This is beginning the sermon with a story but suspending it at the complication (Ugh!) stage. The preacher then unfolds the biblical text either deductively or inductively and concludes with the rest of the story. The second half of the story will demonstrate the central word at the Aha! stage. Here is another student's example that uses a Hong Kong drama serial to "sandwich" her exposition of Exodus 6:2–9. This is about God's reassurance to Moses that God will deliver the Israelites despite Pharaoh's escalating oppression. Her word from the Lord: "Follow God's plan because it is greater than what we can see."

> Have you seen this Hong Kong TV drama? (Shows picture on PowerPoint.) I like this show very much. It is about two lawyers who want to help the poor establish an NGO (non-governmental organization) in their neighborhood. The area is Sham Shui Po, which is the area I grew up in.
>
> The main plot is about an apparently kindhearted tycoon who is actually exploiting the poor through devious means. Two lawyers, Law and Wong, try to find evidence to bring the tycoon to justice, but the tycoon always manages to use his wealth to bend the rules.
>
> In fact, the tycoon gets the two justice-fighters into trouble, and Law is arrested and detained in jail. Wong loses hope in the legal

system, which seems to have been reduced to a tool manipulated by the rich and powerful. There seems to be no justice at all. Although this is just a TV drama, the struggle that it depicts is very real to people in Hong Kong.

(The preacher then transitions to injustice experienced by the Israelites in Exodus 6 and expounds on the person of God and the promises of God. Her deductive outline:

1. Follow God's plan because it begins with the person of God.

2. Follow God's plan because it ends with the purpose of God.

She then returns to the rest of the TV drama.)

Remember the TV show I was telling you about at the beginning of the sermon? I was saying that when Law was in detention, Wong had become disillusioned with the legal system. In the midst of this despair, there is a moving scene. Though Law was in detention, he encouraged Wong saying, "Even though our legal system is imperfect, we should never give up our conviction to do justice. If we don't want the legal system to merely become a tool of the rich and powerful, we must protect it at all cost."

I was deeply convicted by this secular lawyer's unwavering sense of justice despite suffering a miscarriage of justice himself. As Christians and servants of God, should we not have much more trust in our God, despite the injustice of this world and the failings of the church? Can we not trust that God's plan is greater than what we can see? Will you follow God's plan no matter what?

Concluding a suspended story is like an *inclusio*: It gives a satisfying sense of closure and affirms the central word. The only part missing in the above sermon is the denouement of the two lawyers in the drama serial (i.e. the Unfolding or Yeah! stage of Lowry's homiletical plot), but this aptly reflects the angst of the Israelite slaves in Exodus 6. The hearers are left in the same dilemma – Would we follow God no matter what?

Conclusion

We have learned about deductive and inductive forms, but Greidanus warns against forcing these forms on the passage, lest one twists the meaning and intent of the text to fit the forms. He recommends looking for the form in the text itself, and we will turn to this in the next chapter.

7

Shaping the Skeleton III: Textual Forms

A. Why Textual Forms?

When Jesus pronounced "Blessed are the poor in Spirit," Craddock cautions that we are not to preach it as "We must be poor in spirit" because that is mutating a blessing into a command. The Beatitudes are not about doing but realizing our condition and trusting in God. Similarly, Greidanus notes that a narrative text should be preached narratively, a lament ought to guide the tone and mood of the sermon, and a teaching should be didactic in character. The point is not "slavish imitation of the form of the text, but such respect for the textual form that its spirit is not violated by the sermonic form."[1]

However, Craddock also reminds the preacher of his pastoral consideration: Does the function of the text serve the present need of the congregation?[2] A judgment oracle may be too harsh for a committed and struggling congregation. The empathetic preacher can re-shape it as an assurance of the character of God rather than as an indictment against human behavior. Conversely, if one is preaching from a comforting text but the congregation is dull and apathetic, then a more subversive form is called for. For example, if preaching the Beatitudes to nominal Christians, one might consider the opposites of the Beatitudes as a description of modern day Christians.

---

1. Craddock, *Preaching*, 178–179; Greidanus, *Modern Preacher*, 154.
2. Craddock, *Preaching*, 180.

Recognizing the textual forms enables one to preach the text with integrity. A second advantage is the variety available to the preacher. Long notes that "no one form is adequate to display the fullness of the gospel."[3] The third benefit is that uncovering the form of the text presents one with a ready-made sermon outline. In this chapter, I will look at four biblical genres and forms: prophetic literature, apocalyptic literature, psalms, and epistles. The narratives (Old Testament, New Testament, parables) have been covered in the preceding chapter on inductive forms. Greidanus has a more extensive discussion on textual forms in his book, *The Modern Preacher and The Ancient Text*.

B. How to Shape Textual Forms

1. Prophetic Literature

The historical context is indispensable in understanding the relevance of a prophetic book. The prophet was not just informing his audience about what will happen in the future, but his immediate commission was to deliver a word of warning or comfort to his contemporaries. Therefore, it is when we understand the political-cultural milieu of the prophet that we will be able to draw analogies between the issues then and now.

The prophetic literature contains many forms such as reports, speeches, and prayers. Prophetic speeches in turn contain different kinds of oracles, such as judgment or salvation speeches, each with their own subtypes. A judgment speech can take the form of a covenant lawsuit, which takes on the imagery of a court trial (e.g. Mic 6:1–2). It may also take the form of a funeral dirge in which the prophet laments over the people as if they have already died (e.g. Amos 5:1–2). The impact of these forms would be felt if the preacher delivers the sermon according to their modern versions (i.e. a court trial or a funeral service).

I was invited to preach on Amos 6, which contained a *hoy* oracle. Amos 6:1, "Alas (*hoy*) those who are at ease in Zion, and those who feel secure on Mount Samaria, the notables of the first of the nations, to whom the house of Israel resorts!" The exclamation *hoy* is distinguished from *'oy* (woe). While *'oy* is used in a context of lament over death or destruction, *hoy* is a calling to

---

3. Long, *Witness of Preaching*, 135.

someone to get his attention.[4] It is better translated as "hey you" and usually used in a warning to those who are complacent about their sin and the coming consequences. It has a three-part structure:

1. Attention: Amos calls the attention of the idle rich (Amos 6:1–5)
2. Indictment: He charges them with apathy over the ruin of others (Amos 6:6)
3. Consequence: They will be taken into exile (Amos 6:7)

The word from the Lord for my sermon was "Do not live for materialism," and I followed the structure of the *hoy* oracle. The oracle itself has an inductive form, pandering to the audience's sense of self-importance, while questioning it at the same time. It is only at the end of the oracle that an ironic judgment is pronounced: Those who think they are first will be the first to go into exile. Because I was new to the congregation, I did not want to come across in an accusatory manner, so instead of speaking directly as Amos to "you" the congregation, I used the third person "they." This works rhetorically as an overheard conversation until it dawns on the hearers that they are the ones being described.

Attention: God addresses those who pursue materialism.
I draw the analogy between elite Israelites and materialistic Singaporeans.

Indictment: God accuses those who do not care about the needs of others.
I draw analogies between the needy in Israel and the needy in our community whom we have overlooked.

Consequence: God is warning us that everything will pass away.
Just as the Israelites lost everything in the exile, our wealth will also pass away, if not now, then at death or the *eschaton*.

This is an appropriate outline for a well-off congregation that is mainly concerned about their worldly careers and ambitions. For a congregation that is already committed to serving God but that might need a bigger vision of what God is calling them to do, the central word and outline can be modified. The word from the Lord may be to care for the needy. I would then preach

---

4. F. Brown, S. Driver, and C. Briggs, *A Hebrew and English Lexicon of the Old Testament* (Oxford: Clarendon Press, 1907), 222.

the first and third points first (Attention and Consequence). The question can then be asked what is wrong with wealth and why God punishes the rich so severely. The final answer would focus on indictment, that is, the failure to care for the needy. The audience can then be challenged to care for those God cares about, and in fact, to emulate Amos in speaking up for social justice. Pastoral consideration can help tweak a textual outline to convey God's particular word to a particular congregation.

2. Apocalyptic Literature

I once heard a sermon on Daniel 7, which belongs to the latter apocalyptic half of the book. There was the vision of the four beasts that represent the worldly empires until one like the son of man came with the clouds of heaven and was presented to the Ancient One. "To him was given dominion and glory and kingship, that all people, nations, and languages should serve him. His dominion is an everlasting dominion that shall not pass away, and his kingship is one that shall never be destroyed" (Dan 7:14). The young preacher then used this verse to speak of how God's people should establish Christ's kingdom on earth through evangelism, social justice, and ecological responsibility. Great applications, except for one problem – this is not what the text is about!

The apocalyptic genre conveys the message that when human kingdoms (represented by the four beasts) seem to prevail against the church, God's people must remain faithful under persecution because God is still on the throne. This is the truth revealed by apocalyptic writing. Apocalypse in Greek literally means "revelation." Therefore, the purpose of Daniel 7 is not about God's people establishing the kingdom because under an oppressive regime, there is nothing they can do – except to trust in God's ultimate victory.

At another time, one of my Singaporean students was assigned to preach on Daniel 10, as was mentioned in chapter 3 on Exegesis. In this chapter, Daniel was overcome by a vision of an angel that was sent to him in answer to his prayer. The apocalyptic genre uses angelic messengers to show the spiritual reality behind earthly events. The message (in Dan 11) was that despite the massacring rampage of the Seleucid emperor Antiochus Epiphanes IV against Jerusalem in the second century BCE, God is still in control and will triumph in the end. The word from the Lord for his sermon was, "Trust God because he is on top of it all when things go wrong." He used an inductive-deductive outline:

| Inductive: | Illustration about how things work behind the scene even though we are unaware of it. |
| Deductive: | 1. What you must know: God is on top of it all when things go wrong. |

        a. In the biblical context

        b. In today's context

    2. What you must do: Trust God by prayer and fasting.

        a. In the biblical context

        b. In today's context

The two deductive points follow an "indicative-imperative" form (what you must know – what you must do), and the subpoints have a then/today comparison. This is, of course, not the form of Daniel 10, which is a vision report in response to Daniel's prayer. But because this is a complex text, the deductive outline helps to convey the function of the apocalyptic genre.

However, if this sermon were to be preached to a persecuted church, then it may serve the congregation better to preach it according to the structure of the vision report in Daniel 10:

1. Prayer (10:1–4)
2. Angelic vision (10:5–11)
3. Assurance
4. Angelic explanation (10:12–19)
5. Assurance

To integrate this with the contemporary context, one can employ what Long calls a "flashback" form (today/then/back to today).[5] The word from the Lord could be "Stay strong in times of persecution."

1. Prayer (10:1–4)
   a. Persecution today
   b. Persecution then
2. Angelic Vision: Stay strong in God's presence (10:5–11)
   a. Assurance then
   b. Assurance today

---

5. Long, *Witness of Preaching*, 167.

3. Angelic Vision: Stay strong in God's peace (10:12–19)
    a. Assurance then
    b. Assurance today

This is a more inductive approach because the answer climaxes at the end. The preacher begins by giving voice to the congregation's troubles. The sermon delivers a hard truth that God may not deliver the people from persecution, but God is nonetheless with them. As the sermon takes the hearers through the angelic encounter, the aim is that they may hear God's assurance afresh for themselves.

3. Psalms

The Psalter contains many genres such as thanksgiving, lament, praise, wisdom, messianic psalms. Understanding the form of each type of psalm will provide the structure of the sermon, and I will give two examples based on the praise and lament forms.

A praise psalm consists of two key elements: Calls to praise and reasons for praise. There are usually a few categories of reasons for praising God: God's creation, God's character, God's kingship, and God's acts in history. A careful attention to the overall structure of the psalm will also provide further insights into its arrangement. For instance, in Psalm 100, there are two calls to praise that divide the psalm into two halves.

1. Call to praise to all the earth (100:1–2)
2. Reasons for praise: God is our Creator and Provider (100:3)
3. Call to praise in God's temple (100:4)
4. Reason for praise: God's character of goodness, love, faithfulness (100:5)

As can be seen from the above, the textual outline is already a sermon outline and only needs explanations and illustrations.

It is often supposed that praise psalms make up the majority in the Psalter, but that is a mistaken notion. The predominant genre is actually the lament psalm, and it is my lament that we do not use them enough. In our everyday lives, Christians face all kinds of struggles and setbacks in our homes, offices, schools, and even church. But when we turn up in church on Sunday, we are expected to stuff all that aside (or worse, inside), put on a smile, and praise God as a good Christian. That is not real spirituality; it is pseudo-spirituality.

Real spirituality is being honest with God about our questions, doubts, depression, and anger. The lament psalms show us the way to be honest so that we can eventually encounter God. The structure of the lament psalm usually includes all or some of these elements:

1. Complaints about God, enemies, and self
2. Call for help
3. Confession of sin or a contention of innocence
4. Curse of enemies
5. Confidence in God and reasons for such confidence
6. Celebration expressed as a vow of thanksgiving

The lament psalm also works like an inductive form where trouble is first expressed but culminates with an affirmation of faith and thanksgiving. It will not do therefore to preach the psalms in a piecemeal way because one will lose its natural movement towards resolution. It is as we stay with the psalm and express all our emotional dregs that we come to a point of throwing ourselves upon God. And that is the turning point of faith. All forty-two lament psalms bring the reader to this turning point; all, that is, except for Psalm 88, which also reflects the reality of human experience in that we do not always see the light at the end of the tunnel. Nonetheless, the very step of turning to God in prayer, even when one despairs that God will hear and answer, is already an act of faith. Below is a structural analysis of Psalm 13 that I have used for a sermon:

1. Complaints to God (13:1–2)
   a. about God's delay
   b. about the psalmist's despair
   c. about his enemies' disdain
2. Call for help (13:3–4)
   – based on the psalmist's personal relationship with God
3. Confidence in God (13:5)
   – based on God's steadfast love and salvation
4. Celebration (13:6)
   – because God will surely deal bountifully with the psalmist

4. Epistles

An epistle may also be made up of several rhetorical structures such as repetition, *inclusio*, chiasm, climax, diatribe (an imaginary debate with an opponent), hymns, doxologies, prayers, antithesis, and metaphor.[6] Craddock uses 1 Corinthians 11:17–34 on the subject of the Lord's Supper for an example. Here, Paul raises a problem: "I hear that there are divisions among you." He then responds with a solution that is both theological and practical. This problem/solution (or trouble/grace) form can be just as relevant and useful for a sermon today.[7]

Epistles are letters to congregations that usually address some specific issues, whether doctrinal or ethical. Long suggests that the sermon might likewise be composed as a letter addressed to the contemporary congregation. "This form is especially effective in evoking the sense of personal address and in disclosing the affective dimensions of the gospel."[8] Below is the outline of a sermon by an Indonesian student who preached on Philippians 3 as if he were the apostle Paul, but addressing the present rather than the past congregation. This calls for a then/today approach within his textual outline. To keep the sermon clear, the main points were stated in a deductive manner. The word from the Lord was to keep on serving Christ in whatever circumstances you face.

- 3:1–11 Keep on serving Christ by giving up all things for him.
    - a. What this meant for Paul and the Philippians
    - b. What this means for the hearers
- 3:12–14 Keep on serving Christ by depending on him for all things.
    - a. What this meant for Paul and the Philippians
    - b. What this means for the hearers
- 3:15–17 Keep on serving Christ by serving together.
    - a. What this meant for Paul and the Philippians
    - b. What this means for the hearers

This novel approach caught the hearers' attention from the time he started with "This morning, I would like to invite you to open your hearts and listen to what I have to say to you pastors-to-be. I, Paul, exhort you to keep on serving

---

6. Greidanus, *Modern Preacher*, 319–323.
7. Craddock, *Preaching*, 180.
8. Long, *Witness of Preaching*, 168.

Christ in whatever circumstances you face." However, some congregations may not be used to such an approach and may either be confused or even offended, thinking that the preacher is trying to arrogate Paul's authority to himself. The speaker needs to check the context he is in and consider whether it is helpful to give some preliminary explanation. He might say that he wants the hearers to know what it's like for the Philippians to receive a letter from Paul, especially when the apostle was in prison suffering for the gospel and for them. He could then ask the congregation to imagine that he was Paul writing a letter to uplift them in their present situation, just as he sought to hearten the Philippians.

Conclusion

In the last three chapters, we have looked at the deductive, inductive, and textual forms as guides to shaping the skeleton of a sermon. In Part III, we will build the body on the skeletal form.

Part III

Building the Body

8

The Digestive System: Explanations (What?)

A. Why Explain?

Now that you have shaped the skeleton, it's time to build the body. Using the analogy of the human anatomy, the usual three parts of a deductive sermon – explanation, illustration, and application – may be compared to three main body systems – the digestive, nervous, and muscular systems respectively. This will be clear as we discuss the purpose of each part of the sermon.

Robinson argues that to develop a thought, one must do one or more of three things: explain it, prove it, or apply it.[1] These are in response to three questions: What does it mean? Is it true? What difference does it make? Although Robinson was applying these three questions to the exegetical task, they are also helpful guidelines for developing the sermon content. Chapell is also a proponent of these three developmental parts of a sermon, which he suggests may be varied according to the needs and interests of different congregations:

> Youth pastors typically swell the illustrative component of their sermons and drive application behind a few well-chosen explanatory points. . . . Blue-collar congregations often desire solid explanation whose relevance is spelled out more fully in down-to-earth application. . . . When professionals and management types dominate a congregation . . . it may be

---

1. Robinson, *Biblical Preaching*, 50.

important to package explanation in such a way that application becomes largely self-evident.[2]

Nonetheless, Chapell emphasizes that there should be a good mix of the three parts to cater to the congregation and to appeal to the different aspects of a person. He says, "It is often helpful to think that explanations prepare the mind, illustrations prepare the heart, and applications prepare the will to obey God."[3] While that is generally true, it is an oversimplification because explanations, illustrations, and applications can be both logically convincing as well as emotionally motivating.

A typical deductive sermon outline is shown below, using Robinson's questions reduced to just one word (in typical Singlish, which is a mix of English with local dialects and languages):

1. First main point
    - a. What?   Explanation
    - b. Really?   Illustration
    - c. So?   Application
2. Second main point
    - a. What?   Explanation
    - b. Really?   Illustration
    - c. So?   Application
3. Third main point
    - a. What?   Explanation
    - b. Really?   Illustration
    - c. So?   Application

I likened explanation to the digestive system because the preacher is feeding the congregation with the word of God. This is a non-negotiable step in the sermon because nutrition, health, and growth come from God's truth and not just from human wisdom. It is the Spirit-inspired Scripture that gives life, not pop psychology or positive thinking. Listening to the sermons of some popular speakers, both local and global, can be alarming. One verse might be cited at the beginning of a sermon, sometimes a verse that has been ripped out of its context, and then used as a spring-board to a remotely related point, with the original verse left forgotten. The congregation survives on a

---

2. Chapell, *Christ-Centered Preaching*, 91.
3. Ibid., 92.

hodgepodge of experiences, testimonies, and the motivational rhetoric of a charismatic speaker. The people may be all hyped up, but then one gets high on sugar too – the sermon tastes good but proves to be only empty calories. Explaining the meat of the text provides the essential nutrients for the church to grow healthily so that she can fulfill her God-given mission.

Progressing from "What?" to "Really?" is to move the congregation from understanding the text to a conviction of its truth. Proving the truth can be compared to activating the body's nervous system – the brain, the spinal cord, and the nerves. The preacher needs to appeal to both the left and right hemispheres of the brain so that hearers are convinced both rationally (Yes, I understand) and emotionally (Yes, I'm motivated to respond). The nerves will then fire off the message to the body to act. It is when we are convicted of the truth in our minds and hearts that it becomes not just a principle but a passion in our lives, innervating our will to act. So, the nervous system is what activates the muscles to perform the desired actions, leading to the third part of the sermon.

The link between sermon application and the muscular system is obvious, for the muscles are what move the body. As had been spelled out in the first two chapters, preaching (as heralding, teaching, exhorting, and witnessing) is aimed towards a response from the hearers. To miss this is to truncate the pulpit ministry. It is to bring people to the threshold of encountering God and failing to open the door to usher them in. What I mean by application is not a packing list of do's and don'ts to send the congregation off with. Such a list may provide helpful guidelines, but application fundamentally means to do what the Lord calls, out of a relationship with him. It may mean to believe and rest or repent, it may be recalibrating one's values or attitudes, and then working out those implications during the rest of the week as the Spirit prompts.

In this chapter, we will focus on how to explain the text meaningfully. The next two chapters will then give guidelines on using illustrations to prove the text and on making relevant practical applications.

B. How to Explain?

Here are four guidelines when explaining the text: Explain the problematic, explain the passage, explain to the people, and explain the perspectives.

1. Explain the Problematic

If the text raises a question in the minds of the listeners, the preacher should remove that stumbling block so that people can focus on what the text is about. For example, in my sermon on Luke 9:57–62, Jesus gave a startling response to a would-be follower: "Let the dead bury their own dead; but as for you, go and proclaim the kingdom of God." This is problematic to an Asian audience brought up on filial piety and therefore needs explanation (cf. ch. 3 on Exegesis). Of course, the preacher needs to keep such explanations to the point and not detract from the main sermonic thrust. When the bone of contention has been extracted, the preacher can challenge the people to consider what excuses they themselves are giving for not fulfilling God's commission.

2. Explain the Passage

Explaining the text is based on the preacher's exegetical work. The following framework may be used as a guideline when considering what to explain for each main point of the sermon.

1. First main point
   a. Explanation
      i. Historical context (cultural, political, geographical, religious)
      ii. Literary context (of the chapter or book)
      iii. Genre, form, and structure
      iv. Language (grammar, syntax, or word study)
      v. Theological context

The preacher is not expected to fill in all the categories of explanation or to do so in the exact same order. Rather, choose what is relevant for giving the congregation deeper insights. The central word still controls the whole sermon, so choose exegetical explanations that best fit the emphases of the sermon. You are preaching a word from the Lord, not delivering an academic lecture, much less showing off your intellectual ability or exegetical hard work. One fact may well be sufficient to bring home the main point, or perhaps two, but I would think not more than three. If a sermon has three explanatory subpoints for each of the three main points, then the congregation would have already reached the point of satiation or slumber.

For examples of explanations, I will use Psalm 23 as a case in point. In my first main point about a God who provides, I contrasted our idea of a modern shepherd with that in the Bible. An urban congregation may think of shepherds seen on television or in New Zealand, but these ranchers of flocks of thousands are a far cry from the ancient shepherd in Palestine. As told in Jesus's parables, the shepherd in biblical times looked after only about a hundred sheep, each of which he knew by name. The sheep were totally dependent on the shepherd for food, protection, and survival. This is why Psalm 23 is about a God who cares for us personally. For my second main point about a God who protects, I explained that in the ancient Near Eastern culture, the shepherd's rod and staff are metaphors for the mace and scepter of a king. Therefore, it is not just a rustic shepherd that protects us through the valley of the shadow of death, but it is the divine king himself. The third main point about a God who pursues us is based on a linguistic explanation of verse 6, commonly translated as "Surely goodness and mercy shall follow me all the days of my life . . ." The word "follow" is the Hebrew *radaf*, which is almost always used to describe an enemy army in hot pursuit of another army. Hence it is better translated as "pursue" (which is found in the *Tanakh*, an English translation of the Old Testament by the Jewish Publication Society). In the context of the psalm, this gives an ironic reversal of the situation that the psalmist finds himself in – instead of being persecuted by his enemies, God is the one who pursues him with steadfast love. Explaining this linguistic fact gives a stronger assurance of God's determination to care for us.

3. Explain to the People

Preachers need to explain the passage in a way that is relevant to our modern day context so that hearers will grasp it better. One way to do this is to draw parallels between the text and our contemporary situation. I gave the example of a student's sermon on Amos 8 in previous chapters. He wanted to show the similarities between the economic prosperity of Israel during Amos' time and modern day Singapore. He did so by describing the ancient context in current economic terms:

> I mean, Israel was doing really well in Amos time: economic prosperity from international trade, regional peace with neighbors, high net worth individuals, good class bungalows

made of ivory along Sentosa,[4] I mean Samaria, vibrant religious activity. Sound familiar?

In a sermon on Amos 6, I used the opposite approach. Instead of describing the biblical context in modern terms, I compared our current context to the background of the text. After explaining the hedonistic carousings listed by Amos, I pointed out that we in Singapore are just as obsessed with our 5 Cs – namely, our Car, Cash, Credit card, Condo and Country club. In fact, that is already passé because we have upgraded to the 5 Bs – BMW, Billionaire, Bank, Bungalow, and being the Boss.

Besides drawing comparisons between then and now, the preacher can think of using an analogy from nature, science, history, literature, or other spheres of life. This overlaps with the next chapter on illustrations, but an analogy can explain the text by comparing the unfamiliar with something more familiar to the hearers. When preaching on Isaiah 9:1–6, for example, I used an analogy to explain the role of the Wonderful Counselor. Listeners today think of "counselor" as a psychotherapist. He is there to listen to your problems and give you emotional support and encouragement. Such a profession would be foreign to the ancient mind. Rather, a word study of "counselor" in the Hebrew Bible indicates that this refers to the king's court counselors who advise the king on political, military, and other national matters. This is a straightforward explanation, but it doesn't mean much to the hearers. I then used an analogy from our Asian history that people are more familiar with – famous Chinese military strategists such as Sun Tze (544–496 BC) and Zhu Ge Liang (AD 181–234). In fact, Sun Tze's *Art of War* is now ubiquitously applied in the business world. To flesh out this analogy, I cited some specific military tactics they used that made the difference between victory and defeat. Such analogies convey the assurance of what it means to have God as our Wonderful Counselor when we face seemingly insurmountable challenges.

One can also highlight the limit of analogies because no one thing is exactly like another, especially when it comes to the person of God. Despite their brilliance, Sun Tze and Zhu Ge Liang could not control all the variables of life and war, such as terrain, weather, people, or their own death. Only God is the wonder-working Counselor.

---

4. Sentosa is a small leisure island at the southern tip of Singapore where the most expensive private property is located.

4. Explain the Perspectives

Because preachers are focusing on one text in an expository sermon, it is often not possible to cover a controversial topic comprehensively. Therefore, we need to make it clear that we are giving only one perspective and that there are other considerations for a holistic understanding. This is what I have discussed earlier regarding biblical theology in chapter 3 on Exegesis. One, of course, does not have the time to explain everything in a sermon, but one can point towards the larger canon for further study so that hearers do not stumble over what we say or leave with a lop-sided theology.

Robinson gives the example of the baptism of the Holy Spirit in 1 Corinthians 12:13. One needs to be aware of different assumptions that the congregation may have. Non-charismatics may be uncomfortable and think that it entails speaking in tongues and unusual experiences, even though the Corinthian text focuses on unity. On the other hand, charismatics may assume all the outward signs but miss the larger message of the Pauline text. Robinson suggests that the preacher may need to devote some time in the sermon to clarifying what is meant by baptism of the Holy Spirit even though Paul did not have to.[5]

Another controversial subject is that of healing. If you are preaching on a healing narrative, it is important to explain some hermeneutical principles. First, explain the purpose of the miracle in its context. Is it a promise that all will be healed, or is it for a specific historical purpose, such as to show the authority of Jesus and that the kingdom has come? Second, point to the context of the larger canon. There were also occasions when faithful Christians were not healed such as Timothy, Trophimus, and even Paul himself (1 Tim 5:23; 2 Tim 4:20; Gal 4:13). Third, be aware of broader theological considerations. In terms of New Testament theology, the kingdom of God has come but not yet; the full consummation will be at the *eschaton*. Therefore, healing is available but not guaranteed till Christ comes again. So, in the meantime, we ask and pray, believing that God can graciously heal (Jas 4:2; Luke 15:12–13). But we do not demand how and when God should heal. This is a topic that has generated many shelves of popular and academic books and would require at least a whole sermon, if not an entire series, for further discussion. But a few basic guidelines go a long way in educating the congregation towards a mature understanding.

---

5. Robinson, *Biblical Preaching*, 52.

C. Concluding Examples

Below are two sample outlines with explanations consolidated from the foregoing discussion and from chapter 3 on Exegesis. Most of the exegetical matters have already been explained and will not be further elaborated unless necessary. The first is an Old Testament sermon on Psalm 23, and the second is from the New Testament text of Luke 9.

Psalm 23 The God Who Cares for You

Word from the Lord: Come to God because he cares for you personally

1. Come to God because he provides for your needs (23:1–3).

    Explanation of historical background: A contrast between modern rancher and biblical shepherd.

2. Come to God because he protects you from evil (23:4–5).

    a. Explanation of genre: A trust psalm expresses trust in the midst of trouble.

    b. Explanation of historical background: A shepherd is used as a metaphor for a king in the ancient Near Eastern culture.

    c. Explanation of theological context: Although Psalm 23 describes God's protection and victory over enemies, this does not mean that a Christian never experiences suffering or defeat, but God is with us and will ultimately vindicate us.

3. Come to God because he pursues you with goodness and love (23:6).

    Explanation of language: The Hebrew *radaf* is better translated as "pursue" rather than "follow," conveying God's firm intention to bless us.

Luke 9:56–62 Crazy Discipleship

Word from the Lord: Give up all to follow Jesus because of who he is.

1. Give up your possessions because Jesus provides (Luke 9:57–58).

    Explanation of literary context: In the context of Luke 9:10–17 on the feeding of the 5,000, a follower can trust in Jesus's provision.

2. Give up your priorities because Jesus has all authority (Luke 9:59–60).

   a. Explanation of historical context: In the light of Jewish two-stage burial customs, Jesus is not against filial piety.

   b. Explanation of literary context: In the context of Luke 9:34–35 on the transfiguration, a follower is called to give up his temporal pursuits to follow the authority of God's Son.

3. Give up your concerns because Jesus cares (Luke 9:61–62).

   a. Explanation of theological context: In view of other texts (e.g. 1 Tim 5:8), Jesus is not against familial concerns.

   b. Explanation of literary context: In the context of Luke 9:37–42 on the deliverance of the demon-possessed boy, a follower is called to entrust his family to God.

In the expository outline on the Lucan passage, I have made only one cross reference to another text (i.e. 1 Tim 5:8), and that was to explain a truth in its broader theological context. Preachers should avoid excessive cross referencing unless it is absolutely necessary for making the text clearer, otherwise it is simply explaining a text with another text taken out of its context, which may simply be a poor case of proof-texting. Referring to other verses may not make a point any clearer to the listeners, and may, in fact, clutter their attention. I suspect that preachers who pad up a message with cross references have not paid enough exegetical attention to the text at hand and are covering up that deficiency by appearing to have a breadth of biblical knowledge.

Now that you have explained the text and what it means, the preacher will have to anticipate the questions, "Really?" "Is it true?" Having heard the explanations of Psalm 23 and Luke 9, the hearers may still wonder whether God's promises still hold true for us today. This is dealt with in the next chapter on Illustrations.

9

The Nervous System: Illustrations (Really?)

A. Why Illustrations?

I once met a pastor who did not believe in using stories and illustrations. His sermons offered solid explanations and went straight to applications. I suggested that he use illustrations to move the sermon from the head to the heart of the congregation, but he said that he wanted to immerse the hearers in the biblical world and not let stories distract them from the text. I guess this was a reaction to shallow emotive sermons that had caused problems for the church in the past. However, hearers only ended up with a maze of theological doctrines and intellectual principles. As faithful Christians, they very much wanted to live in the kingdom of God but felt confounded by their inability to do so. The pastor was a capable exegete and a caring shepherd, but I felt that his flock might appreciate some succulent grass from time to time in their steady diet of dry hay.

My response was to point out that Jesus was not above telling stories and parables. But the pastor saw his task as expounding biblical stories rather than telling new ones. If so, then those stories should be experienced inductively as stories and not as dry theses. If preaching is also witnessing, then a faithful witness reproduces the effect of biblical stories. A witness also shares about what God has done in one's own life or what one has seen God doing in other people's lives. Just because an inept cook has put too much salt into a dish does not mean that one should not put any salt in at all. Rather, if the herald-preacher is to represent God, then he should be like God who reveals himself through the stories or illustrations in the Bible.

Christianity is distinctive because we worship a monotheistic Trinitarian God who relates to us personally. God does not reveal himself through a set of propositions or a series of commandments and rituals. He relates to us as we relate to our family and friends, and thus, much of the Bible contains the interactions between God and his people. Theologian Alistair McGrath states that "Narrative is the main literary type found in Scripture." David Larsen surmises that 75 percent of the Old Testament is narrative, and besides the Gospels and Acts in the New Testament, Thomas Liske points out that Paul's doctrinal exposition alludes to the history of Israel, the arena, the sports field, the military, the market place, the temple, the home, and the school.[1]

It has been said that everything on earth reminded Jesus of heaven, which is why he could draw so many analogies between ordinary life and the kingdom of heaven. In fact, W. E. Sangster said that with the example of Jesus before us, "Only a combination of vanity and blasphemy could convince a man that the matter was beneath his notice."[2] Christ has come not to be theologized about but to be personally encountered. This needs to be conveyed through how we preach. Are we only making propositional statements as if God is a topic to be lectured on, or do we also invite people into a relationship with God through stories?

Stott notes that throughout the history of preaching in the church, there have always been records of the use of illustrations. This is evidenced by collections of *exempla* for preachers (forerunners of the modern "treasury of sermon illustrations" that are now available on the Internet). It was because these *exempla* became used both as vehicles of false teaching and as substitutes for serious biblical exposition that John Wycliff and his band of preachers determined to concentrate exclusively on the text of Scripture, a path followed by the Reformers.[3] It is not, therefore, that stories are wrong in themselves, but it is when they overshadow the authority of the Bible that they become a problem.

Preachers, therefore, need a clear understanding of the role of illustrations and how to use them. Essentially, they help us to answer the listeners'

---

1. Alistair E. McGrath, "The Biography of God," *Christianity Today* (22 July 1991): 23; David Larsen, *Anatomy of Preaching: Identifying the Issues in Preaching Today* (Grand Rapids, MI: Baker, 1989), 90; Thomas V. Liske, *Effective Preaching*, 2nd ed. (New York: Macmillan, 1960), 185.
2. W. E. Sangster, *The Craft of the Sermon* (London: Epworth, 1954), 211.
3. Stott, *I Believe in Preaching*, 237–238.

question, *Is it true?*[4] I will break this question down into two aspects: First, is it true for a fact? This is answered cognitively with Aristotle's *logos*, using facts, figures, or logic. It lays the foundation for a hearing, but it may not lead to a personal commitment. The second aspect of the question is, "Is it true for us today?" and is answered by testimonies that demonstrate the preached truth in people's lives. According to Aristotle, hearers are more convinced by the *pathos* of such personal and emotional reality than they are by factual *logos*. In preaching, we prove and persuade using both facts and experience.

1. Prove by Facts

Scientific facts, mathematical statistics, and philosophical logic can be part of the preacher's factual illustrations. In a sermon on Psalm 100, I expounded on verse 3 that says, "Know that the LORD is God. It is he that made us, and we are his; we are his people, and the sheep of his pasture." Here is a praise of God as our Creator and Provider. To prove the power of God as Creator, I discussed a 1953 experiment conducted by Stanley Miller, who claimed that life was created by spontaneous chemical reactions. He passed electrical sparks through a mixture of gases and found that amino acids, the building blocks of protein that make up all organisms, were produced from the reaction. However, his experiment produced a mixture of both left-handed and right-handed amino acids. But only left-handed amino acids make up organic life, and there is no natural way to separate the two types of amino acids. In fact, the presence of right-handed amino acids is detrimental to life. So, it takes the power of God rather than random chemical reactions to create life. This same God who created and ordered the amino acids of life is also the same One who takes care of us.

If I wanted to demonstrate the power of God in delivering people from sin and violence, I could turn to various psychological or sociological studies and statistics. For example, a 2005 American study shows that prison inmates expressing belief in a higher power are 73 percent far less likely than those who do not believe to be involved in a fight. A 2011 study found that those participating in religious services were less likely to engage in deviant behavior.[5]

---

4. Robinson, *Biblical Preaching*, 53–57.
5. Andrew S. Denney and Richard Tewksbury, "Motivations and the Need for Fulfillment of Faith-Based Halfway House Volunteers," *Justice Policy Journal* 10, no. 1 (2013): 3–4.

When citing facts, preachers should maintain their credibility by checking the research and not just cite opinions. Numbers are also clearer when rounded up and compared to familiar objects.[6] For example, Goliath's height of 6 feet 9 inches in the Septuagint is the height of an average American NBA basketball player. The Chinese player Yao Ming was one of the tallest NBA players at 7 feet 7 inches. However, if we take the Hebrew Bible's record of Goliath's height at 9 feet 9 inches, then he would be about three heads taller than Yao Ming. This will give a visual idea of his fear-inspiring size.[7]

Sometimes a proof is based on logical arguments. If I wanted to prove the resurrection of Christ, I would have to address the purported theory that his disciples stole the body (Matt 28:11–15). One can demolish this notion by pointing out that the disciples had nothing to gain but everything to lose by claiming that Jesus rose from the dead. For preaching the resurrection, they were ridiculed, persecuted, and eventually martyred (except for John who was sent into exile). People might be willing to die for the truth, but it is incomprehensible that anyone would knowingly die for a lie.

All these factual arguments are useful in convincing the hearers of the veracity of your claims, but whether it moves people to respond is another matter. Besides *logos*, the second means of persuasion is *pathos*. John Reed points out that this is conveyed, first, by the preacher's enthusiastic delivery, and second, through the use of illustrations, especially by "emotion-producing narrations of human experience. In other words, dynamic storytelling can be a powerful force in moving people to the desired response."[8]

2. Persuade by Examples

Illustrations are usually compared to the windows of a house, a description used by Charles Spurgeon. To "illustrate" is to illumine (i.e. to throw light on a dark object). Spurgeon says that a building without windows is a prison not a house. But other homileticians warn about illustrations being too prominent, like windows that draw attention to themselves.[9] However, example-style

---

6. Robinson, *Biblical Preaching*, 102.
7. The question of Goliath's actual height is matter for text-critical analysis.
8. John W. Reed, "Visualizing the Big Idea: Stories That Support Rather than Steal," in *The Big Idea of Biblical Preaching*, eds. K. Willhite and S. Gibson (Grand Rapids, MI: Baker, 1998), 153–154.
9. Charles H. Spurgeon, *Lectures to My Students* (London: Marshall, Morgan & Scott, 1964), 350; Long, *Witness of Preaching*, 202.

illustrations demonstrate another vital function of windows – to look at the world outside. They offer glimpses into another reality and invite hearers to come and revel in it.

Long makes a helpful distinction between analogy-style and example-style illustrations. An analogy works like a simile by comparing a biblical concept to something that is more familiar to the hearers. Therefore, an analogy primarily creates clear and vivid understanding, as discussed in the previous chapter on Explanations. However, examples do more than clarify a thought:

> The preacher does not compare "A" and "B" but instead gives us a little slice of "A." . . . Example-style illustrations are crucial in preaching because they put flesh on theological concepts. Like analogies, they make concepts clearer but that is not their main purpose. They give the hearer a taste, a vicarious experience of the reality being present.[10]

Example-style illustrations may come from the preacher's personal experience, a third-party testimony, or a description of what life in the kingdom would look like in reality.

Stories affect people in various ways such as creating attention and establishing rapport. These two reasons are why some preachers preface their sermon with a joke. But if the joke is not relevant to the sermon, then it merely distracts the listeners, leaving them to wonder about the point of the joke. Chapell also warns that preachers who illustrate primarily to entertain ultimately destroy the foundation of their messages because "an entertainment ethic creates shallow congregations and hollow pulpits."[11]

My pastor friend who shied away from using illustrations had an intuitive understanding of the power of stories. All of us have the experience of remembering a story after a sermon but not the point that the story was meant to illustrate. Stories stay in our memories because of their emotive force, a psychological and neurological fact proven by numerous studies.[12] Rather than be wary of illustrations, the preacher should harness their affective

---

10. Long, *Witness of Preaching*, 208–209, 243.
11. Chapell, *Christ-Centered Preaching*, 179.
12. Bradley et al. "Remembering Pictures: Pleasure and Arousal in Memory," *Journal of Experimental Psychology: Learning, Memory, & Cognition* 18, no. 2 (1991): 379–390, accessed 29 December 2015; S. B. Hamann, "Cognitive and Neural Mechanisms of Emotional Memory," *Trends in Cognitive Sciences* 5, no. 9 (2001): 394–400, accessed 29 December 2015.

power for his purpose. We have heard the usual maxim that students retain 10 percent of what they hear, 30 percent of what they see, and 60 percent of what they do. In the 1970s, researchers also discovered that people learn as much from "fully described" experiences as they do from actual experiences.[13] Thus, just as modern pedagogy emphasizes learning through case studies and real world experience, so also the preacher can help his congregation learn more effectively through vicarious experiences provided by illustrations. It is opening a window and inviting people to venture outside of their box into a greater reality.

Now, it needs to be admitted that just as anecdotes are not proof of a scientific claim, neither are stories proof of a theological claim. We may share stories of healing, but that does not imply that everyone will be healed. Long says they are but "foretastes and anticipations of the new creation." He emphasizes that the promises of the gospel – forgiveness of sin, freedom from bondage, triumph over evil, reconciliation of broken relationships – are just that: promises. However, believing and trusting in these promises do make a difference in how we live now.[14] If we do not use illustrations correctly, then we are presenting a mistaken view that Christians can find full satisfaction in the life here and now. Or, we taint the gospel promises with legalism by implying that the promises may be achieved if only one had more faith, or more positive thinking, or more diligence. If such stories are presented unrealistically, they will lead to skepticism and disillusionment. But if preachers understand their rightful significance, then they are testimonies of hope, enabling us to entrust the outcome to God.

Let me give an analogy and an example to demonstrate their different functions. In explaining the sacrificial nature of God's love, I once used a story about China's massive Sichuan earthquake in 2008 that left 69,000 people dead, over 18,000 missing, 374,000 injured, and about 4.8 million people homeless. In the midst of this catastrophe, a Chinese newspaper reported that a three-month old baby boy was found alive under the rubble of a house. He had been protected by the body of his mother who had crouched over him. She had sacrificed her life for her son. While the authenticity of this news cannot be determined, it makes for what Long calls a wallop-packing

---

13. Chapell, *Christ-Centered Preaching*, 184, citing Val Byron Johnson, "A Media Selection Model for Use with a Homiletical Taxonomy" (PhD diss., Southern Illinois University at Carbondale, 1982).

14. Long, *Witness of Preaching*, 214, 213.

analogy[15] by comparing God's love to maternal love. However, it does not prove God's love *per se*. For that, I would use an example that witnesses to the reality of God's love.

This is a testimony shared by a young woman whose world was shattered at the age of 13 when she found out that her father was having an affair. Her parents continued to stay together for the sake of the children, but that did not protect her from the hurts of their constant quarrels. Her father stopped being around, leaving her with a deep sense of abandonment and insecurity. As a typical Singaporean, she compensated by striving to do well academically to get her parents' attention, but the stress of performance soon overwhelmed her. At her lowest point, she thought of ending her life. But in the midst of her pain, God met her. A friend invited her to a concert where she heard a young man share about how God has a special heart for the fatherless. She was so moved that her tears flowed uncontrollably. Having experienced God's love, she started to rebuild her life and her relationship with her father. Now grown up with a family of her own, she faces the future with hope because of the reality of God in her life. Her life example is a window that beckons hearers to enter into that experience of a relationship with God, based on the truth of the gospel.

Here are three guidelines for using an illustration appropriately: Tell it relevantly to the text, tell it relevantly to the people, and tell it relevantly to the illustration. At the end of the chapter, we will discuss how you can find your own illustrations.

B. How to Tell Illustrations?

1. Tell It Relevantly to the Text

A student was assigned to preach about the woman who anointed Jesus with an alabaster jar of costly ointment in Matthew 26:6–13. She began her sermon with a story of a couple, who instead of throwing a lavish feast for their wedding, had a simple reception and used the money to purchase a truckload of food for the poor. This is a heart-warming story, but unfortunately, it was not what the text was about. In Matthew 26:8–9, the disciples were offended by the waste of ointment and argued that it could have been better used for the poor. But Jesus rebuked them for missing the christological significance

---

15. Ibid., 205.

of the woman's act: "By pouring the ointment on my body she has prepared me for burial." The student's story was precisely what the disciples were advocating and had missed the essence of the pericope. If an illustration does not fit the text, it confuses the listeners, and if it is a particularly emotive story, it will hijack the sermon and take the interpretation of a text in the wrong direction.

The student subsequently changed her story. She told of a shabbily dressed boy who trudged several miles through the snowy streets of Chicago, determined to attend a Bible class that was conducted by D. L. Moody. When he arrived, Moody asked the boy, "Why did you come to a Sunday school so far away? Why don't you go to one of the churches near your home?" The boy answered, "Because you love a fellow over here." This story could still have gone in different directions, such as showing love to those who come to church. But the student linked the story to her focus: "Because he had found love, this boy was willing to brave the cold and the inconvenience. He was willing to go to any length to get near to God." The student has now learned to tell a story relevantly to the text, but her choice of illustration can actually be improved by observing the next guideline.

2. Tell It Relevantly to the People

The problem with the story of the boy going to Sunday school is that it contains too many elements that are foreign to a local congregation. In Southeast Asia, we do not have snow, nor do we know what Chicago is like, and not everyone would have heard of the famous American evangelist D. L. Moody. Nonetheless, the story still works because there is sufficient overlap of experience, such as going to Sunday school and receiving God's love. Robinson presents four different levels of the effectiveness of an illustration, which I discuss below.[16]

a. The most powerful illustrations are based on the common experience between the preacher and the congregation.

When gleaning for illustrations from books, or more commonly, the Internet, I advise my students to avoid those about American football or baseball, sports that mean little to Singaporeans. If a preacher wants to use

---

16. Robinson, *Biblical Preaching*, 111–112.

a sports illustration, then references to the FIFA World Cup soccer matches resonate more with Singaporeans (especially the men).

A lay preacher, who is a football fan, used the problems of the Singapore Sports Hub to illustrate Matthew 6:21: "For where your treasure is, there your heart will be also." Since October 2014, the hybrid turf of the spanking new Sports Hub had been in the headlines for its poor and sandy condition. It was a national embarrassment when Singapore hosted its first international match. This lay preacher gave his personal analysis of what went wrong. He recounted that Singapore is known globally for her efficiency, so the priority of the Sports Hub was to be a world-class facility with air-cooled seats and a massive retractable roof. "Somewhere along the line," he said, "some forgot that the stadium is about sports." He then contrasted the situation with the World Cup Football Final in Brazil held earlier in that same year:

> In the lead up to the event, the concern around the world was that the spectator stands and facilities like transport networks would not be ready in time. There were no concerns about the field. Why? Because the field is the first and most important feature when building the stadium in Brazil. When one thinks Brazil, one thinks "football," despite their humiliating 7 – 1 loss to Germany in the semi-finals that year. The heart of Brazil is football, and the heart of Singapore is efficiency. In Brazil, they laid the field first, then built the rest of the stadium around it. In Singapore, they built the stadium first, then laid the field, after completing the roof. Where your treasure is, there your heart will be also.

After the service, the congregation was talking about this sports analogy in the fellowship hall, but because it was anchored to the text through the key words "treasure" and "heart," the lesson was unmistakably embedded in the story.[17]

---

17. Chapell (*Christ-Centered Preaching*, 197), advises that "an illustration should not merely reflect the concepts of the explanation; it should echo the terminology of the explanation as well. . . . [In] an oral medium, the repetition of key terms orients the ear to what is important and ties thoughts together."

b. The second most powerful illustrations are those that come from the listeners' experience.

Robinson urges pastors of rural churches who have grown up in the city to learn as much as possible about farmers and farming if they expect to illustrate their sermons effectively for their congregation.[18] Though Singapore is a city-state, this is a principle that will serve the preacher well not only when preaching in a cross-cultural context but also when preaching to different segments of the populace. When preaching to youth, talk about the challenges of friendship, the stress of exams, or the problems of bullying. When speaking to the people in the marketplace, seek out testimonies of Christian professionals and entrepreneurs. Use illustrations that appeal to both men and women – from the sporting arena to the home, from the military to the family.

c. The third most effective illustrations are those from the preacher's experience.

In a reverse situation, Robinson points out that a minister who grew up on a farm can tell a story about delivering a calf so vividly that even a city audience can identify with it.[19] In an earlier chapter, I mentioned a Mongolian student who preached on Jonah 3 with the central idea "Arise and go in the power of God." She began with a delightful illustration about colt-racing, telling the congregation that Mongolian preschoolers would race on young horses during festivities. But to ensure that the inexperienced riders and their animals keep going in the right direction, the colts' mares would be brought to the finishing line. On hearing their mother's whinnies, the nervous and exhausted colts will muster up their strength and gallop to the end. So also, said the Mongolian preacher, when we keep our focus on God, we will have the power to arise and go. Although the Singaporean congregation was clueless about horses, they were fascinated by her account. They caught her excitement vicariously, and so the point of that analogy rode home to the listeners.

d. The fourth and least effective illustrations are those that come from outside both the preacher's and congregation's experience.

These are examples that may come from history or other cultures (like American football and baseball). The listeners may understand the illustration

---

18. Robinson, *Biblical Preaching*, 111.
19. Ibid., 112.

but not experience it. However, such illustrations can still be helpful if one can draw parallels between it and our contemporary context. I have always been drawn to the stories of nineteenth-century British evangelist George Mueller's faith in God's provision. He built five orphanages and took care of ten thousand orphans in his lifetime. The best known story is the one where God provided breakfast for three hundred orphans one morning when there was no food left in the orphanage. Mueller had sat the children at the tables and after giving thanks for the food, he simply waited. Within minutes, a baker knocked at the door with a donation of freshly baked bread. Soon, the milkman came by to donate ten large cans of milk because his cart had broken down right in front of the orphanage. It is a faith-building story but rather removed from our contemporary experience. Not many of us run orphanages or even live by faith.

However, I came across another story about Mueller in his younger days. When he told his father he wanted to be a missionary, his father was very upset and refused to give him any more money for school. Mueller went back to college, not knowing how he was going to pay for his tuition fees. He did something he thought was rather silly for a grown man to do. He got down on his knees and asked God to provide. An hour later, a professor knocked on his door and offered him a paid tutoring job. George was amazed! This was the beginning of Mueller's dependence on God.[20]

I used these two accounts in a sermon to demonstrate God's provision, and from the comments after the service, it was clear that people identified more with the second story. "That happened to me, too!" A man said to me. The second story worked better despite it being about a historical person living in a foreign land because the hearers could identify with financial worries, especially finances for higher education. The younger Mueller also came across as more of an average Christian who, like us, had doubts about prayer.

In the same vein, using a Bible story may not be a helpful illustration. Robinson points out that modern congregations do not know their Bible, and even when they do, the stories sound so long ago and far away that people do not identify with them easily.[21] The thinking is that it may have been true in biblical times, but is it true for us today? In making illustrations relevant to the people, Long reminds preachers to employ a rich variety of experiences

---

20. "George Mueller, Orphanages Built by Prayer" accessed 29 September 2015, http://www.christianity.com/church/church-history/church-history-for-kids/george-mueller-orphanages-built-by-prayer-11634869.html.

21. Robinson, *Biblical Preaching*, 112.

that congregants of different ages, genders, vocations, marital status, and life situations can identify with. This might entail using a series of illustrations or showing snapshots of different situations. Long gives an example below:[22]

> But how do we handle the problem of unanswered prayer?
>
> We pray for rain, but the drought continues.
>
> We pray for peace, but the headlines still shout of war.
>
> We pray for healing, but the dark stain remains on the x-ray.
>
> We pray for our children, and the crises continue.
>
> We pray for inner calm, but the anxiety does not diminish.
>
> We pray for light, but the shadows lengthen.
>
> How do we handle the problem of unanswered prayer?

The chances are good, says Long, that most listeners will find themselves somewhere on this list.

The preacher should also be wary of using illustrations that are limited to his own vocational experiences and perspectives. I have heard sermons where illustrations revolve around the challenges of doing ministry or about God's provision for those in the mission field. These may be suitable when speaking to seminary students, pastors, or missionaries, but when speaking to the lay people, such persistent usage will cause people to think that God may not work in and through the lives of ordinary Christians. This undermines the priesthood of all believers and the call to serve God in whatever vocation we are in.

If our examples are windows into the kingdom of God, then another consideration is that "we must be careful to ensure that this worldview reflects the life we have been given in the gospel and not merely the culture close at hand."[23] If most of our examples are about individuals wrestling with personal concerns, then we give an individualistic distortion of the faith. We will overlook the communal and social justice aspects of the gospel. If most are about family life, then we imply that singles are incomplete. If we omit children, then we undermine their value in the kingdom. Illustrations also shape the hearers' faith.

---

22. Long, *Witness of Preaching*, 219.
23. Ibid., 220.

3. Tell It Relevantly to the Illustration

Okay, so perhaps I'm trying too hard to make all my subtitles into parallel sentences, but what I mean is that a story should be told as a story to capture interest. Also, it should be expressed descriptively so that listeners can experience it vicariously.

a. Tell it narratively

The punchline of a joke is delivered only at the end, otherwise it would ruin the joke. So also, a story should build up the tension to a climax so that the resolution comes towards the end. To reveal the spoiler would turn the story into a didactic teaching and preempt the emotional impact. Lowry's narrative loop provides a useful outline to follow: Oops (Conflict), Ugh (Complication or Analysis of the problem), Aha (Resolution), and Yeah (Unfolding). In a sermon based on Isaiah 46:3-4 about God's power to deliver Israel from the Babylonian exile, I wanted to give an example of resting in God's power. I shared the story below, following Lowry's narrative outline:

> Oops: A friend shared that she was having a hard time getting her Primary One daughter to school every morning. While waiting for the school bus, the little girl would burst out crying. Despite all her mother's cajoling, she would refuse to go to school. Then her mother would start crying out of anxiety too, and the two of them ended up sobbing into their tissues by the roadside.
>
> Ugh: I asked my friend whether she prayed with her daughter before going to school. She said, "Yes, I do." I asked, "What do you pray about?" She said, "I pray that she won't be scared, or lonely, or bullied." I realized that the mom was focusing more on her problems than on God. When she got fearful, the daughter sensed it and got even more fearful herself.

Aha: I said to my friend, "Do you believe God is able to take care of your daughter and that he is more powerful than your problems?" She said, "Yes, I do." I said, "Then rest in his power. Instead of focusing on your problems, focus on God in your prayer. Say, 'I know you care for my daughter, you will be with her, you will protect her, you will watch over her.' And thank God that he will be with her." She said, "Okay, I'll try that."

Yeah: A week later, I met the mother again and asked her how things are with her daughter. She gave a big smile and said, "She stopped crying!" The mother has learned to rest in God's power.

Note that the story is linked to the text or the main point by the repetition of the call to "rest in God's power." Now, supposing I had started the story by saying that a mother helped her child to stop crying by focusing on God in her prayer. How would the congregation have responded? Probably with less engagement because the tension is lost. They might even be a little resistant because it already sounds preachy. It is stating the obvious to say that a happy ending should come right at the end, after people have identified with the desperate mom and her problem. In fact, after hearing that story, many mothers have come up to me to remark, "It's true. I would pray like that mother did." And it is not just mothers who identify with that story, but also professionals worried about their jobs, students stressed about their exams, and seniors struggling with their health. A specific story can have universal appeal, which leads us to the next point.

b. Tell it descriptively

The more specifically an incident is described, the better the congregation can identify with the experience. It would be a mistake to generalize an event to make it applicable to everyone. Something that applies to everyone will apply to no one. On the other hand, something that happened to someone could happen to anyone. "There is no such thing," says Long, "as life in general; ironically, illustrations depend upon the honest ring of particularity – *this* life, *these* circumstances – for their ability to speak powerfully to a wide range of hearers."[24] How can a preacher provide a vivid description? Two

---

24. Long, *Witness of Preaching*, 219.

techniques are particularly helpful: (1) Describe actions rather than feelings, and (2) Provide dialogue.

i. Describe actions. Chapell uses the parable of the prodigal son as an example (Luke 15:20–24). "But while he was still a long way off, his father saw him and was filled with compassion for him." How does the audience know that the father was filled with compassion? The next line tells us – "He ran to his son, threw his arms around him and kissed him." A few simple actions portrayed the father's love and forgiveness. Craddock warns against using too many adjectives that coerce the listeners' response rather than evoke their emotions.[25] To exaggerate a description would make it lose its everyday realism. It is not necessary, for example, to say that the father was so filled with compassion that his heart felt like bursting or that a dark oppressive sense of grief was lifted from him. It is the scene of the father's actions that moved the listeners. As they say, "Show, don't tell."

Using the usual questions of who, what, why, when, where, which, and how can help us better depict a scene. For example, my previous story told about (who) a mother and daughter, (what) crying, (why) because of the fear of going to school, (when) while waiting for the bus, (where) by the roadside, (how) sobbing into their tissues. Some local touches add authenticity that hearers can connect with. The reference to tissues is very Singaporean because everyone carries a packet of tissues rather than handkerchiefs.

ii. Provide dialogue. The second technique is to include dialogue. The parable of the prodigal son is also told through dialogue between the father and his two sons. There is even an internal dialogue between the prodigal son and himself at the lowest point of his life. Dialogue creates a sense of immediacy as if the audience were actually there listening in. For example, when I ask the mother, "Do you believe God is able to take care of your daughter?" the listeners are also indirectly challenged. So as you prepare an illustration, narrate it by describing actions and constructing dialogue. Now, where can a busy preacher find illustrations? Everywhere, actually.

C. Where to Find Illustrations?

There are five sources that the preacher can pay attention to: personal experience, pop culture, past events, the natural environment, and the Internet.

---

25. Craddock, *Preaching*, 202–203.

1. The World Within: Personal Experience

This includes the preacher's own experience and those of others. The apostle Paul used examples from his own life, both in terms of his strengths (Phil 3:17 "join in imitating me") and his weaknesses (2 Cor 12:9 "So, I will boast all the more gladly of my weaknesses, so that the power of Christ may dwell in me"). Such personal disclosure is not for promoting oneself but for revealing the glory of Christ. Much advice has been given to ensure that the preacher uses examples from his life judiciously. Some counsel that preachers should share only about their weaknesses, not their strengths, but that runs counter to the example of Paul. Even if preachers share only about their own struggles, that draws attention to themselves and could appear as a plea for sympathy. Thus, it is the preacher's purpose that matters.[26] The congregation will be able to discern whether preachers are merely puffing up themselves or pointing to the grace and power of God. There will be a few traditional folks who are uncomfortable with personal disclosure of any sort from the pulpit and who will let the preacher know how they feel. This is when preachers need to ensure that they have a clear conscience before God, check with a few trusted leaders, and explain their purpose to the critics. However, preachers should always ask permission from their own families if they want to share about them; they should never embarrass their children or spouses. They should also not talk about them in every sermon because that would be narcissistic.

What about using the experience of others? Again, Paul was not averse to mentioning his co-workers such as Timothy (Phil 2:19) and Epaphroditus (Phil 2:25). He also held up the generosity of the Corinthian church as an example to the Macedonians (2 Cor 9:2). Similarly, it is encouraging to hold up examples of people within the congregation because it shows that God is working in and through ordinary people in the church. However, never ever betray what is said in confidence. Doing so will cause untold harm and undermine your own trustworthiness as a pastor. Always ask for permission to share, and it may be better to share anonymously. Even if it were a positive testimony, most people (especially Asians) are shy about being in the spotlight. Naming people could also create a sense of jealousy because it implies that some are more spiritual than others. But as in the case of Timothy and Epaphroditus, it may be appropriate at times to name the person, especially to encourage prayer or support for that person.

---

26. Long, *Witness of Preaching*, 221, advises that "far more important than a list of rules is the matter of intent."

2. The World Around: Popular Culture

Preachers should be familiar with the environment of their congregations. They should keep up with current news, and watch what people are watching on television, movies, advertisements, and YouTube. If we don't influence the flock, the world will. Jesus said in John 17:16–17 that while we are not *of* the world, we are sent *into* the world. The preachers speak about the world in order to show their congregations how they can respond to materialistic or humanistic values. On the other hand, God's creational grace can also be discerned in human cultures because we are all still made in God's image, albeit marred by sin. Therefore, in the world around us we can find verisimilitudes of truth from which we can point towards the ultimate truth.

I once sang a snippet from Teresa Teng's well-loved Mandarin pop song, "The Moon Represents My Heart," during a sermon to illustrate that we are all looking for perfect love. The chorus goes:

> You ask me how deep my love for you is,
> How much I really love you.
> Go think about it; Go take a look.
> The moon represents my heart.

This was a special occasion to which church members had invited their unbelieving parents to attend. My attempt at singing caught the audience's amused attention, especially those of the older generation. They saw that I was not just a religious person out of touch with everyday reality but one that understands them and their world. The point of that illustration was that while we all hunger for perfect love, we are often disappointed by parents, children, friends, and even spouses because no one is flawless, not even ourselves. I gave examples of demanding parents, neglectful children, and fighting spouses. The only one who is perfect and who can love us unconditionally is God, and he proved that through the cross.

While working on this chapter, I watched a popular animated movie, *Inside Out*, produced by Pixar Animation Studios and released by Walt Disney Pictures. It shows five personified emotions (Joy, Sadness, Fear, Anger, and Disgust) in the mind of Riley, an 11-year-old girl trying to adjust to life in a new city. The plot shows that one cannot suppress sadness without losing the capacity to feel and relate socially. Sadness is a component that enables a person to empathize with others. We can affirm these psychological truths, which is why we have lament psalms and why God let Job rant and rail against the unjust suffering in his life. In the end, Riley could turn to her loving family for comfort. But what if one does not have that kind of family to fall back on? This is where the gospel provides something that the world cannot. The book of Hebrews tells us that Jesus is our high priest who is able to sympathize with our weaknesses, and that he too has prayed with loud cries and tears (Heb 4:15; 5:7). In our sadness, we have someone to turn to, even when it seems that no one else understands.

If you prepare your sermon ahead of time by one to two weeks, the right illustrations will find you. Nowadays, we are wading knee-deep, if not drowning, in information from the mass media. If you are mulling over your sermon whether consciously or unconsciously, your antennae will be tuned to pick up a God-sent illustration, whether you are flipping the pages of a magazine or scrolling through a newsfeed.

3. The World Behind: History

Although more removed from the contemporary audience, this is still a useful source. Examples can come both from secular and church history. Using the national or ethnic history of the congregation would help the preacher get their interest and build a rapport with them. Earlier, I mentioned the sixth-century Chinese military strategist Sun Tze. When telling about the lives of church founders and missionaries, the purpose is to point to the work of God in their lives and not to put them on a pedestal, lest we discourage the average Christian with unrealistic ideals. The nineteenth-century evangelist George Mueller is one such example that was mentioned in this chapter.

4. The World of Nature

Jesus's parables were also based on his sharp observations of human behavior and creation. Birds, flowers, shepherds, sheep, sowing, fishing were all used as analogies for the kingdom of God. The natural sciences are also a resource for illustrations. I have referred to Stanley Miller's experiment that attempted to prove the creation of life. Be sure to check your facts as there will be people who will be using their smart phones to verify what you say even as you are preaching.

5. The World Online

There are many websites that provide illustrations. One credible source is www.preachingtoday.com that is produced by the editors of *Leadership Journal*, part of Christianity Today. They can be useful if the preacher is at his wits' end, but he should be careful to apply the preceding guidelines to ensure that he uses them relevantly.

If using a quotation, Craddock has some useful advice.[27] In the first place, quotations should be kept to a minimum because listeners would not be able to follow a long quote, unless it is printed out or flashed on the PowerPoint. If the author is significant, then name him. If it is the content and not the source that is significant, then one could simply say that "it has been said" or "a well-known scholar has written that..." Similarly, while a sermon is not an academic paper, avoid passing off a source or experience as your own. One can simply attribute it to another by saying that this is an account that one has heard, read, or came across.[28] Many a pastor's reputation has been ruined by plagiarism whether committed by pride or negligence.

The sermon has been explained and proven by facts. The people have been persuaded by examples. What's next in building the body of the sermon? Preachers need to answer the third question: So?

---

27. Craddock, *Preaching*, 206.
28. Chapell, *Christ-Centered Preaching*, 194–195.

10

The Muscular System: Applications (So?)

The preacher who fails to confront his congregation with the "so what" question deceives them. He has lulled them into thinking that they are alright simply by sitting in the pews. Such a preacher has failed to understand what he is called to do: as a herald, to call for a response; as a teacher, to ask for a life commitment; as an exhorter, to encourage or warn; and as a witness, to bring people to meet God.

However, application does not mean beleaguering people with a to-do list that either leaves them feeling guilty or weary. The danger of legalism may be the reason why Johnson in *The Glory of Preaching* eschews application. He says that applying the text is not the preacher's responsibility and believes that it is enough to present the biblical worldview.[1] There may be gifted preachers who are able to inspire a change of mindset, and that may be the function of some sermons. But Johnson overstates his case when he applies this principle to all sermons. One only needs to take a look at the prophetic books and epistles to see how practical they are, but such instructions are not dispensed legalistically; they are always a response to God's grace.

It is true that only the Holy Spirit can change lives, but he works incarnationally (i.e. preaching is both a divine and human act). The Spirit works through God's people, endowing them with gifts to build up the body. So, the preacher must also put thought and effort into preparing sermon applications. They form the muscular system enabling people to be doers of the word and not hearers only, lest they deceive themselves (Jas 1:22).

---

1. Johnson, *Glory of Preaching*, 158, 167.

Making relevant applications requires an understanding of the congregation. There are some who only want to be teaching or preaching pastors and not do pastoral ministry. I doubt that they will be effective preachers. They may be exegetically and theologically knowledgeable, but if they don't know the people, how can they draw out suitable applications for their hearers' lives? In this chapter, I will discuss the why, who, what, and how of sermon applications.

A. Why Apply?

When Old Testament prophets spoke, they did so in no uncertain terms about what the hearers are to do or not to do. Amos addressed the hypocritical religiosity of eighth-century Israel by telling them, "For thus says the LORD to the house of Israel: Seek me and live; but do not seek Bethel and do not enter into Gilgal or cross over to Beersheba; for Gilgal shall surely go into exile, and Bethel shall come to nothing" (Amos 5:4–5). Specific places and actions were mentioned. Similarly, Isaiah 58:3–6 takes up a question by the Jews who had returned from exile – "Why do we fast, but you do not see?" The answer is that they served their own interest on the fast day and oppressed all their workers. Then followed the details of what they have done wrong (quarreling and fighting) and a list of imperatives – share bread with the hungry, bring the homeless into your house, etc.

The apostle Paul was no ivory tower theologian but engaged with the nitty-gritty of church concerns. The epistles to the Corinthians dealt with issues of split loyalties, food offered to idols, sexual immorality, spiritual gifts, proper gender conduct, to name a few. Even the more general epistles such as Ephesians and Colossians contained practical exhortations in the areas of marriage, parenting, and work. God is very much interested in every part of our lives, and the preacher should be no less attentive.

Despite the Calvinist presumption of some preachers, John Calvin said, "If we leave it to men's choice to follow [what] is taught them, they will never move one foot. Therefore the doctrine itself can profit nothing at all."[2] It seems that Calvin, while having a very high view of God's grace and sovereignty, also had a very realistic view of human propensity. Some preachers assume

---

2. From John Calvin's sermon on 2 Tim 5:1–2, as translated in *Sermons on the Epistles to Timothy and Titus* (Edinburgh: Banner of Truth Trust, 1983), 945–957, cited in Chapell, *Christ-Centered Preaching*, 210.

that mature and committed Christians should be able to go home and think through the applications for themselves. Let's be honest – how many of us actually do that? How many will even remember the sermon when they arrive home from church? There may have been some deeply moving sermons that we responded to, but probably not on a weekly basis. Rather, the preacher best serves the hearers when he challenges them to commit to a response at the end of the sermon.

Someone asked Karl Barth, "What do you do to prepare your Sunday sermon?" He famously answered, "I take the Bible in one hand and the daily newspaper in the other." Farris explores this statement in the light of Barth's dialectical theology. He notes that Barth's absolute denial of any analogy between God and humanity was a response to a humanistic nineteenth-century liberal theology. However, Barth was open to the analogy of relationship, meaning that some human relationships are analogous to the relationship between God and humanity. Farris goes on to argue for an analogy between Israel, the early church, and ourselves, since God continues to address humanity. The preacher can then explore the possibility of analogies between the world of the text and our world. In other words, God's specific directions to the audience in the time of Amos, Isaiah, Paul, and James, must have some relevance to us and our world today. As Greidanus puts it, "Since the message was first addressed to the ancient church, it requires explication; since that message now needs to be addressed to a contemporary church, it requires application."[3] Farris points out that Barth himself applied Scripture to his own situation in Nazi Germany.

B. Who to Apply To?

A preacher cannot just hide in his office to write a sermon. He needs to be out in the field where his flock is – in the office where his parishioner is being backstabbed, in the home where a single mother is worried about her rebellious teenager, in the coffee shop with the retrenched sole bread-winner. What will your sermon have to say to them? Not to all of them at the same time, but God may have a word for some of them through this week's text. As

---

3. Arthur Michael Ramsay and Leon-Joseph Suenens, *The Future of the Christian Church* (London: SCM, 1971), 13–14, cited in Stott, *I Believe in Preaching*, 149; Farris, *Preaching that Matters*, 25–27; Greidanus, *Modern Preacher*, 183.

you invite people to your home or visit the small Bible study groups in their homes, you will see how your sermon can be brought home to their lives.

Farris proposes a more formal way of analyzing your congregation, using a questionnaire that I adapt below:[4]

Exegesis of the Congregation:
1. Social and economic makeup of the congregation, e.g. types of professions, homes, cars:
2. Social and economic makeup of the surroundings:
3. Age of listeners (rough numbers and percentages of the whole):
   Children (1–12) _____
   Youth (13–20) _____
   Young adults (21–30) _____
   Adults (31–40) _____
   Mature Adults (41–60) _____
   Senior Adults (61+) _____
4. Gender:
   Female _____
   Male _____
5. Marital Status:
   Single _____
   Married _____
   Divorced _____
   Widow/Widower _____
6. Educational Background (highest level attained):
   Primary School _____
   Secondary School _____
   Diploma _____
   Degree _____
   Postgraduate _____
7. In what people or structures does the power lie?

---
4. Farris, *Preaching that Matters*, 31–32.

8. What are the special ideological or theological values? (For example, denomination, conservative, charismatic, cell-groups, outreach, etc.)
9. What issues or circumstances are currently of special concern? (For example, conflicts, fundraising, leadership, etc.)
10. Describe the worship style:
11. What special factors of institutional history might affect the congregation's ability to hear you?
12. What expectations do people have of the minister?
13. What expectations do people have of the pulpit ministry?
14. What are their strengths?
15. What are their needs?
16. What do they hope for the future?
17. In their free time, they like to
    watch:
    read:
    listen to:
    do:

Getting the information may require a period of observation and interactions, but these guidelines alert the preacher to various aspects of the congregation. A new pastor could kick off this study by having conversations with some key leaders.

Yet a third way of understanding the people is suggested by Craddock. He calls it empathetic imagination: "It is an effort of the imagination to bring to a specific human condition all that a person has heard, seen, read, felt, and experienced about that condition." He instructs one to take a blank sheet of paper and write at the top, What's it like to be . . . ? Then write a phrase describing a specific human experience, for example, facing surgery, a major exam, broken relationship, lost job, failed exam, and whatever else may be happening in your congregation. For the next fifteen minutes, scribble every thought, feeling, experience, place, sound, smell, taste, or people that come to mind. With some practice, the preacher will stretch his capacity to empathize.[5] When the preacher shows that he cares and understands, then people are more willing to listen, even to rebukes and warnings, because they

---
5. Craddock, *Preaching*, 97–98.

have the assurance that the preacher is speaking out of love. Now that you have an idea of who you are preaching to, what do you apply?

C. What to Apply?

There are three levels of application to consider – to the congregant, the church, and the community. One does not need to apply a sermon on all three levels, as different texts will have different implications. But keeping the possibilities in mind will forestall the preacher from riding his favorite hobby horse and ensure that the church is holistically challenged.

1. Apply to the Congregant

There are two sides of an individual's relationship to consider – his relationship with God and also with others. In terms of relationship with God, we can think of the total person in terms of her spiritual, emotional, physical, or financial needs. There may be a need for repentance, assurance of forgiveness, deliverance from addiction, and so on. Scripture covers a range of the human condition, from self-worth (Ps 139), peace of mind (Phil 4:7), financial provision (Matt 6:25), to healing from sickness (Jas 5:16).

Relationship with others covers the domestic and vocational spheres. Ephesians and Colossians set out instructions in the Household Codes dealing with husband-wife, parent-child, and master-slave relationships. In the modern context, instead of the master-slave, we need to consider the employer-employee correlation. A Christian spends much of his time in the work place and needs guidance where it comes to unethical practice, unscrupulous bosses, demanding clients, or the prospect of being laid off. If you are seeing bored faces, the problem may be that you have not shown them that God cares about their cares. People come to church hoping to find living water for their parched souls. Do not disappoint them with dry sermons. A brilliant piece of exposition does nothing to slake their thirst unless it makes a difference in their relationship with God and others.

When preaching on Psalm 23 to seminary students, I guided three of my students to pen their own personal adaptation of Psalm 23. One wrote as a student, another as a mother of three boys, and the last as a business executive. At the end of my exposition, I invited them to deliver their compositions that dealt with exam stress, illnesses, office politics, etc. The hearers were so moved that we were inundated with requests for copies of their personal psalms. The hearers now understood what it means to say that "The LORD is *my* shepherd." I reproduce below the one written by a Singaporean about his work experience:

Psalm 23 for the Market Place[6]
By How Choon Onn

The Lord is my CEO,
What more could I want.
He gives me peace of mind and calms my heart when handling projects.
He leads me to the right overseas ventures;
He restores my confidence with words of encouragement;
He leads me to do things with integrity for his name's sake.

Even when the engineering projects are difficult,
and it seems I won't make it,
I fear no failure in meeting tight timelines and budgets
because you are with me.
Your guidance and provision,
they comfort me.

You prepare my career ahead for me,
even when my enemies attempt to stab me from behind.
At board meetings, you anoint my head with foresight;
my discernment overflows.
Surely I shall have goodwill and favor in the office all the days of my employment,
And I shall serve the LORD in the marketplace as long as He leads me.

2. Apply to the Church

In this category, there are also two levels of relationships to consider: relationship within the church and with those outside of the church. Paul wrote the first epistle to Timothy so that he "may know how one might behave in the household of God" (1 Tim 3:15). In Titus 2, Paul gave detailed ethical instructions to different groups in the congregation: older men, younger men, older women, and younger women. All these were first based on sound

---
6. Used by permission.

doctrine, and so like Paul, we must keep doctrines and ethical conduct together in our preaching. Legalism is avoided when the preacher makes it clear that ethics is not a conditional requirement for salvation but a response to unconditional salvation.

In terms of relating to others outside the church, we can direct people towards evangelism and social service. The Great Commission and the second greatest commandment apply to all outside the church. James 1:27 tells us that true religion is to care for orphans and widows. We need to consider who the destitute are in our contemporary society: ex-prisoners, migrant workers, the physically, mentally, or emotionally disabled. Are we aware of meeting their needs and not just giving money?

In chapter 5 on Deductive Forms, I used a student's sermon on Amos 8 as an example. It was a sermon about upholding justice for the poor and needy. The student had done an internship with HealthServe, an NGO that provides medical and legal help for migrant workers in Singapore. In his sermon, he shared the story of Madhu who was fired for "not doing a good job," without being told what he did wrong. He had not been paid for three months, but his employer only offered to give him back half of his salary. He refused and was subsequently beaten up. Madhu made a police report and was given a temporary visa by the Singapore Ministry of Manpower to look for another job. But due to his poor command of English, he did not realize that he had to look for another job himself. He only realized this fact two weeks before the expiry of his visa.

Madhu faced a grim future because he owed three years' worth of salary to come to Singapore and had worked for only three months. He had to support his parents back home, and now he was left with nothing but a mountain of debt. Then the preacher addressed the congregation, "You may be thinking, 'I don't abuse the poor. Is this relevant to me?' Yes, you don't physically abuse the poor, but you know that these abuses are going on. What does God call you to do, knowing that true worship is to uphold justice?"

Then he continued that someone in the drop-in center where he was interning collected a love gift for Madhu. When the gift was presented to him, Madhu exclaimed, "Why are you so good to me?" The HealthServe staff replied, "Madhu, it is not because we are good. It's because we know someone who is good. He is Jesus." This is an example-style illustration that also works as an application of serving the needy. We shall see later how this challenge can be sharpened.

3. Apply to the Community

Is the gospel relevant to socio-political issues when we do not live in a theocracy but in a pluralistic democracy? This is a subject that requires a more extended discussion of public theology, but the fundamental principle is that God is not only God of the church but God of all creation. Genesis 1 and 2 lay down universal principles about human worth, gender equality, creation care, sexuality and marriage. The reach of our applications should go as far as the reign of God's sovereignty.

Today, there is much debate over the institution of marriage. As much as we teach about homosexuality, we should also preach about premarital and extramarital sex, abortion, and divorce. If we do not teach our youth, the mass media will, and faster than you realize. When I give a talk on the biblical view of the LGBT (Lesbian, Gay, Bisexual, and Transgender) issue, I lay out several applications for the church: Build strong families to bring up children with healthy gender identity, form friendships with homosexuals because they, too, need the love of God, provide support and counseling for those who struggle with same-sex attraction, and register our views as citizens against the erosion of family values.

Another area that is seldom taught in the pulpit is economic and social justice. God cares for the poor, and the church ought to be concerned when business corporations exploit the poor for profit. Big businesses rape the earth and pollute the environment for cheap resources, jeopardizing the livelihood of those who depend on the land. The annual haze choking Southeast Asia is one such example. These are complex issues, and the pulpit is not the place to solve such problems. But it is the place where biblical values and principles must be enunciated so that both policy-makers and the ordinary consumers can consider how they should act.

There are many other issues that we face in society: gambling, radicalization, racism, ageism. Preachers are to help people consider these issues in the light of Scripture lest we are blinded by ignorance, apathy, or pragmatism (translated as "I don't know," "I don't care," and "Not my problem"). If we only concentrate on spiritual topics, we make Christianity irrelevant from Monday to Saturday. We need to heed Stott's warning that "We justify Marx's well-known criticism that religion is an opiate which drugs people into acquiescing in their status quo; and we confirm non-Christians in their sneaking suspicion that Christianity is irrelevant. All this is much too high a price to pay for our irresponsibility."[7] So then, how does a preacher help people to apply the sermon?

D. How to Apply?

Some preachers deliver the applications only at the end of their sermon, after they have expounded and illustrated the text. While this may be suitable in an inductive sermon, it is better in a deductive sermon to show the relevance as one goes along. This will keep the audience engaged throughout the sermon. Also, when a practical implication follows a point from the text, people will see the connection better. Instead of a to-do list, they will apprehend (or be apprehended by) the basis for the call to faith and action.

The guidelines below are based on a couple of presumptions: first, that the application is consistent with the central word of the sermon, and second, that the application is drawn from a careful exegesis and comparison between the ancient and modern contexts. A preacher who has gone through the process of exegesis and *lectio divina* should be clear about the sermon's function and apply it to specific situations in the listeners' lives.

The preacher also needs to be aware of similarities and differences between the situations then and now. Robinson gives an example of Paul's exhortations to slaves to submit to their masters.[8] While there are principles that can apply to employer-employee relationships today (like doing one's best irrespective of being watched), to ignore the fact that modern employees are not slaves would lead to gross misapplication of these passages. Is the injunction to "obey your earthly masters" to be applied to every act irrespective of legality or morality? Should one allow oneself to be taken advantage of at the expense of one's health and family commitments? Being a doormat only supports and perpetuates a culture of wrong-doing that does not glorify God. Responding to complex issues requires wisdom that may need to be taught beyond the sermon, but at least the congregation starts the learning and thinking process. Careful hermeneutical consideration is needed in passages such as the wearing of veils, Jephthah's sacrifice of his daughter (which is not meant to be emulated), curbing Christian liberties for the "weaker brother" (which refers to sin-prone rather than judgmental-prone Christians), and others.

---

7. Stott, *I Believe in Preaching*, 162.
8. Robinson, *Biblical Preaching*, 59.

Keeping the central word and analogous contexts in mind, here are four guidelines on effective sermon applications: Apply them to specific people, in specific situations, through specific actions, and with suitable motivations.

1. Apply to Specific People

"The surprising thing is that the more directed and personal a message, the more universal it becomes."[9] Thus Robinson suggests focusing specifically on two or three types of people in a message and changing the focus group each week. He uses a grid devised by Don Sunukjian, which I here adapt from the American context. The preacher is to label the columns at the top of the grid for men, women, singles, married, divorced, and widowed. At the side of the grid are rows for different age groups (youth, young adults, adults, mature adults, senior adults), occupations (unemployed, self-employed, workers, professionals, homemakers, retirees), levels of faith (nominal, committed, seekers), the sick, the hospitalized, and any other groups that are relevant to the congregation. When thinking of specific applications, the preacher can then look for two to four intersections where the message will be especially relevant. When speaking on financial giving for example, the preacher can address the professional who earns more than his family needs as well as the factory worker who barely makes enough to support her family. To the latter we may stress that God looks at the heart and not the amount, but to the former we have to warn that our heart is where our treasure is.

2. Apply in Specific Situations

If the preacher employed an example-style illustration, that may already serve as an application. But if we want to speak to a larger cross-section of the congregation, then we need to give a variety of specific situations for application. How can the preacher do this? Chapell offers a useful model: The preacher should first give the details of a concrete situation for application and then unroll it into other situations that can be mentioned briefly. "The initial situation makes the principle real; the unrolled specifics make it relevant to all."[10]

---

9. Haddon Robinson, "Preaching to Everyone in Particular," *Leadership* (Fall 1994): 100.
10. Chapell, *Christ-Centered Preaching*, 225.

For example, in my aforementioned sermon on Psalm 23 preached to a seminary congregation, one of my main points was that the LORD pursues us with goodness and love. I gave an illustration of a lady who received an amount of money at just the right time to pay for a family member's hospital bill. But since I was preaching to seminary students, I unrolled a few other specific situations that they could identify with:

> Some of you may be worried about your financial needs too. You gave up a regular job with a steady income. You wonder whether you will have enough to finish your studies or to take care of your growing family.
>
> Or you may be anxious about being posted to a new ministry that you feel is beyond your ability.
>
> Or perhaps you received bad news from a doctor either about yourself or a loved one.
>
> Whatever you are facing, the God who pursues you says, "Do not be afraid. I am with you." Whether things work out the way you want them to or not, God is with you in the midst of your difficulties. His goodness and love still pursue you.

Notice that the applications are connected to the main point of God pursuing us and also to the central idea ("Do not be afraid because I am with you") by the repetition of key phrases. I also use the second person pronoun "you" rather than the first person "we." This makes for a more personal application, which is appropriate since Psalm 23 is an individual rather than a corporate psalm. There are times when "we" might be appropriate, for example in a communal response or to avoid an accusatory tone.

3. Apply through Specific Actions

A preacher can guide people to respond by providing realistic steps and structure. I will suggest three levels of specific actions: immediate, intermediate, and church. The immediate level is when hearers are given an opportunity to respond to God after hearing the sermon. There are biblical precedents for this, for example, when Peter called on the people to repent in Acts 2, when the Ethiopian eunuch was baptized in Acts 8, when Peter ordered the baptism of the Gentile household in Acts 10. If the Holy Spirit has convicted the hearers, then they should be allowed to make a commitment accordingly. It will be more difficult to motivate people when the moment has passed and the cares of everyday life kidnap the people when they leave the church. If one has preached about forgiveness, then invite people to forgive those who have hurt them. For those who struggle to forgive, encourage them to see the pastoral staff after the service for further prayer and ministry. Of course, the pastoral team needs to follow up attentively so that such responses do not become a one-off (or even repeated) emotional reflex but the first step towards healing and growth.

Second, the preacher also needs to think about realistic and achievable applications at the intermediate level to help people grow, that is, to suggest applications beyond the present moment to the formation of a habit. They should not be exhortations so general and idealistic that they have no connection to real life, for example, "Love all your neighbors with all your heart" or "Never get angry with your enemies." These platitudes will run like rain off a duck's back. Neither should admonitions be so demanding that people give up before they even begin, such as "Pray for an hour every morning" or "Share the gospel with someone every day."

It is far better to get people to do something they can achieve within a trial period[11] because "Nothing succeeds like success." For example, if encouraging people to pray, then for those who do not have a regular practice of doing so, I would suggest that they pray for just five minutes a day for a week. They can choose a time that works best for them – while driving, or taking the bus or train, etc. After a week, they may find that this brings such vitality to their life that they can renew the commitment or even extend the time of prayer, thus acquiring a life-long habit. For the more mature Christian, challenge them to deepen their growth, such as going on an annual spiritual retreat or having a regular extended time of prayer and fasting. Such suggestions may necessitate further teaching, which leads us to the third level of application.

Third, the church can provide further support for application at its organizational level. For example, it could hold a workshop on spiritual disciplines or conduct a prayer retreat. Another helpful approach would be to integrate the pulpit calendar with the church's small group curriculum. The small group provides the best means for accountability and support. If someone commits to pray for five minutes a day for one week, he can share his ups and downs with his small group. The pastor can consider what level of application is most appropriate for a sermon; sometimes, he could integrate all three levels. All these seem like a flurry of activities. How can applications

---

11. Stanley and Jones, *Communicating for a Change*, 188–189.

be sustained without becoming burdensome or mere programs? For this, we come to the last guideline.

4. Apply with Suitable Motivations

Scripture mandates us to make disciples, to pray, to give thanks, but it is left to us how, where, when, and how often to do it. Thus, all the specific actions should be presented as suggestions and guidelines. If the preacher implies that they are what good Christians should do, then he has gone beyond the Scripture into the quicksand of legalism. Chapell warns, "When preachers take a good suggestion and make it a biblical mandate, they not only arrogate their own thoughts to the canon of Scripture but also inevitably preach a pharisaism implying that people can earn grace by meeting these particular standards."[12]

In my younger days, this legalistic notion insidiously infected my conscience. In those days, there was much stress on doing "Quiet time" (QT) or daily devotion. If one missed their QT for a day, then it was thought that one would miss out on God's blessings. If one neglected it for a week, it would be back-sliding. This made me feel so guilty that I just stayed "back-slidden" until guilt overwhelmed me into repentance. But this roller coaster spirituality would viciously repeat itself again and again. It was only when I was older that I realized that my feelings were based on a totally inadequate idea of God. If God loves me unconditionally, would he stop blessing me just because I missed one QT? If God accepts me as I am, does missing a week of QT make him love me less? It dawned on me that the first word in the Lord's Prayer (in Greek) is "Father" not "Forgive me." So, sinful as we may be, we can still come and call him "Father." I could finally get off the sickening roller coaster. Guilt made me pray less but love drew me to pray more.

Millennials may be less affected by guilt, but our Asian or Confucianistic stress on getting ahead, especially through education, still warps our thinking. Even seminary students assume they have to score A's to be good Christians. They need to be reminded about growing in their relationship with God, not just striving for what they, their parents, or their churches, are expecting. Chapell reminds preachers to "motivate believers primarily by grace, not by guilt or greed."[13]

---

12. Chapell, *Christ-Centered Preaching*, 232.
13. Ibid., 219.

Of course, if one is preaching on repentance, there is a place for guilt. The right kind of guilt is one that is based on the character of God and not on our distorted image of him. Guilt can be based on God's holiness, wrath, and sacrificial love, but it cannot be based on legalism, pettiness, and conditional love. "For godly grief produces a repentance that leads to salvation and brings no regret, but worldly grief produces death" (2 Cor 7:10). I would therefore expand Chapell's motivation by grace to say that applications need to come from a theocentric impetus (i.e. understanding who God is). Guilt and greed are anthropocentric motivations – do it to avoid getting into trouble or do it to gain something for yourself. A theocentric motivation commands people to be holy because God is holy. It calls for submission because God is sovereign, encourages obedience because God enables, and unapologetically demands self-denial because of Christ's sacrifice for us. Such a theocentric basis can usually be found in the text or context of the passage. For instance, the Decalogue is premised on the prologue, "I am the LORD your God, who brought you out of the land of Egypt, out of the house of slavery" (Exod 20:1). Paul's exhortations in Romans 12 were predicated on God's mercies expounded in the preceding chapters.

Having a theocentric motivation also means that the congregation is ultimately accountable to God, not to the preacher. Nothing is more freeing for the preacher and nothing more effective for the hearers than to simply leave space for them to hear and respond to the Spirit. After suggesting specific actions, the preacher can ask, "What does God put upon your heart to do?" God can move the people more deeply than the preacher can.

E. An Example

Earlier, I gave an example of a student's application of his sermon on Amos 8:

> You may be thinking, "I don't abuse the poor. Is this relevant to me?" Yes, you don't physically abuse the poor, but you know that these abuses are going on. What does God call you to do, knowing that true worship is to uphold justice?"

Based on the four guidelines above, try improving the application before turning the page.

Apply to Specific People

Should the sermon be applied to individuals or the church? Just as Amos was preaching to the elites of Israel, so the sermon should be addressed to the church as a whole. Further, is one's congregation analogous to the haves or have-nots in Amos's context? In Singapore, Christians tend to be the middle-class, and so they need to hear the same warning. The preacher could have said, "Just as Amos was warning the materialistic people of Judah, he is also addressing the materialistic people here today. What is God calling us as a Christian community to do?" If one is preaching to the have-nots, then the application may be to trust God to judge the oppressors or to work together to stop exploitation.

Apply in Specific Situations

The example of supporting Madhu the migrant worker provides a concrete application, but not everyone will interact with migrant workers, so the speaker needed to unroll a few more practical situations. He could consider what other disadvantaged groups need help, especially those that are connected to the congregation geographically, denominationally, or through the church members' vocations. It may be a nearby nursing home, a social service center that a church member works in, or the foreign domestic helpers who come to church with the families they work for. How can the church serve these different groups?

Apply through Specific Actions

This sermon was originally preached to a seminary audience, so at the congregant level, the preacher could have exhorted students to do their internship at various social organizations. If this sermon were preached in a church, then at an organizational level, the application can be to volunteer in the church's community outreach. Some members might need a more gradual exposure, so some intermediate level applications can be to visit a home or help in ad hoc projects. A sustained application requires advanced thought and planning so that the church can live according to God's commands.

Apply with Suitable Motivation

The motivation came through the illustration where a staff member told Madhu that the Christians helped him not because they were good but because Jesus is good. In fact, the preacher had pointed out from Amos 8 that God's people are to uphold justice because God is a God of justice who cares for the poor. In the larger context of Amos, God reminded Israel that just as he had delivered them from their bondage to slavery, he expects them to treat one another with the same grace (Amos 2). This is the theocentric basis for motivation. The preacher can spur the people by saying:

> Don't do it out of duty because that will get tiring.
> Don't do it out of pity because that is patronizing.
> Do it because of who God is and what he has done for you.
> God is angry about injustice. Are you?
> God cares for the needy. Do you?
> God acted to save you. Will you act for others?

Conclusion

We cannot always expect instant transformation. As Day said, "Sermons . . . gradually change the way people see the world. . . . Like Holy Communion, the word faithfully preached will do its work – even if the congregation can't remember every detail later."[14] So also, the Word faithfully applied will do its work – even if not everyone responds immediately. We have now built the body of the sermon by explaining (What?), proving and persuading (Really?), and applying (So?). We now need to connect the head (Introduction), feet (Conclusion), and ligaments (Transition) to the body in Part IV.

---

14. Day, *Workbook for Preaching*, 144–145.

Part IV

Connecting the Head, Feet, and Ligaments

11

The Head: Introduction

Today, I would like to share some thoughts from Galatians 5:2–15 about faith, love, and freedom, and how they are linked with one another, with specific attention given to verses 6 and 13. First, I want to draw the connection between faith and love in verse 6 . . .

The above was the introduction in a sermon drafted by a student. Does it bait your interest or are you instantly bored? Are there sermons where you hear the introduction and groan inwardly, take a deep breath and grit your teeth, hoping that the preacher will be kind enough to keep it short and painless? In the meantime, the teenagers in the congregation harbor no such illusory hope and are already glued to their mobile games. What is wrong with that introduction? It is clear about the text and the topic, but it comes across as a cold, lifeless lecture that has nothing to do with the lives of the people. It sounds like the beginning of a biblical treatise that the congregation feels obliged to suffer through, as if doing penance in order to be a good Christian.

While listening for a word from the Lord is the first step for the preacher, listening to the introduction is the primary aspect for the listeners. It will either make or break their attention. We will discuss why an introduction is important, and I will give three guidelines on crafting an effective introduction. As for the introduction above, I did not let the student inflict it on the congregation, not till he came up with a better version that you will find with the third guideline below.

A. Why Introduction?

"If you do not capture attention in the first thirty seconds, you may never gain it at all," Robinson observes. Alternatively, Long believes that despite past disappointments, hearers still come with an air of expectancy and a genuine desire to listen. Long has a hopeful perspective, for why else do God's people come to church week after week, even if they do not hear exciting sermons? There is always that innate hunger for God that sends us looking for scraps under the table. Long says it would be more accurate to say that "sermon introductions must not lose the listeners' attention . . ."[1]

How then is the preacher to keep the attention that has been gifted him? Robinson advocates that an introduction should uncover needs. He cites social scientist Arthur R. Cohen who concludes that when audiences receive information that meets felt needs, two things happen: (1) more learning takes place and (2) opinions change faster and more permanently compared to when information is given first and then applied to life. In other words, an introduction should aim to answer the question, "Tell me why I should listen to this?" Robinson goes on to discuss Abraham H. Maslow's hierarchy of needs that begins with meeting basic physiological and security conditions and moves up to seeking for love, self-esteem, and self-actualization. Maslow's theory has been questioned because, among other things, it does not reflect the priorities of collectivist societies such as those found in Asia. Nonetheless, his list of needs is a useful reference for the preacher to keep in mind.[2]

However, one may ask whether the preacher should pander to felt needs rather than address real needs, such as to repent of sin and to be restored to God. These are needs that people may not realize or refuse to acknowledge. I think making a distinction between felt and real needs is a false dichotomy; rather, felt needs can be understood as symptoms of real needs.[3] A doctor

---

1. Robinson, *Biblical Preaching*, 120. Long, *Witness of Preaching*, 173–174.

2. Robinson, *Biblical Preaching*, 122, citing "Need for Cognition and Order of Communication as Determinants of Opinion Change," in *The Order of Presentation in Persuasion*, ed. Carl I. Horland, et. al. (New Haven: Yale University Press, 1957), 79-97; Mahmoud Wahba and Lawrence Bridwell, "Maslow Reconsidered: A Review of Research on the Need Hierarchy Theory," *Organizational Behavior and Human Performance* 15, no. 2 (1976): 212–240; Patrick Gambrel and Rebecca Cianci, "Maslow's Hierarchy of Needs: Does It Apply in a Collectivist Culture?" *Journal of Applied Management and Entrepreneurship* 8, no. 2 (April 2003): 143–161.

3. Wilson, *Homiletical Theory*, 83–84, similarly cites Herman G. Stuempfle, Jr., *Preaching Law and Gospel* (Philadelphia, PA: Fortress, 1978), who views the law as having vertical and horizontal dimensions. The vertical dimension functions as a hammer of judgment for sin,

listens to the patient's litany of symptoms in order to diagnose the real cause of the disease. Only then can she prescribe an effective cure. During the 2003 SARS (Severe Acute Respiratory Syndrome) outbreak in Singapore, the authorities started screening every one for fever – from the airport to the schools. The fever was not the real problem; the SARS coronavirus was, but the fever was the first clue. Doctors do not begin by asking a patient, "Do you have the SARS virus?" The patient would not know. Rather, the doctor asks whether you have a fever and for how long? Do you have a dry cough or difficulty breathing? Do you have a headache or diarrhea? If you realize that you do, you sit up and pay attention to the treatment.

The preacher, like the doctor, addresses the symptoms of life. Do you have sleepless nights worrying about your finances? Are you feeling lonely even in a relationship? Do you keep losing your temper with your spouse or children? The more specific the symptoms, the more people can identify their real needs. When the preacher has the listeners' attention, he can go on to what the text reveals as the real spiritual need. If the doctor diagnoses you as having the SARS virus, you follow his prescription closely. When people realize their fundamental need, they will pay attention to the answer. Robinson notes that "Christians differ from non-Christians not in their needs but in the ways their needs are met."[4] For example, if preaching on Matthew 6:25–34, the preacher could begin, like Jesus did, with the felt need of worrying about material necessities. She just needs to describe such worries in the context of her contemporary audience. The real need, though, as Jesus points out, is that we are looking to ourselves rather than to our Father who knows that we need these things. The world's solution is to keep working harder and accumulate more, but the real solution is to look to God as our Creator and Father.

Though a sermon may commonly begin with a need, we do not always have to begin with this human-centered approach, lest it conveys the idea that the gospel is only for solving our personal problems. The Westminster Shorter Catechism states that the chief end of man is to glorify God and enjoy him forever. Like releasing a movie trailer to attract moviegoers, the introduction can give a glimpse of who God is and his purpose for us so that we are

---

and the gospel brings forgiveness. The horizontal dimension is the effects of sin on the world, such as anxiety, alienation, doubt, and despair, and the gospel is to address these needs. The horizontal dimension of the law relates to felt needs as the consequences of sin. Similarly, Chapell, *Christ-Centered Preaching*, 242, 51–52, advocates that the FCF should be identified in the introduction, which may be a sin or simply human needs due to our fallen condition.

4. Robinson, *Biblical Preaching*, 123.

enthused to hear more. Or to use a medical analogy, this positive approach is like the practice of Traditional Chinese Medicine (TCM). While Western medicine attacks the disease, TCM seeks to strengthen the body's immune system. One may not have an immediate need, but one could regularly take a variety of herbal tonics to keep the body balanced and healthy. Likewise, besides addressing specific needs, the preacher can build up the congregation by pointing to a vision of God or God's purpose for us.

Paul's epistle to the Ephesians is one such example. Though the apostle may have wanted to address various issues such as unity and putting on a new way of life, he begins his letter by elaborating on the glorious riches that we have in Christ. Why then would anyone want to go back to what they were before? The introduction to a sermon on Ephesians could focus more on what we have in Christ rather than on what we need. For example, the preacher might say, "Can you imagine inheriting a bungalow or a vintage car and never claiming it?"

The world around us can also provide positive analogies for an introduction. Because God is God of all creation, we can find his reflection in what is good, even though it is marred by sin. The wedding vows are a reminder that love is not just a feeling but an act of commitment. This observation can be an introduction to loving God or loving neighbors. Topics on missions, service, holiness, and the glory of God can be introduced positively and powerfully. In *The Chronicles of Narnia*, C. S. Lewis described the lion Aslan as being good but not tame; in fact, he is very dangerous. So also, God is good but dangerous – a dangerously holy God.

Relevance, then, has to do with either addressing a need or a God-given purpose. Both have implications for our lives, and both answer the question "Why should I be interested in this?" Below are three guidelines for writing an arresting introduction – make it relevant to the central word, to the contemporary context, and to the congregation.

B. How to Introduce

1. Make It Relevant to the Central Word

The word from the Lord is the guiding beacon throughout the sermon. It is not necessary to reveal the entire idea but the introduction should at least present the subject so that the congregation will know what the sermon is going to be about.

Some preachers like to begin their sermon with a joke. Humor helps the speaker to build rapport with the audience. It puts the listeners in a positive mood so that they will be receptive to the speaker. However, the joke should be linked to the central idea. For one, it is confusing to leave the audience wondering what the joke has to do with the sermon. For another, it belittles the pulpit, reducing it to the entertainment of the crowd. This is not to say that the preacher must always be serious. The prophets employed humor to convey their message with a punch when the hearers were least expecting it. But the frivolous use of humor, says Chapell, creates distrust as listeners realize that they have been manipulated.[5] So, use humor, but use it seriously.

In an inductive sermon, Robinson points out that the introduction only reveals the first point. Or following Lowry's homiletical loop, the introduction begins with a problem or ambiguity that needs resolution. In a deductive sermon, one has to decide whether to introduce only the subject or the entire statement. Where the word from the Lord and outline are straightforward, then introducing only the subject would leave some tension that beckons the listeners to follow. This also applies to a truth that is hard to swallow or follow.

For example, the word from the Lord for the Amos 8 sermon was to uphold justice and build people up because that is true worship. This is a hard truth to follow, so the student has rightly chosen an inductive introduction. He started with the story of Madhu, the migrant worker, who was cheated and abused by his boss. After recounting the initial part of the story, the student could link it to the subject of worshipping God in the following manner:

> What would God want you to do for someone like Madhu?
> Here we are, sitting in a beautiful sanctuary worshipping God.
> But what does it really mean to worship God?

On the other hand, if the central word and the outline is one that is appealing to the congregation, then it will work to have a preview of the sermon in the introduction. In my first-mentioned sermon on Psalm 23, the word was to come to God who cares for you personally, and the three main points were to come to God who provides for you, protects you, and pursues you. I started with a story about my mother-in-law:

> I preached on Psalm 23 at my mother-in-law's funeral wake some years ago. She was widowed at a young age and had to raise three small children by herself. She worked two jobs to support the

---

5. Chapell, *Christ-Centered Preaching*, 240.

family. She became a Christian when her children brought her to Christ. When she thought she could finally enjoy her golden years as a grandmother, she was diagnosed with lung cancer even though she had never smoked in her life. She often questioned why she had to go before her time.

Psalm 23 says that goodness and love will pursue me. But where was goodness and love for my mother-in-law? Through all her difficulties and doubts, she never wavered in her faith because she knew that goodness and mercy is not found in the *absence* of trouble but in the *presence* of God. God cared for my mother-in-law in her trials, and God cares for you in your trials.

You may be troubled about your family, your finances, or your health. Or you may have struggles in your work or school. Whatever you are facing, God says come to him because he cares for you personally.

How does God care for you? Psalm 23 tells us that God is like a Shepherd who cares for you in three ways: He provides for your needs; he protects you from enemies; and he pursues you with goodness and love.

This introduction previewed the central word and outline in a challenging situation (i.e. early widowhood and mortality), which provided the tension that engaged the hearers' hearts and minds. Notice that this sermon begins with a story rather than with the biblical text, which leads me to the next guideline.

2. Make It Relevant to the Contemporary Context

The example at the beginning of this chapter on Galatians 5 began with the text rather than with the listeners. This is a common approach, and responsible exegetes want to show that they place great importance on the text. They often proceed with a historical or literary explanation of the text, but whether the congregation is following is another question. Chapell writes, "Many people sit in pews assuming that the ancient writings of Scripture have nothing to do with contemporary life, and in the first two minutes of the sermon, the preacher does nothing but convince them they are right." He then cites Jay Adams's advice, "Do not begin with the text; begin with the congregation as Peter and Paul did." In the Bible, God spoke to people in their situation then, so also the preacher should speak on behalf of the living God to people in their situation today. Robinson highlights that preachers should use the Bible to talk to people about themselves rather than to talk to them about the Bible. Or as Stanley and Jones ask more succinctly, "Are you teaching the *Bible* to people, or are you teaching *people* the Bible?" (italics mine). They remind the preacher not to be so focused on teaching the Bible that he forgets the real goal of teaching people.[6]

How can we make introductions contemporary? One could tell a personal story, either from your own or other's experience, refer to current events, or raise contemporary questions. To ensure that the story is not simply told for its own sake, the preacher should link it closely to the text through a repetition of the word from the Lord or other key words.

a. Contemporary stories

Using a story from the preacher's own life is useful not only for its contemporary relevance but also for building rapport and establishing the speaker's *ethos*. Your openness and vulnerability shows that you are a genuine person, and this will help people to relate with you and be more open to what you say. Here are a couple of introductions where the preacher spoke of himself/herself. The guidelines in chapter 9 on using illustrations from one's own life should be kept in mind.

This is a sermon by a Vietnamese student on 2 Kings 18:1–5 about the life of King Hezekiah. The preacher's word from the Lord was to heed godly advice, based on Hezekiah heeding Isaiah's counsel when the Assyrians besieged Jerusalem. She started with a story about herself:

> Can you guess what kind of girl I was nine years ago? I was the youngest of three girls, and I was spoilt rotten. I never said "sorry" when I did wrong, and I always expected to be served. God changed my life through one person. That was my Bible study leader in university.
>
> Though I have been going to church since I was 13, it was only when she patiently mentored me and prayed for me that I started to grow as a Christian. Because of her godly advice, I started to grow and serve others.

---

6. Chapell, *Christ-Centered Preaching*, 248–249, citing Jay E. Adams, *Truth Applied: Application in Preaching* (Grand Rapids, MI: Zondervan, 1990), 71. Robinson, *Biblical Preaching*, 125; Stanley and Jones, *Preaching for a Change*, 95.

Similarly, it was when King Hezekiah heeded the godly advice of the prophet Isaiah in 2 Kings 19 that his faith was strengthened even when his city was threatened.

For those who knew the preacher, the revelation that she was a spoilt brat was amusing because she was one of the easiest persons to get along with in the seminary. Her introduction is clearly connected to the text through a repetition of the central word (heed godly advice). However, it can be strengthened by following the third guideline to be discussed below.

Another student, a Singaporean pastor-to-be, wrote a sermon on Genesis 15 about Abraham trusting God to provide him with an heir. His word from the Lord was to trust God's promises when facing discouragement. This is his introduction:

> Not too long ago, I became very discouraged in ministry. I complained constantly to my wife and filled her poor ears with so much misery. Finally, she had enough and said, "I don't know what to make of you. When you are preaching in the Service, you talk about faith, the power of the Holy Spirit, and what Jesus can do in one's life. Are those just words, or do you really mean it?"
>
> "Of course I mean it," I replied.
>
> She said, "But you're not acting like it. You hold it like an intellectual belief. Haven't you really been converted?"
>
> "Of course I'm really converted," I said indignantly.
>
> "Well, it's not showing," she said. "Now, you surrender your life, ministry, future, everything to Jesus Christ."
>
> I was convicted. My wife woke up my ideas[7] and reminded me to trust God even when facing discouragement.
>
> Abraham's story occupies a significant portion of Genesis . . .

I am sure you enjoyed the story, though it needed to be improved in a few places. First, I encouraged the student to be more specific about the issues that he faced so that hearers could identify with him. He expanded his first paragraph thus:

> Not too long ago, I became very discouraged. I complained constantly to my wife about how badly things were going. There was the unreasonable expectation of achieving results, doing the legwork despite empowering leaders, being used as a permanent

---

7. A Singaporean slang for rebuking someone.

doormat, listening to gripes about how things should have been done, and, of course, the "constructive feedback." I filled my wife's poor ears with so much misery.

With the above elaboration, listeners can now imagine being in the preacher's shoes. This sermon is not just about what happened to Abraham 4,000 years ago; it is also about what is happening today.

The second area for improvement is to connect the story more tightly to the text, so he added a connecting paragraph:

Pastors, just like Abraham, can get discouraged and disheartened. Even though we may have experienced God's favor and leading, our trust in God seems to dissipate when we run into another brick wall. In Genesis 15, Abraham was discouraged that God still hadn't given him a son, and his trust in God's promise was sorely tested.

The keywords "discourage" and "trust in God's promise" now connect the story to the text. Besides stories, one can also make observations from contemporary events.

b. Contemporary situations

If a significant event took place around the time you preach, then it would be timely if you can make a reference to it. A week before I was due to preach on Psalm 13, a lament psalm, a tragedy struck a group of young Singaporeans who were climbing a mountain: seven twelve-year-old students, their two teachers, and one adventure guide were killed in a landslide on Mt Kinabalu in Sarawak. This was triggered by a rare 6.0 magnitude earthquake. The nation shared a collective grief for the victims and their families. I began my sermon by asking what any parent might ask, "Where is God at a time like this? How could God allow such a tragedy to occur?" These were questions that the psalmist also hurled at God in Psalm 13. The congregation listened in riveted silence.

If one is preaching in a different political, social, and cultural context, then one should sensitively make reference to the context of the hearers. Another Vietnamese student used her own context to introduce her sermon on 1 Peter 3:8–12 about living under restrictions:

In my Socialism class, the lecturer was ridiculing religions. When he spoke about Christianity, he said, "It is a stupid religion

> because it advises its believers that when they are slapped on one cheek, they should turn the other one also."
>
> I sat quietly, with scornful eyes burning into me. I silently asked God, "Yes God, why are we so silly?"
>
> Do you struggle with this command too? The passage from 1 Peter 3 reminds us of the reason why we should live "foolishly" in the eyes of the world.

Here is another heartfelt introduction to a sermon on God's comfort in tribulations from 2 Corinthians 1:1–11. This was delivered by a student from Myanmar before political reforms had started to take place.

> Lord! Why? Why did God allow all the sufferings in my country when he is the God-of-all-comfort? All of Myanmar suffered under the brutal military regime for over four decades, regardless of religion or ethnicity. However, Christians were especially targeted for persecution with many shot or imprisoned. I asked God "Why must we suffer like this? We have suffered in silence for so long." Yet 2 Corinthians 1:1–11 tells us that even in tribulations, God comforts us. How does the God-of-all-comfort comfort us?

These students are conscious of the challenges their national churches face, and a Singaporean preaching there needs to be similarly aware of the challenges. However, since these students were preaching in Singapore, they needed to connect to their hearers by analogous local challenges, even though such may be less severe. The comparison may be made, for example, by saying:

> Even in Singapore, there are people who do not understand why you should give up a good job to go into ministry, or why you want to bother them with the gospel. Though you may not be persecuted in the same way as the early Christians, God's encouragement for them applies just as much to you.

One more contemporary situation to note is the calendar, both liturgical and secular. If people are celebrating some event in the church or in the world, then a reference to that event, if relevant to the sermon, would make it contemporary. Even a secular occasion, like the Lunar New Year or Valentine's Day, is an opportunity to impart the biblical perspective of such celebrations. If the church does not teach about them, then the world will rush in to fill the vacuum, especially via the deluge of social media. Besides a contemporary story or situation, the preacher can also raise contemporary questions.

c. Contemporary questions

Lowry points out that an audience becomes engaged when they are faced with an ambiguity that they want solved. But it must be an ambiguity that is not merely an intellectual matter – "It is a mental ambiguity which is existentially felt." Lowry gives various examples, one of which is David H. C. Read's sermon on prayer, which started with the question, "When you pray, is there anyone there listening?" Lowry points out that in such an ambiguity, something is left "hanging," and it is this sense of incompletion that holds the listeners' attention.[8]

Preachers can think back to questions they themselves have raised or wrestled with in the course of their exegetical preparation or during the *lectio divina*. Questions that have to do with our lives or with God are likely to echo the congregation's thinking. When preaching on the subject of praise, I asked why we are urged to magnify and exalt the Lord.

> Why does God need to be praised? If I were to ask people to praise me, wouldn't I sound self-centered? Is God being narcissistic? Perhaps the real question is not why God needs to be praised, but why *we* need to praise God. Why do we use a magnifying glass? We usually assume that it is because the object is too small to be seen with the naked eye. But there is another reason why we need magnifying glasses, especially for older folks. It is not because the object is too small but because our eyes are too weak.
>
> Is God too small to be seen? That cannot be the case. Then what is the real problem? It is because we are myopic. This is why we are to praise and magnify God: so that we can see how great God really is. And when we see how great God is, then all our problems will seem small in comparison. This is what the psalmist urges us to do.

Having made the introduction relevant to the central word and to the contemporary context, we go on to the third guideline.

---

8. Lowry, *Homiletical Plot*, 35–37.

3. Make It Relevant to the Congregation

A contemporary introduction means that the congregation sees the general relevance of the sermon to their own time, but they need to be engaged by its specific relevance to their own lives. This is when the preacher can refer to the listeners' needs (felt and real) or to their God-given purpose that is found in the text.

Here is a sermon that moved from a contemporary to a congregational relevance. The text is Genesis 1:1–19, and the word from the Lord is to trust in a God who establishes order out of chaos:

> A quick look at the news on any given day reveals the chaos in the world, both natural and man-made. For example, the floods in Thailand and the regime in Syria result in much suffering and loss of lives. Earthquakes, plane crashes, terrorist bombings are common news these days.
>
> Chaos also strikes our personal lives: when we suddenly lose our jobs and our families are depending on us or when a loved one is diagnosed with cancer.
>
> What can we do when we find our lives in a chaos? In fact, chaos is found in the very first page of the Bible in Genesis 1:2...

The first paragraph makes the introduction contemporary, while the second paragraph makes a more personal connection to the congregation. The third paragraph then connects the subject to the text. All three paragraphs revolve around the central idea of chaos.

In the earlier story of the girl who heeded the godly advice of her mentor, I had referred to the need to make the introduction more effective by applying this third guideline. This can be done by adding a paragraph like the one below:

> Was there someone who made a difference in your life? A Sunday school teacher, a pastor, a family member, a lecturer, or a colleague? Thank God for that person and his or her godly advice.

Notice that this introduction does not address a felt need. Rather, it focuses on a positive God-given purpose, which is to grow in our faith by heeding godly advice. It is made relevant to the congregation by asking them to reflect on godly advice they have received in their own lives and experience. Now we will apply these three guidelines (be relevant to the central word, the contemporary context, and the congregation) to the sample introductions below.

C. Examples

Worked Example

It's time to rework the introduction to Galatians 5:2–15 at the beginning of this chapter. The word from the Lord is "Serve out of love not legalism." The student revised his introduction in the following manner:

Relevance to the contemporary context (by situation):

> We live in a world where we are constantly inundated with requirements and expectations about how we should live. We must get good grades or meet quotas and KPIs.[9]

Relevance to the congregation (through felt needs):

> This also applies to the church where many expectations are placed on pastors and ministry staff, such as having to be available seven days a week to attend to every meeting or matter that is less than urgent, as if you and I did not have our own private life.

Relevance to the contemporary context (by question):

> From time to time, in the midst of the pressures of life and ministry, I wonder if I am serving simply to meet the expectations of others, or am I serving out of an overflow of God's love?
>
> On the outside, it may not look any different. But if I do ministry simply to meet expectations, then it would just be self-serving legalism. I would just be seeking to obtain the approval of God or man through works.

Relevance to the congregation (through felt needs):

> Do you have the same struggles too? Do you feel a need to show good academic results to your church sponsors? Are you anxious about the outcome of your ministry?

Connecting to the text:

> We are like the Galatians who started with grace but fell back into legalism. Like the Galatians, Paul is admonishing us to recover the joy of serving God out of love not legalism.

From the above example, we see that an introduction can blend different aspects of contemporary and congregational relevance. Key words ("serve,"

---

9. Key Performance Index.

"love," "legalism") connect the introduction to the text. Specific details are also given so that hearers can identify with the contemporary situations and questions.

Practice Example

This is the original introduction to a sermon on Esther 2:19–36 in which Mordecai foiled an assassination plot against the life of the Persian king, but Haman, the enemy of the Jews, then planned to kill Mordecai and all the Jews in Persia. The word from the Lord is to trust in God's providence, though unseen. How would you critique the student's work below using the three guidelines?

> Before plunging into the text, it would be good to know a little about the background of the book. While the books of Ezra and Nehemiah focus on the return of Israel to Jerusalem, the book of Esther shows no such interest. Rather, in the book of Esther, life goes on in the heart of the Persian Empire. It describes the life of the Jewish people scattered among the non-Jewish nations, much like the existence of Christianity in the world today.
>
> Another distinctive of the book of Esther is that it shares with the Song of Songs the distinction of being the only one of two books that fails to mention God by name. However, through the eyes of faith, one can see the providence of God at work.
>
> When reading the book of Esther, the major motif of reversals is noticed. The social and political structures of this world, epitomized by Persia, seek to drown God's people in its system, but these efforts are overcome as the Lord intervenes and reverses the course of events, reminding us that he is God. Though nameless and unseen, Yahweh is very much the central character of the book of Esther, for only the intervention of God could result in such a radical reversal of circumstances. God's intervention is evident in chapter 2 where Mordecai happens to be at the right place at the right time to overhear an assassination plot.

Write your critique and improvement before looking at the next page.

1. Is the introduction relevant to the central word?

    Yes, because he did mention God's providence in the second paragraph, but he should pare out unrelated information, such as the mention of Ezra and Nehemiah. These only bloat his paragraph and give his hearers mental indigestion. Even when pointing out the motif of reversals (which actually needs explanation), he needs to relate it to the idea of providence.

2. Is the introduction relevant to the contemporary context?

    This is the biggest problem. The sermon begins with the historical background of the text and includes foreign names that would either baffle or alienate the congregation. There is only a slight relation to the scattering of Christianity in the world today, but that is not even related to the central idea. The preacher needs to find a contemporary parallel for the threat that Mordecai and the Jews faced.

3. Is the introduction relevant to the congregation?

    No. There is no reason why listeners should care about what happened to Mordecai and the Jews if they cannot identify with them at all.

The student rewrote the introduction in the following manner:

Relevance to contemporary context (by situation and question):

The 2004 Indian Ocean earthquake triggered a series of devastating tsunamis, killing over 230,000 people in fourteen countries. It was one of the deadliest natural disasters in recorded history. In times like these, we wonder, where is God?

Relevance to congregation (through felt needs):

When we face personal tsunamis in our lives, we may also wonder, where is God? When we fail an exam, when we have financial needs, or when we or a loved one is diagnosed with a fatal illness, we wonder whether God is really with us. Where is his providence?

Connection to the text:

God's people in the book of Esther also faced a political tsunami in the fifth century BC. They were threatened by genocide in Persia. They, too, must have wondered, where is God? God's name is not even mentioned at all in the book of Esther. But in chapter 2, we see how God is providentially at work behind the scenes.

This is a more relevant introduction than the original bookish version.[10] Key phrases ("providence," "Where is God?") connect the paragraphs to the text. The contemporary situation and felt needs are also specifically described.

If introductions are of first importance to hearers, then conclusions are of even greater consequence because they are the last thing that a congregation will go home with. To this we turn in the next chapter.

---

10. I would not have used the 2004 tsunami, though, because it raises questions that the sermon does not really address. I would have referred to persecutions of Christians, which is a closer parallel to the threat in the book of Esther. For example, one could ask, Where is God when the Malaysian highest court banned the name "Allah" in the Malay Bible, or where is God when churches in Aceh, Indonesia, are burned or torn down?

While the Jews in the book of Esther were spared, many Christians in other parts of the world have suffered martyrdom. For such a question on unrequited suffering, one has to consider the broader theological question of theodicy. Nonetheless, Esther reminds us that the unseen God is still at work providentially, though we may not always understand how and when.

12

The Feet: Conclusion

Concluding a sermon is like landing a plane. Most air crashes occur during two crucial periods: take-off and landing. A poor pilot either lands too soon, leading to a crash landing, or he lands too late, circling the airport several times till he runs out of fuel. An inexperienced preacher may be so relieved that his sermon is over that he beats a hasty retreat by delivering a generic conclusion that could be tacked on to any sermon. There is the ubiquitous "Let us take a few moments to reflect on the message" to the more positive "May the Lord transform our attitudes and lives as we listen to his Word." And then there are those preachers who keep flying around in circles, not knowing how to land. As a passenger, I just want to get off at my destination. For the sermon, that destination is the word from the Lord.

And what do people do when the plane lands? Every passenger is eager to get off, often unfastening the seatbelt even before the captain turns off the "unbuckle seatbelt" sign. We just want to get on with our lives. So also, when the sermon ends, the congregation should be excited about getting on their feet and moving on. The conclusion needs to propel them to live for God. Chapell lists the parts of a sermon that listeners will remember most in order of priority:[1]

1. Their perception of the speaker
2. Some striking aspect of delivery
3. Concluding material

---

1. Chapell, *Using Illustrations to Preach with Power*, rev. ed. (Wheaton, IL: Crossway, 2001), 141–142.

4. Introductory material
5. Illustrations
6. Specific applications
7. Basic idea of the message
8. An interesting thought in the message
9. A main-point statement
10. An expositional concept

Therefore, apart from the speaker and his or her delivery, what the hearers will leave with is the conclusion. What do you want your hearers to take home? I want to point out two things: Let them (1) recall the word of the Lord and (2) be motivated to respond.

A. Why Conclude?

1. Recall the Word of the Lord

Recapitulation announces the destination lest some in the congregation had forgotten or missed it. Almost every homiletical book reminds the preacher not to add any new material in the conclusion. To announce during the descent that the plane is going to divert to a new destination will cause chaos. To deviate from the word from the Lord in a conclusion will confuse the hearers and leave them befuddled. Here is one such example from Genesis 15 cited in the previous chapter on Introduction. The central word was to trust God's promises when facing discouragement.

> Abraham believed God despite all his doubts. He did have a child by Sarah; he did become the father of a multitude; he is the father in faith to Jews, Christians, and Muslims. He was blessed by God to be a blessing.
>
> The Christian faith enables us to face life or meet death. We do not have all the answers, but we trust that God does. Like Abraham, we may doubt and waver in our faith. It often seems that God's promises are not being fulfilled. Yet God does not expect us to transcend our humanity. What God simply wants is for us to believe the promises given us. God wants us to grow in our faith and understanding. In Christ, God has promised us forgiveness of sin and the hope of eternal life. We need not fear,

for God is with us. "Do not be afraid, I am your shield; your reward shall be very great." He says that to us too. You are blessed to be a blessing.

Did you find the central word in the above conclusion? It is there but hidden amidst a clutter of not one but two new ideas. Can you pick them out? One new idea is that Abraham and the hearers are "blessed to be a blessing." That is true, but it is in Genesis 12 not Genesis 15. The second idea is about salvation by faith in terms of facing death and the hope of eternal life, an idea that comes from the Pauline interpretation of Abraham in Romans and Galatians. But this is not the central word for the student's sermon; that word is to trust God's promises when facing discouragement. I advised the writer to reiterate this idea and suggested that he conclude by finishing up the introductory story about complaining to his wife. This is what he rewrote:

> Abraham believed God despite all his doubts. Life is not always fair. Life hurts, life is unjust, life bites us back hard and leaves us maimed, distraught, confused, and fearful. In times of discouragement, trust in God's promises like Abraham did. He did have a child by Sarah; he did become the father of a multitude; he is the father in faith to Jews, Christians, and Muslims.
>
> After my wife "woke up my idea,"[2] I spent time in communion with God. I cried to him and hung on to his promise. "Father God, help me not grow weary in doing good, for your Word says that I shall reap in due season if I do not lose heart." I spent time talking to my mentors and prayer partners. They encouraged me to trust in God's promises. We are to focus not on ourselves or the facts of what is impossible but to trust in God who will fulfill his promise.
>
> Are you feeling discouraged in your ministry, hopeless about your problems, or fearful of expectations? Look to God not yourself. Trust in his promises.

Did you get the central word this time? You couldn't avoid it; it is repeated three times: First, Abraham trusted God, then the preacher himself learned to do so, and finally, the listener is exhorted to do likewise. The word of the Lord has been delivered – no distraction, no deviation – straight to the heart.

---

2. A Singaporean slang meaning "rebuked me."

Having recapitulated the sermon, the second purpose of a conclusion is to call for a response.

2. Call to Respond

John A. Broadus remarked pithily, "If there is no summons, there is no sermon."[3] Jesus said, "If you know these things, blessed are you if you do them" (John 13:17). James's admonition to be "doers of the word, and not hearers only" (Jas 1:22–25) is well known. The Puritans spoke of the need to "preach through to the heart," something that John Wesley also strived for in his preaching.[4] From chapter 1, we've learned that each of the four models of preaching requires a response. There are three kinds of response that a sermon can call for: Why respond? What to do in response? How to respond? All of these need to spring from a theocentric basis.

a. Why respond?

When we tell people why they are to respond to God, it must be based on who God is and what he has done. We respond not to *be* loved but because we *are* loved. Chapell warns against three "Deadly Be's" in preaching: These are exhortations to "be good," "be like," and "be disciplined."[5] Basically they exhort believers to strive to "be" something in order to be loved by God. While sounding biblical, these messages are cancer cells that mutate faith into works, leaving Christians with the burden of meeting up to expectations to earn God's love. Such Christians in turn become as demanding of others as they are of themselves. Or some may give up trying altogether to earn what they can't achieve and so become apathetic or rebellious. Besides God's redemptive grace, motivation can also be based on God as creator, his sovereign kingship, and holy nature.

b. What to do in response?

When we are telling people *what* they are to do in response to God, then a theocentric focus would be on God's kingdom and purpose. This requires the preacher to distinguish between divine and earthly goals, and between biblical and cultural perspectives. In a Singaporean context, a good student

---

3. John A. Broadus, *On the Preparation and Delivery of Sermons*, ed. J. B. Weatherspoon (New York: Harper & Row, 1944), 210.

4. Stott, *I Believe in Preaching*, 246–251.

5. Chapell, *Christ-Centered Preaching*, 288–295.

is one who obtains good grades. This gets spilled over into the Christian life such that being a good seminarian means getting A's and being a good pastor means getting results. But what does God really call us to? He calls us to love (1 Cor 13:1–3), to serve with our gifts (1 Pet 4:10–11), and to grow in the knowledge of himself (Col 1:10).

The preacher also needs to distinguish between God's kingdom and the pastor's own kingdom. Although a preacher may give specific suggestions to encourage concrete applications, only the Spirit knows the relevant step for each congregant to take. For example, not everyone is called to be a full-time missionary, although all are called to be witnesses of Christ. When people are directly and ultimately accountable to God, they will work out their salvation with fear and trembling (Phil 2:12) even when no one is looking.

c. How to respond?
Sometimes, the congregation needs to know the how rather than the why and what of a response. In Philippians 2:12, though Paul calls on his readers to work out their own salvation, he adds that "it is God who is at work in you, enabling you both to will and to work for his good pleasure" (2:13). What an assurance! Often Christians forget that it is God who enables, and like the foolish Galatians who started by depending on the Spirit (Gal 3:3), we fall back into working by our own flesh. We find that we can only keep this up for so long before we fail yet again, and so we struggle under a sense of guilt or give up in defeat.

Biographical preaching in which congregations are exhorted to follow the examples of heroic biblical or historical characters often sets an unrealistic standard. How many of us can pray for hours on end, witness to strangers, or memorize the entire Bible? Not me. Different people have differing gifts and callings. "Preachers should teach God's people to esteem and emulate the righteous actions of godly people . . ., but preachers must also make it plain that such godliness can come only as a response to God's unconditional love and as a result of his enabling Spirit (Phil 1:19–21)."[6] Therefore, we act according to the grace we have, for example, we pray as long as God enables, and that will be more pleasing than trying to match the spiritual giants by our own strength.

Similarly, Chapell warns about the pitfalls of the "be disciplined" messages, which exhort congregations to pray more, give more, serve more:

---

6. Chapell, *Christ-Centered Preaching*, 291.

> Preachers should encourage more prayer, stewardship, study, and fellowship not to manufacture blessing but so that believers can experience more fully the benefits of union with Christ that God freely offers. . . . The same disciplines, however will become distasteful duty and bitter pride for those who think that their devotion keeps them on the good side of a God whose measure of love is determined by the grade of their performance.[7]

In the end, it is the Spirit who enables us to practice the disciplines, whether to pray or to study the Word (Rom 8:26; 1 Cor 2:14–16).

So then, all aspects of a motivation need to be theocentric: the "why" or basis of our response, the "what" or goal that we are responding to, and the "how" or means that enable our response. A conclusion does not necessarily need to include all these three aspects of motivation but should be determined by the word of the Lord or the needs of the congregation. The rest of this chapter will discuss four practical ways to conclude: by telling illustrations, giving directions, inspiring a vision, or extending an invitation.

B. How to Conclude

1. Tell an Illustration

Stories are a powerful way of persuasion through the emotions, but an emotional high is not a substitute for truth based on proper exegesis. "But nearly as great an offense is committed by failing to engage the heart, stimulate the will, excite the mind, and elevate the soul concerning eternal truths at this most crucial stage," says Chapell.[8] I suggest the following guidelines to help the preacher use stories in his conclusion: Tell illustrations that are theocentric and climactic; it may be a personal story, and it may be suspended like an *inclusio* at the beginning and end of the sermon.

a. Tell a theocentric story

In a sermon based on Exodus 32:7–14, a Singaporean student used Moses' intercession for the Israelites as an example of servant leadership. His word from the Lord was: "Intercede for God's people because of God's faithfulness." He ended with the following story:

---

7. Ibid., 293.
8. Ibid., 257.

> In the 1930s, a man also interceded for his people and changed the course of history. The people were in a sea of sin: opium smoking, gambling, prostitution. They were all seeping into the doors of the church. That man fearlessly denounced all sin and hypocrisy wherever he found it, just like Moses did. Sometimes he even pointed his finger at someone and declared, "There is sin in your heart!"
>
> But that man's heart for the people was in the right place. He constantly prayed for the people. He prayed daily over an extensive list of people, usually carrying small photographs of the people wherever he went. He got up regularly at 5 a.m. and prayed for two to three hours. He often prayed till sweat poured down his face. At times he would literally collapse upon his bed, weeping and sobbing under the burden of prayer.
>
> That was Song Shang Jie, John Sung. Through his unflinching stance against sin and his constant intercession for his people, thousands of Chinese were delivered from sin and experienced renewal.
>
> You have been called to serve God's people, will you denounce sin and will you intercede for the people?

This is an inspiring story. It is largely consistent with the word from the Lord, but what is your reaction to the story? I wished I could be like Sung, rising up at 5 a.m. regularly to intercede, but it is unlikely that I will do it because it sounds too demanding. The conclusion needs a theocentric tweaking: People should be responding to God rather than to an exceptional human being. What would motivate ordinary people to intercede more? Not by comparison with others or by self-effort, but like Moses, by focusing on the faithfulness of God himself. It would be better for the preacher to say in conclusion:

> Not all of us are like John Sung. God may not call each of you to rise up early in the morning to pray the way he did. But God's servants are called to intercede. What is God calling you to do? What commitment will you make this week as the Spirit prompts you? Because of his faithfulness and love for his people, God is waiting to answer your prayers.

This ends the sermon with a theocentric basis for response.

b. Tell a climatic story

Another student, mentioned earlier, preached on Genesis 1:1–9 with the word: "Trust God to work in the chaos of your lives." This is his conclusion:

> In closing, I would like to share a song composed by Steven Curtis Chapman when he faced his own chaos in the year 2008. His five-year-old adopted daughter from China was accidentally knocked down by the car driven by his own biological son at the family home. Maria did not survive. This song stemmed from his determination to see God's order despite the chaos of his pain.
>
> [Student plays the song, "Our God is in Control." Part of the lyrics goes:
> *This is not how it should be.*
> *This is not how it could be.*
> *This is how it is.*
> *And our God is in control . . .*]
>
> After Maria's death, Chapman and his wife Mary-Beth started a medical care center in China for orphans with special needs from newborn to age five. They named it Maria's Big House of Hope. The center celebrated its second anniversary last July in 2010 and have cared for more than 500 children with special needs.
>
> Will you, like Chapman and his wife, trust God to work in the chaos of your lives today?

This story has a theocentric motivation based on God as creator. Although it highlights the incredible faith of a man, it rests not on his own strength, but through his song, the focus was on God's sovereignty. The story is so emotive that the preacher only needed to add one last sentence when applying it to the audience. The force of that story rippled through the minds and hearts of the hearers that day.

If you had already used a compelling story in your third or last point, it can segue into the conclusion so that you do not have to narrate another story that will distract from the climax.[9] This is what I did in my Psalm 23 sermon that was preached to a church congregation. The word was: "Come to God who cares for you personally." In my third and last point, I gave the example of how God provided for the financial needs of a lady even before

---
9. See also ibid., 258.

she asked. The congregation's expression showed their amazement. There was no need for me to end with another story. I simply closed with a summary and restated the word from the Lord:

> God's goodness and love was chasing after her though she did not know it. God's goodness and love is also chasing after you though you may not realize it. God knows your needs and will provide for you. God sees the dangers and will protect you. Come to God who cares for you personally.

c. Tell a personal story

If a preacher shares a personal story, listeners usually perk up. This is the *ethos* of persuasion and what the witnessing model is about. We listen because we feel that the preacher is letting us in on a personal secret; we pay attention because if the sermon made a difference to the speaker, then there must be something real to it. In a sermon on Romans 15:1–6, a young Vietnamese student spoke of pleasing others rather than ourselves for the sake of glorifying God. Her original ending was simply a series of rhetorical questions, ending with the mundane, "Let us take a moment to reflect on the message today. What would you do differently to glorify God?"

I gave her the feedback that she needed more specific applications. I asked what difference this sermon had made to her personally. She came back with some applications that sounded like a to-do list, for example, having fellowship or praying in small groups. I urged her to share a personal experience, and she finally opened up with something refreshingly honest:

> What about us? Are we willing to make sacrifices for the sake of building each other up? Have we been living, studying and doing ministry to glorify God or is it really about ourselves?
>
> For me as an introvert, I love to be alone by myself. I don't like to go for community gatherings or fellowship meetings. I see it as a duty that I have to do but do not enjoy. I thought I'm already pleasing God as long as I do well in my studies, treat others nicely, read the Bible and pray every day.
>
> Now when I meditate on this passage, I realized that all I have been doing is about me and myself. I didn't care about what was going on in the community. Even the good things that I did were not to glorify God but myself. I realized I was wrong.

> Brothers and sisters, do we care only for ourselves, or are we willing to step out of our comfort zone for the sake of others? Let us look to the example of Jesus and glorify God.

Her testimony was more effective than the rhetorical questions because through her, we faced our own behavior as well.

d. Tell an *inclusio* story

If you began with a story that introduced a problem, then you can tie up the loose ends in the conclusion. "This wrapping up of the sermon gives the message a sense of being packaged and thus communicates craft, thoughtfulness, and conscientious preparation."[10] Here is an example I used when preaching on Psalm 13, a lament psalm:

> A young man I know seemed to have everything going wrong in his life. As a student, he failed and had to repeat his "O" level exams. When he started working, there was an economic crash, and he lost his job. His girlfriend broke up with him via a phone text. Soon after, his mother was diagnosed with cancer and eventually passed away. As if that wasn't bad enough, his father was also diagnosed with cancer and also passed away soon after. He was devastated and felt that God had abandoned him.

After expounding the psalm, I concluded the sermon with the rest of the story:

> Remember that young man I told you about in the beginning? Like the psalmist he poured out his complaints to God. Despite everything, he kept his confidence in God's steadfast love and trusted God to deal bountifully with him (Ps 13:6).
>
> His parents had always objected to Christianity. But as the church ministered to his mother during her illness, she saw God's love and became a Christian before she passed away. His father witnessed the same love and care, and he too became a Christian before he died. The young man found a more stable job after losing his first job. In fact, it was at that previous job that he was introduced to his present wife. The lady who broke up with him was simply not ready for a relationship, and God provided

---

10. Ibid., 259.

someone more suitable for him. Today, he is the proud father of a son.

We may not get what we want, but we can trust God to deal bountifully with us according to his will. Like the psalmist, this young man kept his eyes on God in the midst of his pain. Whatever you are going through, keep your eyes on God in the midst of your pain. Trust him to deal bountifully with you.

Just as the psalmist resolved his struggle at the end of the psalm, so did the above story, thus testifying to the reality of the psalm. Besides ending with a story, a second way to conclude is to give directions for applications.

2. Give Directions

Some sermons are specifically aimed at application. The parable of the Good Samaritan ends with "Go and do likewise" (Luke 10:27). Jesus's last words to the woman caught in adultery were "Go and sin no more" (John 8:11). Preaching as *didasko* (teaching) means changing behavior. Preachers can conclude by giving directions that are specific, relevant, and theocentric.

a. Give specific directions

Remember the Galatians 5 sermon, "Serve out of Love not Legalism," in the previous chapter? Below is his original conclusion:

> The heart that is acceptable to God is not one that depends on works but rather one that is transformed by God's grace that results in a life of work. We may be growing in theological knowledge, but are we growing in love? We may be growing in ministry skills, but are we growing in love?

I asked the student to give examples of how the hearers can act in love. He came back with one good example, but for greater variety and a sense of completion, I add a couple more below:

> Could we, for example, during this Chinese New Year season, consider how we may offer hospitality to one or two needy families within and outside our faith communities by visiting them or inviting them to our homes? Or perhaps it is to drop a note to someone who hasn't been to church for some time. Sometimes, it can just be offering to pray for a colleague's problems. What is God calling you to do because of his love?

General directions in the "before" version are like vapors that evaporate from the minds of the hearers. Specific directions, on the other hand, help listeners to put feet on the sermon after hearing it.

b. Give relevant directions

When giving directions, the preacher needs to keep the context of the congregation in mind. What difference would the sermon make to the married, the single, the divorced, or bereaved? How would it be relevant to students, working adults, homemakers, or retirees? How can it address their varying problems in the areas of health, finances, work, relationships, or family? Stott gives an example preached by a young man on the seventh commandment not to commit adultery. The preacher ended with the following applications: to single young people, to keep themselves pure; to people in an adulterous relationship, to decide to break up despite their pain; to married couples, to work at their marriage and be a model to others; and to the local church, to have the courage to confront and discipline offenders according to biblical teaching.[11] These are thoughtful and practical directions.

c. Give theocentric directions

Lest applications become a mere to-do list, preachers need to focus on the why, what, or how of a theocentric motivation. For a congregation that is resistant to change, then one has to explain more of the why. Another group might be willing to change but needs to know what to do. If a congregation knows what to do but are fearful or discouraged, then the preacher can emphasize the how.

Stott's example of a sermon on adultery, for example, focused on *what* people should do, though I suspect that most people already know what is morally right but have to contend with straying desires. Some theocentric explanation of *why* they should obey may be needed. An explanation of the historical context of the Decalogue would show that the commandments were given after God has set the Israelites free from slavery; the law, therefore, is not a bondage but a guide to living in true freedom. The preacher can explain how sexual sins rob us of living fulfilled lives. If the congregation needs the *how* or means to do what is right, then the preacher can point to God: Just as he freed the Israelites from slavery, so also he is able to deliver us from our

---

11. Stott, *I Believe in Preaching*, 253, citing a sermon preached by Roger Simpson in All Souls Church.

temptations and bondages. Besides illustrations and directions, a third way to conclude is to inspire the imagination.

3. Inspire a Vision

A vision shows what the kingdom of God is like: It is the Sermon on the Mount lived out in the reality of our world; it is the local church continuing the life of the Pentecostal church; it is the eschatological vision both of judgment and salvation found in Jesus's parables and in John's visions in Revelation. Nor is such a vision found only in the New Testament: Isaiah envisions that in days to come, many peoples will come to the mountain of the Lord, for "out of Zion shall go forth instruction, and the word of the LORD from Jerusalem. He shall judge between the nations, and shall arbitrate for many peoples; they shall beat their swords into ploughshares, and their spears into pruning hooks; nations shall not lift up sword against nations, neither shall they learn war anymore" (Isa 2:3–4). This vision was recorded at a time when Israel was threatened by foreign domination; it seems like a fantasy, but it is seeing what is really real with eyes of faith. This is what we also need today in our world. I describe two ways below to present an inspirational conclusion through visualization and through poetry.

a. Inspire through visualization

Robinson defines this as "a method that projects a congregation into the future and pictures a situation in which it might apply the truth that we have preached."[12] He adds that visualization takes on force if the situation it envisions is possible, or better still, probable. In other words, make the scene as realistic as possible. He gives an example of concluding a sermon with the central word of "Keep the workday holy":

> If you take this truth seriously, you may face difficult days ahead. Sometime in the future, you will have a boss tell you to do something that you know is wrong. He or she may urge you to falsify your spending account. "It's all right to be honest," your boss tells you, "but your overactive conscience is making other people in the department look bad." You know, however, that you ultimately will not account to others in the department; you will recognize that you'll give an account to God. In as polite and

---

12. Robinson, *Biblical Preaching*, 131.

gracious a way that you know how, you say, "I'm sorry. I simply cannot do that."

You may discover that your boss does not appreciate your commitment to honesty. In a short time, through trumped-up charges, you may lose your job. If that happens, you will feel overwhelmed. You will not be tempted to sing a cheery chorus. You'll be threatened. You'll wonder about your future.

Perhaps in those grim hours, you'll remember the truth of this text. Your master is in heaven. He does not pay on the first or fifteenth of the month. But he promises that he will reward you for any good thing you do on your job. You will come to a place in your life when you have staked your job, your security, and even your future on what God has said. What a commitment! What a witness! What courage! In the confidence that God can be trusted, even with your job, you have remembered the workday and kept it holy.[13]

Going beyond individual applications, Stanley and Jones recommend ending a sermon by casting a vision for the church. "In this closing moment you call on your audience to imagine what the church, the community, families, maybe even the world would be like if Christians everywhere embraced your one idea." Imagine what a church would be like, they ask, if "love one another" was a lifestyle rather than a memory verse. Imagine homes where husbands and wives submit to one another as unto the Lord; imagine young people committed to purity and service; imagine what would happen if for three months Christians managed their money as if everything really belongs to God.[14] However, for imagination to work effectively, it ironically also needs to be realistic. Below I explore how to provide a realistic as well as a communal vision.

i. Realistic Imagination. One may have heard about the positive effects of visualization, especially in improving sports performance.[15] However, when it comes to motivating people to pursue their goals, psychologist Gabriele Oettingen shows that visualizing about a positive future alone actually

---

13. Robinson, *Biblical Preaching*, 131–132.
14. Stanley and Jones, *Communicating*, 129–130.
15. Vinoth K. Ranganathan et al, "From Mental Power to Muscle Power: Gaining Strength by Using the Mind," *Neuropsychologia* 42, no. 7 (2004): 944–956. Researchers at Cleveland Clinic Foundation in Ohio found that subjects who only visualized doing biceps curls, five times a week, for two weeks, increased their strength by 13.5 percent.

demotivates people. In a 2011 study, she had thirsty participants imagine drinking a large, cool glass of water. This was found to reduce their blood pressure, indicating relaxation and reduced energy. In other words, simply imagining quenching your thirst will make you less likely to get water. Such imaginations are fantasies that conceal the need to invest effort to obtain the goal. This result is borne out in many other studies carried out by Oettingen and her colleagues. Whether the wish was to find a date, recover from hip-replacement surgery, look for a job, lose weight, or get good grades, the outcome was clear: Positive thinking alone did not help.

Oettingen shows that positive thinking must be combined with "realism" (i.e. to also imagine the obstacles that stand in one's way and how they can be overcome). She calls this process "mental contrasting." Laboratory experiments that involved healthy eating and exercising, recovering from chronic back pain, getting better grades, and managing stress showed that mental contrasting helped people achieve far better results.[16]

Robinson's vision above of keeping the workday holy incorporated mental contrasting when he walked hearers through the possibility of losing a job for the sake of doing the right thing. Below is another sermon based on Genesis 15:1–6 written by an Indonesian student. Her word from the Lord is to trust in God our shield and reward even in the midst of crisis. Look out for the elements of a good motivational vision in this conclusion:

> You may be feeling like Abram today. Despite all the good things that are happening in your life, you know that deep within your heart, something is bothering you.
>
> You may have seen your ministry flourish, but you may ask, "Oh Lord God, what good is a successful ministry if my parents are still unbelievers?"
>
> For graduating students, you may ask, "Oh Lord God, what good are all my A's if I am not effective in ministry?"
>
> For lecturers you may say, "Oh Lord God, what good is my scholarly reputation if my own children go wayward."
>
> Whatever your anxieties or crises may be, you can find assurance in God our shield and very great reward. He who has

---

16. Gabriele Oettingen, "The Problem with Positive Thinking," *The New York Times*, 24 October 2014; Lowry, *Homiletical Plot*, 84–47, puts it in another way, which is that one can motivate change by reducing fears. He cites Kurt Lewin, "Quasi-stationary Social Equilibria and the Problem of Permanent Change," in *The Planning of Change*, eds. Warren Bennis, Kenneth Benne, and Robert Chin (New York: Holt Rinehart, and Winston, 1961), 235-238.

> granted you divine grace in ministry will open a way for you to minister to your family. He who equipped you with divine strength in your study will also fight alongside you in the ministry. He who has entrusted you to train his servants will enable you to teach your children. Let us put our trust in God our shield and our very great reward.

In the above conclusion the preacher acknowledges the hearers' anxieties, yet gives the hope of a positive future. Though the hearers have to play their part in working out this future, the outcome and the means is possible by trusting God.

ii. Corporate vision. Stanley and Jones remind preachers that visions are not just for individuals but also for the body of Christ to corporately "shine like a beacon of hope in our communities, our neighborhoods, and in the market place."[17] In a sermon on being the servant of all like Christ (Mark 9), I challenged the church to serve and welcome not just the respectable but also the rejected. I pointed out the opportunities for service inside and outside the walls of the church. My key verse was Mark 9:37: "Whoever welcomes one such child in my name welcomes me," where a child represents those without rights and status. If I were to preach it again, I would conclude it with the following vision:

> When this church welcomes a child in Jesus's Name, you welcome Christ. When an ex-prisoner sits next to a professional who helps him find a job, Christ is moving in this church. When a migrant worker gets a meal and a listening ear, Christ is listening in this church. When a domestic helper finds fellowship and prayer support, Christ is here in this church.
>
> Sure, it's messy. Children are messy. People may take advantage of us. We need the patience and wisdom of the Spirit. But we are promised the presence of God in this church. "Whoever welcomes a child in my name welcomes me, and whoever welcomes me welcomes not me but the one who sent me."

In the above conclusion, I focused on the theocentric why of motivation, which is Christ's presence with us. A vision should be a pull rather than a push factor so that people will respond to God and not to a pushy pastor.

---

17. Stanley and Jones, *Communicating*, 130.

A vision acknowledges the needs and difficulties but draws the congregation beyond that to focus on Christ.

b. Inspire through poetry

When I say poetry, I don't merely mean lines that rhyme but carefully chosen words that move the heart and mind. In a prior example of a first-person narrative based on the call of Elisha in 1 Kings 19, the concluding challenge was to give up all to follow God's call. The preacher recounted his struggles with worldly desires until God spoke to him:

During one Sunday service, a hymn was sung:

> *O soul, are you weary and troubled?*
>   *No light in the darkness you see?*
> *There's light for a look at the Savior,*
>   *And life more abundant and free.*
> *Turn your eyes upon Jesus,*
>   *look full in his wonderful face,*
> *And the things on earth will grow strangely dim,*
>   *in the light of his glory and grace.*[18]

God knows my weakness. He understands my struggles. He knows that my eyes have been captured by the fancies of this world. I need to turn my eyes back to Jesus. Then all these things will become dim in the light of his glory and grace.

You may have committed yourself to serve the Lord, but have the currents of the world eroded your heart? You may have burned your plough, but are you now digging through the ashes to find it again? How can we keep following in difficult times?

> *Turn your eyes upon Jesus,*
>   *look full in his wonderful face.*
> *And the things on earth will grow strangely dim,*
>   *in the light of his glory and grace.*

The hymn has conveyed the message more movingly than prose. The sermon can then end with the congregational singing of the quoted hymn. At the end of the sermon, the usual procedure is to close with prayer or to offer a few moments of silence for reflection. There is yet a fourth method of conclusion that takes the appeal into the time of prayer.

---

18. Words and music by Helen H. Lemmel, 1922.

4. Extend an Invitation

You may have told a moving story, or given specific directions, asked challenging questions, or painted an inspirational vision. The Spirit may prompt you to challenge the people there and then, whether to repent of sin, to cast a burden on God, or to decide a direction in life. Some extreme Calvinists believe that the preacher only needs to present the gospel and leave the conviction to the Holy Spirit. R. Alan Streett lays out the biblical, historical, practical, and psychological arguments for a public invitation.[19]

The public invitation can be found as early as the Golden Calf incident in Exodus 32 when Moses called out, "Who is on the LORD's side? Come to me!" Jesus often used the word "come" to call people to himself, for example, "Come to me, all you that are weary . . ." (Matt 11:28). In the final chapter of the Bible, the Spirit and the Bride say, "Come." Says Streett, "Here is a picture of God and man working together to bring the lost into the kingdom. As the evangelist or pastor extends the invitation for sinners to come to Christ, the Holy Spirit is also invisibly drawing them to the Savior."[20]

I find it helpful to issue the invitation during the closing prayer. This is so that the hearers may focus not on the preacher or other people around them but on God alone. In order to give time for the invitation, I keep the conclusion short and prepare the people by telling them that I will be giving them an opportunity to respond to God, whether by raising hands or coming to the front. Below are three guidelines in issuing an invitation: Invite personally, theocentrically, and progressively.[21]

a. Invite personally

Address the hearers in a personal way by addressing different groups, their specific needs, and particular fears. I usually spend time in prayer before I work out the invitation, asking the Spirit to show me if there are groups or needs to be surfaced. Below is the invitation that I gave after preaching on Psalm 23 in a church setting with the word to come to God who cares for you personally. I had cued the musicians to play the closing song quietly during

---

19. R. Alan Streett, *The Effective Invitation* (Old Tappan, NJ: Revell, 1984).
20. Ibid., 66.
21. I learned some of these guidelines by observing Rev Lawrence Khong, a pastor whom I grew up with. Each week he would give an invitation to receive Christ, and each week I witnessed many people, both Christians and non-Christians, responding, streaming down the aisles to be prayed for and counseled.

the prayer time. Worshipful music helps people to focus on God and touches them emotionally. It is not about being manipulative but being persuasive based on a preached truth.

> The Lord knows you by name; he knows your needs, and he cares for you personally. This morning, come, receive a touch from the Lord. I invite you to come up for prayer during the closing hymn.
>
> If you need the Lord's provision, if you are weighed down with worries about your work, studies, family, or health, come and ask for what you need.
>
> If you need the Lord's protection for you or your family, if there is anything you are afraid of, whether your enemies are human or spiritual, come, because his rod and staff will comfort you.
>
> If you feel far from God, he is still your Shepherd; his goodness and love pursue you. Come to God your Shepherd and King because he cares for you personally.
>
> As we sing the closing song, just walk right up here to the front. I will be here to pray for you. The pastors and elders will be here to pray for you. Don't let embarrassment stop you. All of us need him. Don't let pride stop you from receiving all that God wants to do in your life. He cares for you.
>
> Let's all rise now to sing this song prayerfully. As we sing, if you need prayer, if the Spirit is prompting you, just come.

I handed the time over to the worship leader, and soon, people started making their way to the front. Just as it takes time for the first corn to pop, one may have to wait a while for people to pluck up their courage. That Sunday we prayed for many, beyond the end of the closing song.

Note that in the beginning, I addressed specific needs, based on the sermon preached. Later, I verbalized the fears that hold people back. The fears are addressed both positively and negatively: positively in that we need God and he cares for us; negatively in warning people that if they ignore God, they might miss out on God's work in their lives. For those who are too shy, one could invite them to come forward with a friend, or to seek counsel privately. But the invitation gives people an opportunity to ask for prayer that they might never have done so, and indeed, I referred several congregants to their own pastor for follow-up.

b. Invite theocentrically

An invitation is given on behalf of God to call people to God (basis), to do God's calling (goal), and by God's enabling (means). Hearers may not be ready to make a life-changing decision on the spot, but they are usually willing to be prayed for, which itself is a theocentric means. Below is an example from a sermon I preached on Genesis 12:1–3 with the word to "step out in faith for God to bless you and to make you a blessing." I provide an analysis to highlight the theocentric elements:

Invite theocentrically (basis of response):

> God is here to call you to be a blessing. Will you say, "Yes, I am willing"?

Invite personally (addressing different categories of people):

> Will you step out in faith to be a blessing in your family, office, school, or church? You are never too old or too young. You may be a student, a working adult, a stay-home mom, a retiree. You may be a young Christian or a mature disciple. God wants to use you as you are.

Invite theocentrically (goal of response):

> What has God put in your heart to do?

Preparation:

> In a moment, I will give you an opportunity to demonstrate your response to God by raising your hand.

Invite personally (addressing fears):

> But you say, "But, Pastor, I'm not sure I can do it. I'm not good enough."
>
> Friend, you don't have to be good enough. You only have to be willing.

Invite theocentrically (means of response)

> If you want to be a blessing, raise your hand so that I can pray for you. I want to pray that you will experience God's blessings – his provision, fruitfulness, and power, just as he blessed Abraham.
>
> So raise your hands now, where you are seated, if you want to say, "Lord, I want to be a blessing. Lord, bless me to be a blessing." Raise your hands so that I can pray for you even now.

The preacher should verbally acknowledge those who raise their hands, and this also encourages others to follow. When there are no more responses, close the time with prayer. There is no need to keep the people waiting as a form of emotional blackmail. The preacher can encourage those who raised their hands to stay behind so that they can be prayed for specifically. The pastoral team should be ready to counsel and guide those who respond. This ensures that people do not merely make a spur-of-the-moment decision that is conveniently forgotten soon after.

What if there is no response? We are afraid of feeling like a failure, but an invitation, even without a response, can serve a purpose. It is a reminder to hearers that they face a choice, something that they might ponder in the days to come. They can be encouraged to speak to a Christian friend on their own even if they are not ready to respond at that point in time. If it was an evangelistic invitation, the congregation may think about inviting their non-Christian friends to church next time. If the Spirit has led you to give an invitation, then entrust the outcome to God to work in his own time and way.

c. Invite progressively

A progressive invitation is particularly helpful for an evangelistic appeal. I am not referring to the usual practice of asking people to repeat a prayer quietly, and then to raise their hands, and finally to stand and walk to the front. While the intention is to make it easier for people to move from a private to a public decision, it seems like a form of behavior control. If the preacher is going to prepare people, then he needs to tell them just the one action to indicate their decision. He can choose any method that the church may be most comfortable with. Even just filling in a response card at the end of the service is a helpful means for follow-up.

What I mean by progressive is to give an invitation first to Christians followed by one to non-Christians. Because Christians are more likely to respond, this will create a positive atmosphere and avoid making non-Christians feel that they are especially singled out. Below is an invitation that I gave after an evangelistic Christmas message based on Isaiah 9:1–7. The central word was to come to Jesus as our Wonderful Counselor, Mighty God, Everlasting Father, and Prince of Peace. After giving an invitation first to Christians, I addressed those who were not Christians:

Invite personally:

> For those of you who are not Christians, you are not here by accident. Jesus came for you 2,000 years ago at Christmas. Perhaps God has been speaking to you for a long time.

Preparation:

> Jesus is here for you, and if you want to come to him, then I'll ask you in a moment to raise your hand and put it down again, as an indication of your desire and so that I can pray for you.

Invite personally (specific categories of people):

> I do not know your name, but God does. You may be a young man or woman who thinks that no one cares. You may be a father or mother who carried your burdens here. Or you may just simply be tired of always having to prove yourself, to keep on doing better.

Invite theocentrically (basis of response):

> Today, you don't have to walk out alone. You can walk out with God. Jesus is here to be your Wonderful Counselor, your Mighty God, your Everlasting Father, your Prince of Peace. If you want God's presence in your life, raise your hands and put it down, and I will pray for you.

Invite personally (addressing fears):

> Don't be worried about what your friends will think because this is between you and God. Don't let fear hold you back because God's perfect love will cast out your fear. Don't let pride hold you back because God opposes the proud but raises up the humble.

Invite theocentrically (basis of response):

> I will ask for the last time today. Jesus is here waiting to set you free from your sin, your fears and burdens. If you want to say, "Yes, Jesus, I want you to be Lord of my life," then raise your hand and put it down, and I will pray for you.

The preacher should do his or her best to prepare the invitation, but ultimately, it is prayer that makes a difference. Billy Graham shares that he experiences a great spiritual battle after closing the invitation. Often doubts flood his soul as he wonders if anyone will come. But he says that the Spirit will sweep away those doubts and fill his heart with faith. He then enters into a state of total concentration in prayer, explaining, "It's at this point that I feel a real struggle with the enemy. . . . Not only do I feel the need to pray, but I ask my associates and others to be much in prayer at this time as the battle rages for the souls of men."[22] You have sown the seed, and the Spirit will bring the harvest, whether it's now or later, whether it's one or many.

Conclusion

When a pilot is going to land a plane, he has to switch from auto to manual control. If he was catching a nap while his co-pilot was flying, he has to take-over, communicate with the control tower, get his flight crew ready, and look out for the right runway. Ending a sermon requires the same effort and attention. Usually the preacher has expended so much energy on studying and preparing the sermon that he usually has no energy left to work on the conclusion. But the failure to prepare an effective conclusion could undermine all the effort that the preacher has put in. I have learned to set aside time just for preparing the conclusion. I need freshness of mind to pray and to hear the Spirit, to envision the kingdom of God, or to plan the invitation.

Now that the preacher has prepared all the parts of a sermon from the skeleton to the body and added the head and feet, he or she needs to ensure that they all move together by being properly connected through the ligaments. This is what we will look at in the next chapter.

---

22. Billy Graham, "Insights to the Invitation," *Proclaim* (Oct 1977): 5, cited in Streett, *Invitation*, 35.

13

The Ligaments: Transitions

When you sprain your ankle and tear a ligament, you suffer in pain and end up limping. When a sermon lacks tight transitions, hearers suffer in confusion, and your sermon ends up limping. You may have a word from the Lord, but strong transitions ensure that everyone gets it too. The outline for a deductive sermon usually looks like this:

Introduction

Transition

1. First main point
    a. Explanation
    b. Illustration
    c. Application

Transition

2. Second main point
    a. Explanation
    b. Illustration
    c. Application

Transition

3. Third main point
    a. Explanation
    b. Illustration
    c. Application

Transition

Conclusion

I will focus only on the major transitions indicated above, but the same principles will also apply to minor transitions between the explanation, illustration, and application under each main point.

A. Why Transition?

Homileticians usually agree on four purposes:
1. To review the preceding point
2. To preview the following point
3. To explain the connection between two points
4. To connect to the central idea

Oral communication differs from the written word. If a reader didn't understand a point, he can always go back and read it again, but if a listener missed what was said, there is no rewind button and the connection is lost. This is why Robinson says that "it takes at least three or four statements and restatements of a point to make it clear to an audience. Carefully constructed transitions help your listeners to think with you so that together you and they move through the sermon." And from Broadus: "Skilled transitions are often the distinguishing mark between mundane messages and excellent sermons." The four purposes listed above indicate the guidelines for crafting transitions. I will start with explaining the connection between two points first, for that is the major ligament that holds the sermon together.[1]

---

1. Robinson, *Biblical Preaching*, 94; Broadus, *On the Preparation*, 120, cited in Chapell, *Christ-Centered Preaching*, 261.

B. How to Transition?

1. Reason for Connections

There are three ways to make connections: by enumeration, by logic, and by shift of perspectives.[2] Enumeration is simply to number the points – first, second, third, etc. The weakness is that enumeration does not explain the connections between the points, but if used with other connections, they help the hearers to follow the progress of the sermon. One should not overdo the numbering though, for example, "the third subpoint of the second main point," as that would be hard to follow and would make a sermon sound overly long, tedious, and stilted. The logical connection and change of perspectives are what the speaker should provide for the hearers.

a. Logical connection

These are marked by the conjunctions "and" and "but" (and their related variations such as "not only . . . but also," "on the other hand," etc.). In my sermon on Psalm 23, I wanted to explain the historical context of the shepherd before getting into the psalm itself. I could have simply said:

> Now, let me explain the historical context of the shepherd metaphor in the text.

Or, I could use a logical connection:

> What kind of shepherd are we talking about in Psalm 23? He is not the sheep rancher you may have seen in New Zealand, who keeps thousands of sheep roaming over rolling green hills. The animals are just money-making livestock to him. It doesn't really make a difference if one of them gets lost.
>
> But the kind of shepherd we are talking about in Psalm 23 is a Palestinian shepherd, one who takes care of only about a hundred sheep, each of which he knows by name. He has to watch over them in a dangerous and rocky terrain. God is like that Palestinian shepherd who cares for each and every one of you. He keeps an eye on you personally.

---

2. David Buttrick, *Homiletic Moves and Structures* (Philadelphia, PA: Fortress, 1987), 70–71, categorizes the types of connections.

The above transition uses the logical connection of a contrast (not this but that). It allows the preacher to begin with something that the hearers are familiar with and lead them to a new realization.

In the same sermon, I wanted to move from the first point that God provides for your needs to the second point that God protects you from enemies. Making the "and" connection, I could have just said:

> Besides providing for your needs, the second point is that God also protects you from your enemies.

That is simply enumeration, but giving a reason for the connection would make the sermon more interesting. Such connection can usually be gleaned from the exegesis. The shepherd imagery is not only about God as a personal and attentive shepherd, it is also a metaphor for God as a sovereign and authoritative king. Therefore, I can transit in the following way:

> Come to God. He is the Shepherd who personally provides for your needs because he cares for you. But you may ask, "I know God cares. But can he deliver in difficult times?" The psalmist tells us that God is not only a caring shepherd but a powerful one. This is the second point in verses 4–5, that God protects you from your enemies.

This transition uses the "and" connection in the form of "not only but also." Long provides a few other useful logical connections: The "if . . . then" category that can be expressed as "because . . . therefore," or the "imperative . . . indicative" outline that was discussed in chapter 5 on Deductive Forms. The "reconsider" connection provides another point of view with words such as "look again" or "in a deeper sense" that would be relevant to an inductive outline.[3]

b. Change of perspectives

Perspectives may be shifted by moving from a broad to a narrow view or from the past to the present and the future. Chapter 11 on Introduction provided some guidelines for connecting the introduction to the text. Usually this includes a shift in time, moving from the historical context to the contemporary context or vice versa. To make the introduction even more relevant, the preacher can also shift from a broad to a narrow perspective (i.e. from the general contemporary context to one that is personally relevant to

---

3. Long, *Witness of Preaching*, 190.

the hearers). The shifts have to be connected by the use of key words so that the perspectives are tied together.

In my last point on Psalm 23, I explained verse 6, first illustrating it in its historical context and then shifting to a contemporary and personal context:

> Almost every English translation of verse 6 says goodness and love shall "follow" me. It sounds like a leisurely walk. But in Hebrew, the verb is *radaf*. *Radaf* is used 143 times in the OT, usually of one army pursuing or chasing after another army. So it would be more accurate to translate verse 6 as "goodness and love shall pursue or chase after me." Instead of enemies hunting us to harm us, God is hounding us with goodness and steadfast love.
>
> But God's goodness and love may seem to take a long time to catch up with people. That's because we don't see how God is actively working behind the scene. David had to wait eight years as a fugitive in the wilderness before he finally became king as God promised. Where was God's goodness and love in those wilderness years? He was actively training David to be the greatest King of Israel.
>
> Are you wondering where God's goodness and love are in your life? Are you wondering why God hasn't caught up with you yet? A lady shared with me about a financial need she was worried about . . .

I then explained how God was already working to meet that need even before the lady prayed. The key words are "God's goodness and love" and "catching up." The change in perspective in the last paragraph was introduced by a couple of questions, which is another way of making connection.

2. Raise Questions

In the two examples from Psalm 23, I had already incorporated the use of questions: "What kind of shepherd are we talking about?" and "Can he deliver in difficult times?" The second question is framed as one that may be asked internally by the hearers. This is what Chapell calls a dialogic question:

> A preacher who can hear the questions playing on listeners' minds and then asks these questions *out loud* employs a powerful rhetorical tool. The dialogue a preacher initiates on listeners' behalf not only convinces them that the preacher respects

their thought and is sensitive to their concerns but also invites listeners to continue progressing through the message to satisfy their concerns.[4]

My transition from the second to the third point of the Psalm 23 sermon also employed a question:

> Come to God who cares for you by providing for your needs and protecting you from enemies. But you may be asking, "Why is God not answering my prayer? Why doesn't he seem to care?" Verse 6 gives us the assurance that we need – that God is pursuing you with his goodness and love.

Use questions that you yourself asked during your exegesis or *lectio*. Most likely they are also questions that your listeners would also ask. Questions may also arise as you think about how the message would apply to different members of the congregation or as you minister to people in your pastoral work. Don't ignore difficult questions but struggle through them in the light of the text or the broader framework of theology. If we sweep the hearers' questions under the carpet, then they will remain unconvinced by the message. The congregation will leave church thinking that the preached truths are mere idealism that have no place in their lives outside the church. It is true that the perfect will arrive only at the *eschaton*, but it is also true that the kingdom of God was inaugurated at Christ's first coming, and so his teachings are meant for us in the here and now empowered by the Spirit, although not without opposition and sacrifice.

3. Review and Preview

A well-known rule for clear communication advises speakers to "Tell them what you are going to tell them. Tell them. Then tell them what you have told them."[5] This, of course, applies to deductive rather than inductive sermons. Long notes that reviewing and previewing provide assurance to the listeners that they have indeed received the message. For those who got lost, whether it was the preacher's fault or their own, it gives them an opportunity to reenter

---

4. Chapell, *Christ-Centered Preaching*, 263.

5. This maxim has been traced to Aristotle and popularized by Dale Carnegie, an American writer and lecturer in self-improvement, sales, and public speaking.

the sermon and get back on track.[6] Here is an analysis of the transition between the first and second main points of my Psalm 23 sermon:

Review of the first point:

> Come to God. He is the shepherd who provides for your needs because he cares for you.

Transition question:

> But you may ask: "I know God cares. But can he deliver in difficult times?"

Transition by logic:

> The psalmist tells us that God is not only a caring shepherd but a powerful one.

Preview of second point:

> This is the second point, in verses 4 and 5, that God protects you from enemies.

When it comes to the third point, it is also helpful to review the first two points so that the congregation can recall what you said around 20 minutes earlier.

In the conclusion, a brief summary also functions as a transition from the last point to the conclusion. The preacher would usually say, "In conclusion, we have learned that . . ." If transitioning to directions, he could ask, "What difference will this make in our lives?" Or, if ending with a vision, the preacher can ask, "What will it look like if we all took this truth seriously?"

4. Repeat the Central Word

In the Psalm 23 example, I repeated the central word "Come to God who cares for you personally" in the review of the preceding point. The word from the Lord is the scarlet thread that runs through the whole sermon, especially if it is not fully incorporated into the main points. This ensures that the word is clearly heard and that people are constantly persuaded to respond. Even if they don't answer God's call immediately after the sermon, at least they carry it with them when they leave. At the same time, do not belabor the point if the central word is already stated shortly before or after the transition.

---

6. Long, *Witness of Preaching*, 189.

C. An Example

Recalling the sermon based on Genesis 1:26–2:4 with the call to enjoy our work and to rest like God, the student had two main points: Enjoy work like God, and enjoy rest like God. She transitioned from the last paragraph of the first point as follows:

> Do you enjoy your work? Can you say *hinneh* – I am satisfied with my work; I am pleased with my reading; I am happy with my writing? We can, if we know we are working for God and the good of God's world. We can, if we ask God to help us work like him.
>
> Now we need to define what rest is. Is it watching Sunday night football as much as we like? Is it sleeping the whole day without thinking about our assignments, jobs, or future? Is it taking a long holiday to a beautiful island and enjoying delicious food?

What is your assessment of the above transition, and how would you rewrite it using the guidelines in this chapter? You may adapt the outline below as you see fit. Try it on your own, and then compare it to the suggested answer that follows.

Notice that in the example, the student had not provided any transition at all. She made a sudden switch to a new point that could have caught a hearer unawares.

Review of previous point, and repeat central word (if necessary):

> Genesis 1 showed us that God enjoyed his work, and we are also called to enjoy our work like God.

Raise question:

> But is life all about working?

Reason for connection by logic (but):

> The final thing that God did was to rest on the seventh day. In fact, rest was the culmination of God's work. It is the only day that God blessed and sanctified.

Reason for connection by shift of perspectives (from biblical to contemporary):

> Do we know how to rest like God?

Preview of next point, and repeat central word (if necessary):

> This is the second point, that you are called to enjoy rest like God.

Raise question (to connect from main point to explanation):

> But what do we usually mean by rest? Is it watching Sunday night football . . .

This is an example of a full-blown transition, which may be overdone and wooden if applied at every turn. It worked in the above sermon because there were only two main contrasting points that required a strong connection.

We now have all the components for the content of a full sermon. But a sermon that is not delivered or poorly delivered cannot bring life to hearers. In the fifth and last part of this book, we will focus on oral delivery that enlivens through ears, eyes, and voice.

Part V

Delivering with Ears, Eyes, and Voice

14

The Ears: Oral Style

When reading the book of Esther, the major motif of reversals is noticed. The social and political structures of this world, epitomized by Persia, seek to drown God's people in its system, but these efforts are overcome as the Lord intervenes and reverses the course of events, reminding us that he is God. Though nameless and working behind the scenes, Yahweh is very much the central character of the book of Esther, for only the intervention of God could result in such radical reversals of circumstances.

The above paragraph may sound familiar; it's the sample introduction used in chapter 11 for practice. Was it easy to understand? Were there too many clauses swimming around in your head? You can go over what is written on a page, but if it is orally delivered, the audience might have drowned in the verbosity. A sermon has to be written for the ear and not for the eye. In other words, write the way you talk.

A. Why Words?

Why should a preacher be concerned with his or her choice of words, or what is called "style"? Are we relying on rhetoric to convince people rather than on the power of the Word and the Spirit? Certainly we do not seek to work people up with emotional words, but if we are convinced that we are preaching the truth, then we must do our utmost to engrave those truths on the minds and hearts of the hearers. This is what the sage did in writing the book of Ecclesiastes, he "sought to find pleasing words, and he wrote words of truth plainly" (Eccl 12:10). King Solomon believed that "A word fitly spoken is like apples of gold in a setting of silver" (Prov 25:11). The prophets were wordsmiths who used poetry, parallelism, puns, and metaphors to deliver their oracles. The means is as important as the message because the preacher must do his best to communicate when lives are at stake.

For example, the prophet Amos was a master of puns. In Amos 6:1 he addressed those who considered themselves the elites of the *leading* (Hebrew *re'shit* from the root *ro'sh*) nation and warned that they will be at the *lead* (*ro'sh*) of the exile. The prophet makes his message of poetic justice stick by means of verbal irony – the consequences fit the crime. Carefully chosen words can capture the mind, ears, and will of the hearers. I will list the most common feedback that I give to my students about style and demonstrate how it made a difference to their sermons. The four guidelines are be plain, be poetic, be personal, and be powerful.

B. How to Use Words?

1. Be Plain

This does not mean to be boring; it means to be clear, and clarity comes through simplicity. To be simple is not to be simplistic. "Simplistic" implies giving a shallow explanation, but "simple" means communicating an idea in such a way that everyone can understand. This usually requires brief sentences and short words. If you have tried explaining theology to a child, this can be harder than you think. Shakespeare said, "Brevity is the soul of wit."

While good writing advocates varying sentence length and vocabulary, an oral style calls for short sentences and words so that hearers do not get bogged down in a jungle of multiple clauses and polysyllabic words. If they stumble over a sentence, they are not able to retrace the same route as a reader could. A preacher should have his or her own style in terms of expressions, but as Stanley and Jones argue, "If you want to be an effective communicator, you must allow communication principles to *shape* your style. At the end of the day, . . . clarity trumps style. Clarity trumps just about everything."[1]

Below is what a student wrote in his sermon:

---

1. Stanley and Jones, *Communicating*, 175.

> Thus we see that Genesis 1 portrays the idea of pre-existent chaos at creation, which would have been obvious to any ancient Near Eastern citizen, and now, I hope is clear to us also.

This sentence may be alright with seminary students but is probably not clear to a church audience. First, the preacher needs to get rid of scholarly jargon, like "pre-existent" and "ancient Near Eastern." Either explain them, or if they are not crucial to the sermon, omit them. "Chaos" is central to the sermon and is a word that people can understand, but its practical implication needs to be unpacked. Second, there are three clauses combined into one sentence (which is not as bad as the five clauses in the opening paragraph of this chapter). Two clauses in a sentence should suffice. Below is my edited paragraph:

> Before God acted, there was only darkness and chaos. Without God, nothing could live. Without God, everything would fall apart.
>
> What about the chaos in our personal lives? How many of us had to put up a brave front to hide our fears? How many of you had to pretend on the outside that everything is going well when on the inside you are falling apart?

The first paragraph explains chaos in a way that everyone can understand, and the second paragraph spells out its relevance to the hearers' lives. The above two edited paragraphs also illustrate the next guideline.

2. Be Poetic

Before you skip this guideline because you think you can't be poetic, let me tell you that half of the Old Testament is composed of poetry, not only in the Psalter, but also in the prophetic and wisdom books. Our God is a poetic God, and he can inspire his preachers to preach in a creative manner. Applying Hebrew poetry techniques, such as parallelism, make your sermon more memorable and emotive. I also recommend applying "the rule of three" (see below).

a. Parallelism

Unlike other poetry, Hebrew verses do not rhyme by sounds; rather, they rhyme by ideas. The second line usually expands on the content of the first line, and it may do so in several different ways: synonymously, antithetically, or synthetically.[2] Synonymous parallelism means that the second parallel line contains a similar idea; antithetical means that it has a contrasting idea; while synthetic adds a new idea. Such repetition impresses the message on the hearers both aesthetically because it is well-crafted, and also cognitively because it adds depth and emphasis. Hebrew parallelism is indicated by similar words and syntax to tighten the comparison or contrast. These techniques translate well in English. For instance, in the preceding example based on Genesis 1, there is a pair of synonymous parallelism:

> Without God, nothing could live.
> Without God, everything would fall apart.

The idea in the two sentences is similar, but the second line includes even inanimate matter in creation. There is a parallel syntax beginning with "without God" and a play on the word "thing" that encompasses the extremes of "nothing" and "everything."

An antithetical parallelism is also useful for emphasis. In a sermon based on Matthew 26:6–13, the preacher wanted to focus on how the woman with the alabaster jar poured the perfume on Jesus.

> How do you put on perfume? You dab a little here and there behind your ears or on your wrists.
>
> This woman, she did not merely dip her finger into the perfume and dab a little here and there on Jesus's head.
>
> No, she poured it all out over her Lord.

The first two parallel lines about "dabbing a little here and there" are a contrast between how perfume is usually applied and what the woman did. The last sentence about pouring it all out is a contrast with the preceding sentences in terms of length, thus calling attention to the woman's deed. The short sentence reflects her stark action that dumbfounded the observers.

b. The rule of three

For an even more climatic emphasis, there is the rule of three. Day writes that this rule is used in jokes and everyday communication. For example, we are familiar with "The Three Little Pigs," "The Three Blind Mice," and "The Three Wise Men" (though we weren't told there were three of them in the biblical

---

2. David L. Petersen, *Interpreting Hebrew Poetry* (Minneapolis, MN: Augsburg Fortress, 1992), 24, discusses the categories originally devised by Robert Lowth.

narrative). A Chinese nursery rhyme also sings about "Three Tigers," one of which was blind and two of which were deaf. An explanation for this rule of three may be found in recent cognitive psychological studies suggesting that our working memory has a capacity of about four "chunks" of information (which is less than the seven that was previously thought). For children and older adults, the number is less than four. Thus, the human memory would be most comfortable with three ideas.[3] Besides memory capacity, three would also be the smallest number needed to form a pattern. "The first time you say something, it's an incident; the second time you say something, it's a co-incidence; but the third time you say something, it becomes a pattern."[4] A pattern would be more interesting to the ear and mind than just bits of information.

The Bible also uses the rule of three. The greatest commandment in Deuteronomy 6:6 exhorts God's people to love the Lord your God with three parts: "With all your heart, with all your soul, and with all your might." In the Old Testament wisdom literature, numerical proverbs use the structure "three . . . and even four . . ." as a way of building up to a full listing. For example, Proverbs 30:15–16 say, "Three things are never satisfied, four never say, 'Enough': Sheol, the barren womb, the earth ever thirsty for water, and the fire that never says, 'Enough!'" Interestingly, this structure is used four times in Proverbs 30. In the New Testament, Paul climatically ended his chapter on love by writing, "And faith, hope, and love abide these three; but the greatest of these is love" (1 Cor 13:13). In the last book of the Bible, God is described in a threefold way as the one "who is and who was and who is to come" (Rev 1:4, 8; 4:8).

Of course, one should not overdo the rule of three lest the sermon sounds too pretentious. Imagine listening to a piece of music that is played *sforzando* (forcefully) from beginning to end. Listeners will throb with a headache from the constant banging. Employ the rule of three where necessary for emphasis, to get attention, or to make something stick. (There, I just used the rule.) Or, the rule can be applied with some variation in structure to break the

---

3. Nelson Cowan, "The Magical Number 4 in Short-Term Memory: A Reconsideration of the Mental Storage Capacity," *Behavioral and Brain Sciences* 24, no. 1 (2001): 87–114; George A. Miller, "The Magical Number Seven, Plus or Minus Two," *Psychological Review* 63, no. 2 (1956): 81–97.

4. Lisa B. Marshall, "How to Communicate Better Using the Rule of Three," quoting Kristin Schier.

monotony. In the example from Genesis 1, the synonymous parallelism also uses the rule of three with the last two lines loosely based on the first:

> Before God acted, there was only darkness and chaos.
> Without God, nothing could live.
> Without God, everything would fall apart.

The change of syntax reflects a change of perspective: The first line introduces the idea of chaos at creation, while the last two lines unpack what chaos would mean.

3. Be Personal

Preaching is not delivering an impersonal philosophical treatise. It is representing a personal God who seeks out his people individually and communally. To Robinson, preaching "should sound like lively conversation.... The feeling of good preaching is that you are talking to and with your hearers."[5] Therefore, writing a sermon is more casual and direct than writing. For example, in speaking we use contractions, such as "can't" rather than "cannot" or "didn't" rather than "did not." Some characteristics of conversational speech involve the use of slang, humor, and the second person pronoun "you."

a. Use slang

When we speak informally with fellow Singaporeans, we lapse into Singlish. Clarity, though, should always take precedence, and so we should be careful about slang words because not everyone may understand what we are saying. However, an occasional, deliberate use may create rapport between the speaker and the audience. In an earlier example, a student recounted, "After my wife woke up my idea, I spent time in communion with God." "Woke up my idea" is a Singlish phrase meaning to rebuke someone and bring him to his senses. Singlish has the advantage of saying something in a dramatic and pithy way. Hearers will gravitate towards this down-to-earth person, and his humor gets them to also "wake up their ideas."

---

5. Robinson, *Biblical Preaching*, 142.

b. Use humor

Well-known British preacher Stuart Briscoe writes that one of his church members told him that listening to his sermons is like finding a knife stuck in his rib only after he gets home. Finally, he figured how the knife got there, and he told Briscoe, "You got me laughing, and while I was laughing, you slipped the point home." Briscoe explains that "humor puts us off guard, and at those times we are highly receptive to penetration by the Word."[6] Scientists have now proven that laughing produces the feel-good brain chemical endorphins. This promotes bonding in social groups,[7] meaning that when you use humor, the hearers feel good; when you make them feel good, they like you; and when they like you, they will listen to you. But at all times, humor must serve the truth.[8]

Ken Davis helps us understand that there are three kinds of humor: exaggeration, stating an overlooked truth, and surprise.[9] The right kind of humor can help us see certain truths about ourselves and our world. In the sermon on Amos 8, the preacher made a deliberate slip of the tongue when he described the wealthy people of Samaria:

> Israel was doing really well in Amos' time: Economic prosperity from international trade, regional peace with neighbors, high net worth individuals, vibrant religious activity, good class bungalows made of ivory along Sentosa, I mean, Samaria. Sound familiar?

Sentosa, a leisure island at the southern tip of Singapore, is where the most expensive condominiums are located. The humor is a little bit of surprise, in that while talking about ancient Samaria, modern Sentosa slipped in. It unmasked the hearers' smugness and makes them realize that they are no different from the Samaritans.

c. Use second person pronouns

When we have a conversation, we use "you" to refer to the other person. We don't refer to hearers in the third person, such as "Christians" or "one" or

---

6. Stuart Briscoe, "Interesting Preaching: How to Avoid Talking in Someone Else's Sleep," Preaching Today, online.

7. R. I. M. Dunbar et. al., "Social Laughter Is Correlated with an Elevated Pain Threshold," *Proceedings of the Royal Society B* (14 Sept 2011).

8. Haddon Robinson, "Strengths and Seductions of Humor (Part I)," Preaching Today, online.

9. Ken Davis, "Humor That Connects," Preaching Today, online.

"people." "You" fosters relationship, but preachers are reticent of using it in negative statements. We retreat to the collective first person "we" so that we do not sound too critical, for example, "We are all sinners," or "We should repent." However, if we are too afraid of hurting people's feelings, then we may be dulling the edge of the sermon. One way of handling this is to intersperse some "you's" among the "we's" to sharpen the challenge without sounding preachy. After all, we are speaking as heralds and as witnesses: We deliver the message on behalf of God, but we are also members of the congregation. Paul also mixes "you" and "we" in his epistles, for example in Galatians 6:7–9.

> Do not be deceived; God is not mocked, for *you* reap whatever *you* sow. If *you* sow to *your* own flesh, *you* will reap corruption from the flesh; but if *you* sow to the Spirit, *you* will reap eternal life from the Spirit. So let *us* not grow weary in doing what is right, for *we* will reap at harvest time, if *we* do not give up. (italics mine)

"You" conveys a pointed challenge, while "we" expresses Paul's unity with his hearers.

In an earlier sermon on the call of Elisha, the student had originally written in his conclusion:

> We may have committed ourselves to serve the Lord, but have the currents of the world eroded our hearts?
>
> We may have burned our ploughs, but are we now digging through the ashes to find them again?
>
> How can we keep following in difficult times without turning back?

(Note the use of parallelism and the rule of three above.) I then replaced some of the "we" with "you" as well as "you and I."

> *You* may have committed *yourself* to serve the Lord, but have the currents of the world eroded *your* heart?
>
> *We* may have burned our ploughs, but are *we* now digging through the ashes to find them again?
>
> How can *you and I* keep following in difficult times without turning back?

What difference do you sense between the above two challenges? In the first, there is a sense of distance and safety in numbers with the blanket "we."

The hearers can think, "This applies to other people and not necessarily to me." The rewritten paragraph will not let hearers excuse themselves, but the second line shows that the preacher is also part of them because, as the third line states, we are all engaged in a common struggle.

4. Be Powerful

The most powerful words in a speech are the verbs. They provide the action and energy. Robert Jacks in his book on writing for the ear has fifty rules, and below are those that focus on verbs:

> Rule 6. Active voice is more alive than passive.
>
> Rule 16. Verbs are more alive than nouns.
>
> Rule 27. Don't overuse adjectives or adverbs.
>
> Rule 28. Where possible, replace adjective with strong, more colorful verbs.[10]

Robinson gives some examples of strong verbs. "Say he *bellowed*, not he *talked very loudly*; . . . She *went* gets her there, but not as clearly as *crawled, stumbled, shuffled, lurched*."[11]

In a narrative sermon on God wrestling with Jacob and dislocating his hip, I wanted to describe the pain. I could have stated, "His hip was dislocated, and he felt terrible pain." That would be quite a boring statement for such a dramatic moment. But if we change the passive to active verb and choose stronger verbs (see italics), we heighten the effect:

> The stranger *touches*[12] his hip. It's just a pat, not a punch, but a force *rips* out his thigh bone from its socket. He *howls* in pain. He almost *blacks out*. But Jacob *latches* on to his tormentor and *clings* on for dear life.

I've also changed the past tense to the historical present tense to convey immediacy, enabling the hearers to participate with Jacob as the story unfolds.

---

10. Robert Jacks, *Just Say the Word! Writing for the Ear* (Grand Rapids, MI: Eerdmans, 1996), 92–95.

11. Robinson, *Biblical Preaching*, 145.

12. The Hebrew is literally "touch" rather than "struck."

C. An Example

Now that you are armed with these guidelines about being plain, poetic, personal, and powerful, try rewriting the opening paragraph of this chapter before looking at my suggestion on the next page. The central word is to trust in God's providence (in the book of Esther). You are free to expand on it but keep the emphasis.

The book of Esther is full of reversals. *(Change passive to active. Leave out jargon, i.e. "motif.")*

The proud are brought down and the humble are lifted up. *(Use antithetical parallelism to explain reversal. Passives are used to imply God's hidden work. Rules can be broken if you have a good reason.)*

The Persian emperor thought he could do whatever he wanted. In the end, he did whatever a woman wanted. *(Use short sentences and simple words. Employ antithetical parallelism to demonstrate reversal. Use humor.)*

So who is the real hero in the book? *(Direct question makes it personal.)*

It's not Mordecai.

It's not Esther.

It's someone whose name is not even mentioned in the book. *(Use rule of three to build up anticipation.)*

The real hero is God. *(Use plain language to amplify the main point.)*

Though we may not see him, he is at work behind the scene. Though you may feel lost and threatened, you can still trust in God's providence. *(Use parallelism. Use first person and second person pronouns.)*

It takes time and effort to craft our words and sentences. I use an online thesaurus to help me find, not the most impressive, but the most apt word. Stott mentions that putting in such effort will ensure that instead of memorization, the words will readily come back to our mind even when we take only notes into the pulpit.[13] Parallel structures and the rule of three will etch the phrases in your mind so that you can speak without detouring to your notes.

However, the most important goal in choosing the right word is what is said of the Preacher in Ecclesiastes: "The sayings of the wise are like goads, and like nails firmly fixed are the collected sayings that are given by one shepherd" (Eccl 12:11). Goads are pricks that prod cattle to plough in the right direction. They may hurt, but they get the right response. We need to

---

13. Stott, *I Believe in Preaching*, 231.

ask God for wisdom to find the right words to deliver his Word. When we have the words for the ears, we now need to deliver them effectually with our eyes and voice.

15

Eyes and Voice: Delivery

A. Why Deliver?

In a well-known study, speech communication theorist Albert Mehrabian showed that 55 percent of meaning comes from body language, 38 percent from the voice, and only 7 percent comes from the actual words spoken. This means that if the nonverbal message contradicts the verbal, listeners will believe the nonverbal. As Robinson says, if you insist, "This is important," but your voice is listless and your body stands limp, the hearers will not believe you.[1] Or if you mumble, "God hates sin," with an apologetic smile, people will not be convicted. Conversely, if you holler, "God loves you," and shake your fists at the hearers, then it seems that God is a policeman with a big stick.

Although we cannot see and hear God physically, his body language and voice are conveyed through metaphors in the Old Testament. Hosea 2 describes God's wrath as a husband who strips his wife Israel for her adultery and yet woos her back later by speaking to her tenderly.[2] The love of God is also embodied through the parental acts of carrying, feeding, and teaching a child to walk in Hosea 11. In the New Testament, we can see the acts and voice of God communicated through the incarnate Christ. We witness his anger through his table-throwing in the temple (Matt 21:12), his grief when

---

1. Albert Mehrabian, *Silent Messages: Implicit Communication of Emotions and Attitudes* (Belmont, CA: Wadsworth, 1971), 43–44; Robinson, *Biblical Preaching*, 151.

2. The language of stripping needs to be understood in its historical context as legal punishment for adultery and not as spousal violence. See Maggie Low, *Mother Zion in Deutero-Isaiah: A Metaphor for Zion Theology*, SBL 155 (New York: Peter Lang, 2013), 14–15.

he weeps for Lazarus (John 11:35), and his love when he touched those considered unclean: a leper (Luke 5:13), a dead daughter (Luke 8:54), and a bier with the body of a widow's only son (Luke 7:14). Delivery is not an act to communicate a message, it *is* the message. The preacher who has heard a message from the Lord cannot help but preach it with his body and voice. In this chapter, I share some pointers that have made the most difference to my students' preaching.

B. How to Deliver?

1. Deliver with Your Eyes

How do you feel when you talk to someone, and the other person doesn't look at you? Irritated, neglected, suspicious? We react negatively because the reasons for avoiding eye contact are usually negative: The spouse who is glued to his mobile device while you talk to him values his news more than you; the student who looks down when the teacher asks a question is avoiding the query; someone who suffers from autism is simply unable to respond in a normal way. Establishing eye contact shows that you are confident, friendly, open, and have regard for the other person. The eyes indicate to the audience what the preacher regards as his focus – is he paying attention to the ceiling, the wall, or the floor? Or is he genuinely concerned about the hearers and how they respond to God's word? People want to know that the preacher, as God spokesperson, cares for them. The psalmist cries out to God to *look* upon him and to answer his prayer (Ps 13:4), and another pleads that God will *see* and have regard for his people (Ps 80:15).

Robinson gives the best advice on eye contact. He suggests looking at different individuals and talking to each one for a second or two. Throughout the sermon, the preacher picks different persons in every section of the sanctuary to have a conversation with.[3] The effect of this is that hearers will feel that the preacher wants to address each of them personally and that this is a message for them and their lives.

Keeping eye contact raises the question of whether to preach with a full manuscript. Today's congregations have a preference for preaching without notes because that comes across as more direct and genuine. However, this ability is also over-emphasized. During the Great Awakening in the eighteenth

---

3. Robinson, *Biblical Preaching*, 158.

century, Jonathan Edwards read his sermon, "Sinners in the Hands of an Angry God," and men and women repented with tears and groanings.[4] Of course, we live in a different time and context, but God can work whether a preacher reads his sermon or not. What is more important is whether the preacher has what Edwards had – an all-consuming passion for the glory of God and the souls of men and women. But assuming that the preacher has that kind of passion, he can then consider how he can best serve his people.

Jeffrey Arthurs discusses the pros and cons of extemporaneous and manuscript delivery. The first enhances communication and persuasion, while the later provides security and precision. Arthurs explains that "extemporaneous" does not mean "impromptu," which is to speak without preparation; rather it depends on careful preparation but chooses much of the language at the moment of delivery. However not every preacher has the gift of the gab. Some resort to memorization, but this leads one to focus on the words rather than on the content, and the speaker still ends up sounding like he is reading off a script, just one that is invisibly in his head. The labor of memorizing a script, warns Stott, "is enormous, the risk of forgetting our lines considerable, and the necessary mental energy so great" that it is not worth the preacher's time and effort.[5] What then is a preacher to do? The secret is not in memorization but in internalization.

Internalization is essential whether one preaches with or without notes. Charles W. Koller points out in his book, *Exposition Preaching without Notes*, that when one has immersed oneself in exegesis and prayer during sermon preparation, then one has naturally internalized the message.[6] This is halfway to preaching with no notes. The other half is to organize the flow of the sermon so that it connects simply and logically in a way that is easy to recall. Having good transitions (ch. 13) therefore helps one to keep the main points of a sermon linked together in one's mind. All the speaker needs to do then is a mental review or rehearsal of the sermon before delivery.

Even for a preacher who prefers to use a manuscript, Mark Mitchell advises preachers to read and reread their script before delivery. He says, "Don't try to memorize it, but internalize the flow and train the eye to where

---

4. Stott, *I Believe in Preaching*, 255.

5. Jeffrey Arthurs, "No Notes, Lots of Notes, Brief Notes," Preaching Today, online; Stott, *I Believe in Preaching*, 256.

6. Charles W. Koller, *Expository Preaching without Notes and Sermons Preached without Notes* (Grand Rapids, MI: Baker, 1962), 85–97. For further guidance on this method, see Joseph M. Webb, *Preaching without Notes* (Nashville, TN: Abingdon, 2001).

the material is on the page so you don't struggle to find your place each time you look down." Mitchell understands that for introverts like himself, having a manuscript frees him up to be himself instead of scrambling for words. He advises, though, that the preacher should write for the ear (see previous chapter). It also helps to format the page so that it's easy for the eye to pick up. Use a large font size, plenty of spacing, and bold the key points. Johnson recommends writing in "breath bites" (i.e. write in phrases that you can deliver in one breath). Write each phrase on a separate line and indent each phrase till the end of the sentence.[7] Here is an example taken from chapter 12 on sharing a concluding vision (I will explain the italics in the following paragraph):

> When this **church** *welcomes* a child
>   in Jesus's Name,
>   you *welcome* Christ.
>
> When an **ex-*prisoner*** sits next to a *professional*
>   who helps him find a job,
>   Christ is *present* in this church.
>
> When a **migrant worker** gets a meal
>   and a *listening* ear,
>   Christ is *listening* in this church.
>
> When a **domestic *helper*** finds *help*
>   and prayer support,
>   Christ is *here* in this church.

I use font size 14 for my notes so that I can read them without fumbling for my reading glasses. As you can see, parallel lines aid memory because they follow a pattern. Parallelism is found between the different sentences and also within each sentence, highlighted by the italics. For example,

---

7. Mark Mitchell, "Confessions of a Manuscript Preacher," accessed 27 November 2015; Johnson, *Glory of Preaching*, 152.

"welcome" is repeated in the first line, "listening" is repeated in the third line, while alliterations are used in the second and fourth line. Not only are such crafted sentences helpful for the preacher's memory, they will also stay better in the hearers' minds. One should, of course, not overdo such literary devices otherwise they will seem artificial, but since the above is part of the conclusion, the parallelism and rule of three lifts the sermon to a climatic end.

Most preachers combine the best of both worlds by reducing the manuscript to notes. This gives speakers the assurance that they won't forget their outline or key points, and they are then free to concentrate on communicating with the congregation. However, preachers should be well acquainted with the lines that they want to emphasize so that they can look directly at the people and speak from their heart to their listeners. I also urge my students to deliver three other aspects of a sermon with strong eye contact: the illustrations, the introduction, and the conclusion.

One should be able to tell stories without resorting to notes. Using Lowry's homiletical plot, stories start with a problem, leading to a complication, and then a climax that ends in a resolution. The storyteller just needs to be familiar with the plot, but he will want to be very clear about the turning point, for if one fumbles at that crucial point, it will be like forgetting the punchline of a joke, and the story will fall flat. The most familiar story to share would be one from the preacher's own life because he or she can relive what has been experienced and tell it naturally with emotions. If you were asked to share about a childhood achievement, a bereavement, an accident, or the day you met your spouse, you wouldn't need notes, would you?

The preacher should also deliver the introduction and conclusion without reading. Eye contact at the beginning of a sermon is crucial for establishing rapport with the audience. In the moments before I get up to preach, I mentally run through my opening sentences so that I'm ready to greet the congregation and engage them the moment I'm at the pulpit. Eye contact at the end of a sermon is just as important. You want to make sure that the hearers are paying attention to the final challenge. You persuade with both words and eyes. In chapter 12 on Conclusion, I listed four ways to conclude. If preachers believe that they are calling people to respond to God, then their closing illustration, directions, vision, or invitation would already be internalized. Stanley and Jones write that there is "something very disingenuous about the speaker who says, 'This is very, very important,' and then reads something from his notes. Constantly referring to notes communicates, 'I have not internalized this message. I want everybody else to internalize it, but I haven't."[8] When preparing directions or a vision, the preacher would have imagined what it would be like for people to put the sermon into practice in their lives. This process of prayerful visualization would then make it possible to deliver those thoughts and hopes without reading. The invitation, especially, has to be delivered with eye contact because the preacher is appealing directly to the listeners, unless the appeal is made during prayer. As a herald, you are speaking on behalf of the King and delivering a life-changing message, one that you should have already experienced for yourself, one that has percolated in your mind as you crafted the words, and one therefore that you can share from your heart, even if you happened to lose your notes.

2. Deliver with Your Voice

There are four aspects of your voice that you can control to deliver your message: pace, pause, punch, and pitch. For Asian speakers, I will add one more aspect: pronunciation.

a. Pace

Most times, I have to tell my students to slow down when delivering their sermons. They not only speed through the sentences but also ignore the commas and periods. It's probably nerves driving them to finish the sermon as quickly as possible. I have the same speeding problem because I want to tell people as many things as I can in the limited time. I have to remind myself that it is more important to make a few points to the heart than many points that whiz past the head.

On the other hand, there are some speakers who need to step on the accelerator. Stanley and Jones highlight that the human brain can process words much faster than the mouth can talk. Studies have shown that the average rate of speed for English-speaking Westerners is about 150 words per minute.[9] They quote Jeff Miller in a piece for *Leadership Magazine* that speaking slightly above 150 words per minute adds an element of dignity to one's message. "Faster speakers – up to 190 words per minute – were rated as more objective, knowledgeable, and persuasive than slower speakers."[10]

---

8. Stanley and Jones, *Communicating*, 135.

9. James R. Williams, "Guidelines for the Use of Multimedia in Instruction," *Proceedings of the Human Factors and Ergonomics Society 42nd Annual Meeting* (1998), 1447–1451.

10. Stanley and Jones, *Communicating*, 156.

Speaking faster conveys the conviction that you know your subject matter well and are eager to share about it. This means that public speakers need to speak faster than a normal conversation so that people will stay engaged.

However, variety is the spice of life. The preacher needs to know when to speed up and when to slow down. For example, a story can start at a conversational pace, quicken towards the climax to convey excitement or tension, and then slow down in the resolution in order to emphasize the lesson.[11] Slowing down alerts the listener to the importance of what is being said and gives people time to digest what they hear.

b. Pause

Related to pace is the pause. There is a reason why people refer to "the pregnant pause." A well placed moment of silence can be full of meaning. One can pause *before* a word or phrase in order to create suspense or to allow people to deduce the answer for themselves. Pausing *after* a word will let that word echo in the minds of the hearers. If the preacher poses a series of challenging questions to the hearers, then he should pause after each question to give people time to reflect.

Preachers are usually afraid of silence. They feel awkward being stared at, or they need to show that they haven't forgotten their lines. However, silence is letting the Spirit convict or comfort each heart according to its needs. So don't interrupt. A pause will usually seem longer to the speaker than to the listeners because nervous energy speeds up our sense of time. "The pause should be long enough to call attention to the thought, but not so long that the silence calls attention to the pause."[12]

c. Punch

The opposite of silence, that is, punch or loudness, also brings a word or phrase to the attention of the hearers. The preacher should accentuate the word or idea that is either emphasized or advanced in the line. Consider the example given below by Jana Childers from John 14:27.[13] First, read it in a monotone and consider the effect:

---

11. Keith Willhite, "Matching Delivery to Content," Preaching Today, online.
12. Robinson, *Biblical Preaching*, 163.
13. Jana Childers, *Performing the Word: Preaching as Theatre* (Nashville, TN: Abingdon, 1998), 86.

> Peace I leave with you,
> My peace I give to you.
> Not as the world gives, give I unto you.

Do the words sink in and assure? Now consider which words you would emphasize to advance the idea in each line and also to show what is contrasted. Try reading the lines again by emphasizing the italicized words below:

> *Peace* I leave with you,
> *My* peace I give to you.
> *Not* as the world gives, give *I* unto you.

Is the meaning clearer? The first line emphasizes *what* we all need; the second line points to the *source*, and the third line contrasts the *nature* of such peace. The original Greek or Hebrew can help us locate what to emphasize. For example, in the above verse, the "I" in the third line is underscored by the independent first person pronoun (*ego*) in the Greek text.

There should also be variations in your volume. It does not mean that the louder we are, the more inspired we are. Unfortunately, there are preachers from both conservative and charismatic churches who seem bent on persuading by shouting at the listeners. However, overexposure to a constant high volume will damage our ability to hear. Some discerning hearers will be turned off, while others will be conditioned into thinking that truth is determined by decibels. God thundered at Mt Sinai when he delivered the Ten Commandments but also spoke in a still small voice to a tired prophet on the same mountain. Robinson suggests that "dropping your voice to a mere whisper can put an idea into italics as effectively as a loud shout."[14] Meanwhile, the preacher also needs to project his voice (not shout) to the back of the room, even if using a mic, so that he can be heard distinctly. We need to speak louder than in a normal conversation and maintain that energy to the end of the sermon so that people will not be soothed into slumber.[15]

d. Pitch

Another aspect of the voice that needs variation is pitch (i.e. whether our voice is high or low). Different pitches convey different emotions. Watch a parent talking with his child, and you see how it works. If the parent is speaking in a high pitch, he is stimulating the child for play. But if a parent

---
14. Robinson, *Biblical Preaching*, 162.
15. Craig Brian Larson, "Holding Hearers Captive," Preaching Today, online.

wants to put a child to bed, he speaks in low tones to calm the baby. Similarly, a speaker who raises his voice infects the listeners with excitement, but a low tone will bring a note of comfort.

The pitch needs to match the point, so there should be variety in the delivery. A constant high pitch becomes grating, like fingernails on a chalkboard. A low tone lulls listeners like a lullaby. A public speaker tends to speak at a higher pitch because his nervousness constricts his throat. Take deep breaths before going up to the pulpit to relax the muscles and to sustain the breath. A recent study shows that men and women perceive low-pitched voices as more authoritative, so lower your tone when emphasizing something important.[16]

e. Pronunciation

Most people have a few quirks when speaking English. For instance, Singaporeans, like some Asians, tend to swallow the last consonants of words. Most of the time we can understand what is said, but occasionally a poorly enunciated word may be lost on the hearers or, worse, be heard as something else. For example, if you say, "I wan(t) a wife" without enunciating the "t" in "want," then it would sound like "I won a wife."

Besides the last consonants of words, the letter "s" at the end of plural nouns and singular verbs also tend to get dropped. One needs to be careful if this might create confusion. Does the preacher want to refer to "the God of this world" or "the gods of this world"?

Another problem for some is a disregard for the "th" sound in words. It can be reduced to "t," because the "th" requires more effort by having to stick the tongue slightly out between the teeth. The speaker has to be careful when this might make a distinction in meaning, for example, the difference between "three" and "tree."

A third issue is a tendency to flatten all multisyllabic words instead of stressing the correct syllable. If uncertain of the pronunciation, it's helpful to look up the word online and listen to the correct way of saying it. However, one should keep to one's local accent instead of trying to sound like an American or British speaker, that is, unless one was actually brought up or educated in that foreign context. The principle is to be naturally and consistently oneself, otherwise to use a different accent, voice, or style of speaking behind the

---

16. Rindy C. Anderson, and Casey A. Klofstad, "Preference for Leaders with Masculine Voices Holds in the Case of Feminine Leadership Roles," *PLoS One* 7, no. 12 (2012).

pulpit would come across as pretentious. Either you are trying too hard to impress, or you lack the confidence to be who you are.

Using a special voice to sound "holy" at the pulpit also divides the sacred from the secular, undoing the Reformation's claim that we are to live every sphere of our lives for God. So be real by having an attitude of talking *to*, or better yet, talking *with* the listeners, but never talking *at* them.

Now to put all that you've learned about using your voice into practice, how would you deliver the lines below, taken from the conclusion of the sermon on Elisha? There may be more than one right way of delivery as long as you understand what you are doing and why.

> You may have committed yourselves to serve the Lord,
> but have the currents of the world eroded your hearts?
> We may have burned our ploughs,
> but are we now digging through the ashes to find them again?
> How can you and I keep following in difficult times without turning back?

This is my proposal below:

> You may have committed yourselves to serve the *Lord*,
> but have the currents of the *world* eroded your hearts? *(short pause)*
> *(Punch for contrast. Short pause for reflection.)*
> We may have burned our ploughs,
> but are we now digging through the *ashes* to find it again? *(short pause)*
> *(Punch for irony. Short pause for reflection)*
> *How* can you and I keep following in difficult times <u>without turning back</u>? *(pause)*
> *(Punch for new idea. Slower pace for last three words for emphasis. Longer pause for consideration.)*

All these effects may seem dramatic, but at the pulpit, the preacher has to exaggerate a little in order to carry his message across to a large group. The goal is to improve the clarity and persuasiveness of our delivery. However, the most important effect comes from the heart. In the above example, the preacher went through a personal struggle in giving up the things of the world to follow Jesus, so he was a witness of what he testified. What he urged hearers to do was not a platitude but a pathway to God that he himself had trod.

Craig Brian Larson talks about three kinds of energy in sermons that "grab" listeners: emotional, intellectual, and vocal energy. Vocal energy has to do with all that we've discussed about using the voice. He points out that some speakers tend to wind down when it comes to the conclusion, as if they have run out of energy. That is unfortunate when the conclusion needs to be the most convicting part of the sermon. He shares the following experience about listening to an audio tape of a sermon. This means that it was only the speaker's voice that came across. Still, he recounted, "When I pulled into the driveway, the message had not yet finished, but I put the car in park and kept listening, my cheeks wet with tears. . . . The Spirit and the Word changed me to be more like Christ through a sermon that had an energy I could not escape."[17] But Larson agrees that vocal energy comes from emotional energy, which leads us to the final guideline.

3. Deliver with Your Heart

My students get overwhelmed with trying to remember all they need to do with their eyes and voice, while also trying to internalize the content of the introduction, conclusion, etc. They end up getting more stressed and awkward. My last word to them after the feedback and practice is usually, "Now forget everything, and just go preach from your heart!" Forget everything because it is not the technicalities of delivery that count in the end; it is whether you believe God has given you a word to deliver – a word that burns like fire in your bones. If you have that conviction, then the message will be convicting, and it will come across naturally in your voice, eyes, and body. The way to be convincing is first to be convinced. Rules are to serve not enslave the preacher.

While acknowledging that people have different temperaments and expressiveness, Stott boils earnestness down to the quality of Christians who care. First, Christians care about God. He points out that Paul cared so much about the glory of God that he was provoked by the Athenian idolatry (Acts 17:16), and he was in tears that many Philippians disregarded the cross of Christ (Phil 3:18). The second thing that Christians should care about is people and their lostness. Stott points out that Jesus wept over the impenitent city of Jerusalem (Matt 23:37; Luke 19:41–42) and that for three years in Ephesus, Paul was admonishing everyone with tears (Acts 20:31).[18]

---

17. Larson, "Holding Hearers Captive."
18. Stott, *I Believe in Preaching*, 275–276.

Likewise, Craddock finds it difficult to believe that the message of the gospel could be preached as though nothing were at stake. On the contrary, much is at stake – perhaps for a young adult who is giving God one last chance before giving up on religion, or for a couple who is contemplating divorce, or for a visitor drowning in depression and wondering if God cares. However, Craddock notes that some preachers may simply want to avoid the excesses of passion, thinking that people need to be convicted by objective truths and rationality alone. He clarifies that we are not to manufacture passion but that "there is a passion appropriate to the significance and the urgency of the gospel, and there is no valid reason to conceal that passion." Stott calls for the same synthesis of reason and emotion, exposition and exhortation, as was demonstrated by Jesus and Paul.[19]

Similarly, Jeffrey Arthurs argues that we should not pit *pathos* against *logos*: "Pathos is primary in human decision making because God made us to respond to emotional appeals, and he himself uses pathos. He motivates us through awe of his immensity, fear of his holiness, confidence of his goodness, and joy of his grace." In fact, Arthurs quotes Jonathan Edwards who responded to charges of sensationalism in the Great Awakening. Edwards thought it his duty "to raise the affections of my hearers as high as I possibly can, provided they are affected with nothing but the truth."[20]

How does one raise affections? Not by affectations but by being affected by God and his Word. The truth will shine through our whole being when we speak, much like the instruction attributed to Spurgeon, "When you speak of heaven, let your face light up with a heavenly gleam. Let your eyes shine with reflected glory. But when you speak of hell – well, then your usual face will do."

Before we end this chapter, there is one emotion in the pulpit that we need to address – anger. Pastors who have been hurt by church leaders or members may be tempted to use the pulpit to vent their frustrations. They think that this is righteous anger directed at bringing the culprits to repentance and teaching people how they ought to behave. Such an attitude only brings a backlash. People get defensive when they are publicly scolded, and this will provoke more recriminations that the pastor is abusing the pulpit. Here is the best advice that I received from my Old Testament professor when he was teaching on the prophets: Never preach out of anger but out of anger *and love*.

---

19. Craddock, *Preaching*, 220–222; Stott, *I Believe in Preaching*, 283.
20. Jeffrey Arthurs, "Place of Pathos in Preaching," Preaching Today, online.

The prophets pronounced God's wrath without fear, yet they also assured of God's salvation with tears. If we would speak for God, then we must represent both his holy judgment and his painful longing for his people.

James warns us to be slow to anger because the anger of man does not produce God's righteousness (Jas 1:19–20). So we need to examine our anger before preparing to preach, even as Jesus said to remove the log in one's own eye so that we can see clearly to take the speck out of our neighbor's eye (Matt 7:3–5). Are we willing to repent of our own fault? Do we forgive those who hurt us and even seek their good? Have we tried to resolve the issue at a personal level? Are we trying to justify ourselves, or do we really care about God's glory and the church's good? There are times when we should be angry, but like Jonathan Edwards' sermon, the sermon should be about sinners in the hands of an angry God and not in the hands of an angry preacher![21]

We should be angry about the things that anger God. Jesus denounced the Pharisees for their hypocrisy and for hindering others from entering the kingdom of God (Matt 23:13). Paul rebuked the Galatians for their foolishness in abandoning the gospel of grace (Gal 3:1). We need to be outraged when God's truth and people's lives are at stake. But those who would rebuke, like the prophets, Jesus, and Paul, must also earn the right to do so by their lives of sacrifice for the people. Paul appealed to the Galatians as his little children "for whom I am again in the pain of childbirth until Christ is formed in you" (Gal 4:19). It is with reluctance, he says, that he used his harsh tone with them (Gal 4:20). We are ready to preach with anger when we are reluctant to do so.

However, anger is a difficult emotion to control and may erupt unintentionally. What should the preacher do when that happens? Bill White advises that an apology is always called for, either after the sermon when it has been brought to the preacher's attention, or even during the sermon when the Holy Spirit convicts the preacher. He shares about a time when he was frustrated by his congregation's lack of openness. As he was concluding a sermon with an invitation to married couples to come forward for prayer, none responded, and he gave in to his anger. With sarcasm, he said, "What, do you think you have a perfect marriage, and you don't need prayer?"

White said that the Holy Spirit gently convicted him there and then, and swallowing his pride, he said, "That comment was sarcastic and not helpful. Would you forgive me for that?" Then with the same gentle firmness that he had sensed from the Spirit, he said, "Let's try that again – wouldn't it be

---

21. A. J. Swoboda, "Sinners in the Hands of an Angry Preacher," Preaching Today, online.

helpful to have your marriage prayed over?" White reported that they had a good time of prayer ministry at the altar after that.[22] The openness of the preacher leads to the openness of the congregation. Let there be sanctified emotions in the pulpit!

---

22. Bill White, "Sinning in the Pulpit," Preaching Today, online.

Epilogue

The sermon is constructed, scripted, and rehearsed. But just as there was no breath in the reconstituted bodies of Ezekiel's vision until God's Spirit gave them life (Ezek 37:14), so also there is no life in a sermon until the Spirit gives it breath. The preacher needs to pray, both before and after the sermon, that the Spirit will cause his preaching to come alive.

Pre-Sermon Prayer

Before the sermon, the preacher needs to pray for his or her preparation, for the people, and for protection. First, on preparation, Zechariah 4:6 directs us to focus on God and not on ourselves. "Not by might, nor by power, but by the Spirit of God." I also pray, based on a quote that I read long ago, that the congregation will hear not a great sermon nor a great speaker, but a great Savior. The preacher's goal is not to draw attention to the messenger but to his master. So pray for yourself and for the congregation that they will know God, draw near to him, be comforted or convicted as needed, and live for the glory of God.

If every act of preaching is heralding a kingdom that brings life and establishing that kingdom through teaching, exhortation, and witnessing, then we engage not in a mere human endeavor. "Our struggle is not against enemies of blood and flesh, but against the rulers, against the authorities, against the cosmic powers of this present darkness, against the spiritual forces of evil in the heavenly places" (Eph 6:12). Paul then exhorts his readers to put on the armour of God and to "pray in the Spirit at all times in every prayer and supplication. . . . Pray also for me, so that when I speak, a message may be given to me to make known with boldness the mystery of the gospel, for which I am an ambassador in chains. Pray that I may declare it boldly, as I must speak" (Eph 6:18–20). Preaching the gospel is a spiritual battle, and we advance by prayer.

A fresh graduate shared with me that his wife had fallen quite seriously ill not once but twice before he was due to preach. One time he had to send her to a hospital, and the second time, which was when he happened to meet me, he told me that the doctor could not diagnose what was wrong except that she had some kind of infection. I asked him whether he prays for protection before he preaches. He said, "No, but I think I should start doing that." I prayed for him and his wife that day, and when I met him again after his preaching, he told me that she had recovered the day after we prayed for her. When she went to see the doctor the following week to get her test results, everything turned out normal. Jesus taught us to pray, "And do not bring us to the time of trial, but rescue us from the evil one" (Matt 6:13). We can be confident that we have victory in Christ at whose name "every knee should bend, in heaven and on earth and under the earth, and every tongue should confess that Jesus Christ is Lord, to the glory of God the Father" (Phil 2:10–11).

The prayer for deliverance in the Lord's Prayer is preceded by a prayer of confession: "Forgive us our debts, as we also have forgiven our debtors" (Matt 6:12). Sin and unforgiveness will hinder our ministry and allow the evil one to distract us from ministry. In the days leading up to your preaching, do you find more misunderstandings with your spouse? Do your children aggravate you more than usual? You blow a fuse just as you are on your way to the worship service and exchange words that you regret. You wonder how God can use you when you have failed so miserably. "What a hypocrite!" we think to ourselves.

This is why a preacher needs to pray for protection not only from external attacks but from internal ones as well. Conflicts are more likely to ignite when one is tense from the stress of sermon preparation. But we are called to maintain the unity of the Spirit in the bond of peace (Eph 2:3), so pray that the Spirit will give us the grace to forgive and to repent. When we hear our self-accusations paralyzing us, we can claim the promise of God's forgiveness (1 John 1:9) and be thankful that God uses flawed servants. You'll find them in the Bible and behind the pulpits. The message does not depend on the goodness of the speaker or the sermon, but on the goodness and power of the Spirit.

Post-Sermon Prayer

So you've delivered the sermon with all you've got. You come down from the pulpit, flushed with adrenaline. You shake hands with the congregants as they proceed out the church door. You hear "Thank you, Pastor" and "Good sermon, Reverend" and wonder whether they're just mouthing them. The rest of the Sunday, you play your sermon in your mind over and over like a broken record or an audio file on a loop, obsessing over what you forgot to say, or said wrongly, or could have said better. You are your own worst critic. I used to ask my husband for his feedback with both anticipation and anxiety: anticipation because I needed his affirmation, and anxiety lest he points out some embarrassing mistakes. My husband is always honest and kind, but the human tendency is to dwell more on the negatives than the positives. How do we deal with post-sermon blues?

The root of the problem lies in our insecurity, a problem that Henri Nouwen was well acquainted with. He wrote, "I was caught in a web of strange paradoxes. While complaining about too many demands, I felt uneasy when none were made. While speaking about the burden of letter writing, an empty mailbox made me sad. While fretting about tiring lecture tours, I felt disappointed when there were no invitations." The paradox pulling the preacher apart is that while longing to hear positive feedback, he is afraid to ask lest compliments puff him up, yet he is disappointed if he does not get any, thinking that the congregation thinks poorly of him, all the while fearful that he might hear a criticism that marks him as a failure. Nouwen came to the realization that he had put his whole identity at stake each time he works with or encounters other people.[1]

I learned the same lesson during my first sabbatical. I had put my self-worth in the hands of other people rather than in the hands of God. That's why I over-prepared for each sermon and became over wrought over what people thought. I longed to ask but was afraid to find out their opinions. Asians are generally reticent; even if they thought well of your sermon, they are too shy to come up and tell you. When I learned to accept myself, my gift, and my calling before the Lord, the anxieties lost their megaphone. I was less obsessed with what people thought. God has called me to do only one thing, and that is to deliver his word for his congregation. Knowing that I have preached the word from the Lord gave me the assurance that he is pleased with me, whether anyone said anything or not.

But when people do give feedback, we need to know how to respond. So let me discuss what to do with compliments and criticisms. Sometimes, compliments are merely cursory, like what people say on their way out of the church, so treat them as mere social niceties. If there is the opportunity to do so, I like to ask what the hearers found helpful for their lives so that I can pray for them. Spurgeon exhorts his students to continue in prayer after they have preached for "God will not send a harvest of souls to those who never

---

1. Henri Nouwen, *The Genesee Diary: Report from a Trappist Monastery* (Garden City, NY: Image Books, 1981), 14, 171.

watch or water the fields which they have sown."[2] This is a reminder that the ministry does not begin or end with the sermon, as if preaching were a performance. But if the preacher has a heart not just for himself but for the people, then he would pray for the continuing work of the Spirit in the life of the church. When you hear a constructive compliment, thank the giver for his encouragement, and thank God for speaking to them. Thanksgiving directs the glory to God and saves us from pride. "Let not the wise boast of their wisdom . . . But let those who boast boast in this, that they understand and know me . . ." (Jer 9:23–24).

And now on the thorny issue of criticisms, both of the constructive and destructive kinds. Ask for wisdom to sieve the helpful from the harmful. For constructive criticisms, be grateful for the opportunity to improve. Spurgeon spoke appreciatively about an anonymous person who regularly sent him a list of his mispronunciations and other slips of speech.[3] When I was a guest preacher in another church, the pastor told me later that his congregation found it distracting that I walked around on the chancel rather than plant myself behind the large pulpit. My own church is less formal, and I occasionally walk around because I want to connect with the congregation of mostly young people. But I realized that I needed to adapt to different church cultures (even within the same denomination) so that nothing hinders the preaching of the Word.

This is a minor incident compared to a comment from a member who invited a non-Christian friend to church and worriedly told me after the service that his friend was offended when I shared about a Chinese temple medium who acknowledged the supremacy of Christ over the Chinese gods. I also get the same reaction when I share testimonies from converts, such as a former drug addict who said that he tried many religions, but only Jesus could set him free. On the one hand, the gospel is offensive, and we need to preach it boldly, but on the other hand, we need to be sensitive to the hearers and present our message as considerately as possible. We live in a pluralistic Asian context, and in some countries there is a growing sense of nationalism or even extremism. The preacher should never deride other religions whether in content or tone, but affirm our respect for their moral teachings and charitable works. We can say that all the major religions are good, but we cannot say that all religions are the same. To say that Christianity is different

---

2. Spurgeon, *Lectures*, 308.
3. Ibid., 331.

is a more agreeable starting point than to say that all other religions are wrong. When citing the testimonies of converts from other religions, do so in a factual manner. The truth can be stated, but let it be the truth that offends, not the preacher's derogatory attitude or words.

For these criticisms, I could have drowned myself in a mire of embarrassment and guilt, but God is great enough to handle any mistakes I make. So instead of locking myself into the past with self-incriminations, I look towards the hope of what God can do or undo. Despite my missteps, I take comfort in what is of first importance – that I have preached the word from the Lord.

This assurance is even more crucial when facing a destructive criticism. Not everyone liked Jesus when he was on earth, even though he was perfect in every way. I have been accused of currying favor by name dropping when I was trying to build rapport with the congregation. I have been criticized for promoting myself when I was trying to motivate the church by sharing about the fruits of a ministry. It is a reminder to examine oneself and check with other trusted leaders if one might have given the wrong impression. But if your motives are clear, then chalk it up to experience. You can now be wiser by anticipating possible reactions. For instance, in describing the results of a ministry, affirm that it is God who gives the growth through the contributions of many, and acknowledge the importance of other ministries. Speak with love to your critics. If they do not listen, trust God to vindicate, but who knows whether you might turn an enemy into an ally. Spurgeon spoke of treating a harsh critic "as one who was a friend to my Lord, if not to me, gave him some work to do which implied confidence in him, made him feel at home, and by degrees won him to be an attached friend as well as a fellow-worker."[4]

So let me leave you, my fellow preachers, with my simple post-sermon prayer that I have distilled after many years of post-sermon blues. It now saves me from myself:

> Lord, for what was good, thank you and bless it to your people.
> For what was wrong, forgive me.
> Overrule my mistakes.
> Supplement my failures.
> And help me to do better next time.
> In the Savior's Name,
> Amen.

---

[4]. Ibid., 327.

Bibliography

Adams, Jay E. *Preaching with Purpose: A Comprehensive Textbook on Biblical Preaching.* Grand Rapids, MI: Baker, 1982.

———. *Truth Applied: Application in Preaching.* Grand Rapids, MI: Zondervan, 1990.

Anderson, Bernhard W. *From Creation to New Creation: Old Testament Perspectives.* Minneapolis, MN: Fortress, 1994.

———. *Contours of Old Testament Theology.* Minneapolis, MN: Fortress, 1999.

Anderson, Rindy C., and Casey A. Klofstad. "Preference for Leaders with Masculine Voices Holds in the Case of Feminine Leadership Roles." PLoS One 7, no. 12 (2012). http://dx.doi.org/10.1371/journal.pone.0051216.

Aristotle, *Rhetorics.* Book 1. Translated by W. Rhys Roberts. New York, Modern Library, 1954.

Arthurs, Jeffrey. "No Notes, Lots of Notes, Brief Notes: The Pros and Cons of Extemporaneous and Manuscript Delivery." Preaching Today, online. Accessed 27 November 2015. http://www.preachingtoday.com/skills/2006/october/169--arthurs.html.

———. "Place of Pathos in Preaching." Preaching Today, online. Accessed 30 November 2015. http://www.preachingtoday.com/skills/themes/preachingwithpassion/200102.27.html.

Bechara, Antoine, Hanna Damasio, Antonio R. Damasio, and Gregory P. Lee. "Different Contributions of the Human Amygdala and Ventromedial Prefrontal Cortex to Decision-Making." *Journal of Neuroscience* 19, no. 13 (1999): 5473–5481.

Bockmuehl, Klaus. *Listening to the God Who Speaks: Reflections on God's Guidance from Scripture and the Lives of God's People.* Colorado Springs, CO: Helmers & Howard, 1990.

Bockmuehl, Markus. "*Creatio ex nihilo* in Palestinian Judaism and Early Christianity." *Scottish Journal of Theology* 65, no. 3 (2012): 253–270.

Bradley, Margaret M., Mark K. Greenwald, Margaret C. Petry, and Peter J. Lang. "Remembering Pictures: Pleasure and Arousal in Memory." *Journal of Experimental Psychology: Learning, Memory, & Cognition* 18, no. 2 (1991): 379–390.

Briscoe, Stuart. "Interesting Preaching: How to Avoid Talking in Someone Else's Sleep." Preaching Today, online. Accessed 24 November 2015. http://www.preachingtoday.com/skills/2005/August/104--briscoe.html.

Broadus, John A. *On the Preparation and Delivery of Sermons.* Edited by J. B. Weatherspoon. New York: Harper & Row, 1944.

Brooks, Phillips. *Lectures on Preaching.* New York: Dutton, 1877.

Brown, F., S. Driver, and C. Briggs. *A Hebrew and English Lexicon of the Old Testament.* Oxford: Clarendon Press, 1907.

Bullock, C. Hassel. *Encountering the Book of Psalms: A Literary and Theological Introduction*. Grand Rapids, MI: Baker, 2001.

Buttrick, David. *Homiletic Moves and Structures*. Philadelphia, PA: Fortress, 1987.

Calvin, John. *Sermons on the Epistles to Timothy and Titus*. Edinburgh: Banner of Truth Trust, 1983.

Casey, Michael. *Sacred Reading: The Ancient Art of Lectio Divina*. Ligouri, MO: Ligouri/Triumph, 1995.

Chapell, Bryan. *Christ-Centered Preaching: Redeeming the Expository Sermon*, 2nd edition. Grand Rapids, MI: Baker Academic, 2005.

———. *Using Illustrations to Preach with Power*, revised edition. Wheaton, IL: Crossway, 2001.

Childs, Brevard S. *Biblical Theology of the Old and New Testaments: Theological Reflection in the Christian Bible*. Minneapolis, MN: Fortress, 1993.

Childers, Jana. *Performing the Word: Preaching as Theatre*. Nashville, TN: Abingdon, 1998.

Cowan, Nelson. "The Magical Number 4 in Short-Term Memory: A Reconsideration of the Mental Storage Capacity." *Behavioral and Brain Sciences* 24, no. 1 (2001): 87–114.

Craddock, Fred B. *As One without Authority*. Nashville, TN: Abingdon, 1971.

———. *Overhearing the Gospel*. Nashville, TN: Abingdon, 1978.

———. *Preaching*, 25th Anniversary Edition. Nashville, TN: Abingdon, 2010.

Crum, Milton, Jr. *Manual on Preaching: A New Process of Sermon Development*. Valley Forge, PA: Judson, 1977.

Daly, Patrick. "Traditional Chinese Martial Arts and the Transmission of Intangible Cultural Heritage." In *Routledge Handbook of Heritage in Asia*, edited by Daly and Winter. London: Routledge, 2012.

Davis, H. Grady. *Design for Preaching*. Philadelphia, PA: Muhlenberg, 1958.

Davis, Ken. "Humor That Connects." Preaching Today, online. Accessed 24 November 2015. http://www.preachingtoday.com/skills/themes/humor/200403.2.html.

Day, David. *Embodying the Word: A Preacher's Guide*. London: SPCK, 2005.

———. *A Preaching Workbook*. London: SPCK, 1998.

Denney, Andrew S. and Richard Tewksbury. "Motivations and the Need for Fulfillment of Faith-Based Halfway House Volunteers." *Justice Policy Journal* 10, no. 1 (2013): 3–4.

Dunbar, R. I. M., R. Baron, A. Frangou, E. Pearce, E. van Leeuwen, J. Stow, G. Partridge, I. MacDonald, V. Barra, M. van Vugt. "Social Laughter Is Correlated with an Elevated Pain Threshold." *Proceedings of the Royal Society B* (14 Sept 2011). Accessed 24 November 2015. http://rspb.royalsocietypublishing.org/content/279/1731/1161.

Dwight, Sereno. "A Memoir of Jonathan Edwards." In *The Works of Jonathan Edwards*, vol. 1. Edited by Edward Hickman. Edinburgh: Banner of Truth, 1974.

Farris, Stephen. *Preaching That Matters: The Bible and Our Lives*. Louisville, KY: Westminster John Knox, 1998.

Fee, Gordon D. *New Testament Exegesis: A Handbook for Students and Pastors*. Louisville, KY: Westminster John Knox, 2002.

Fee, Gordon D., and Douglas Stuart. *How to Read the Bible for All Its Worth*, 4th edition. Grand Rapids, MI: Zondervan, 2014.

Gambrel, Patrick A., and Rebecca Cianci. "Maslow's Hierarchy of Needs: Does It Apply in a Collectivist Culture?" *Journal of Applied Management and Entrepreneurship* 8, no. 2 (Apr 2003): 143–161.

Graham, Billy. "Insights to the Invitation." *Proclaim* (Oct 1977): 5.

Green, Joel B. *The Gospel of Luke*. New International Commentary on the New Testament Series. Grand Rapids, MI: Eerdmans, 1997.

Greidanus, Sidney. *The Modern Preacher and the Ancient Text: Interpreting and Preaching Biblical Literature*. Grand Rapids, MI: Eerdmans, 1988.

Hamann, S. B. "Cognitive and Neural Mechanisms of Emotional Memory." *Trends in Cognitive Sciences* 5, no. 9 (2001): 394–400. Accessed 29 December 2015. http://dx.doi.org/10.1016/S1364-6613(00)01707-1.

Hasel, Gerhard. *Old Testament Theology: Basic Issues in the Current Debate*, 4th edition. Grand Rapids, MI: Eerdmans, 1991.

Jacks, Robert. *Just Say the Word! Writing for the Ear*. Grand Rapids, MI: Eerdmans, 1996.

Jensen, Richard A. *Telling the Story: Variety and Imagination in Preaching*. Minneapolis, MN: Augsburg, 1980.

Johnson, Darrel W. *The Glory of Preaching: Participating in God's Transformation of the World*. Downers Grove, IL: InterVarsity, 2009.

Johnson, Val Byron. "A Media Selection Model for Use with a Homiletical Taxonomy." PhD diss., Southern Illinois University at Carbondale, 1982.

Jowett, J. H. *The Preacher: His Life and Work*. New York: Hodder & Stoughton, 1912.

Kittel, G., and G. Friedrich, eds. *Theological Dictionary of the New Testament*. Translated by G. W. Bromiley. 10 vols. Grand Rapids, MI: Eerdmans, 1964–1976.

Koller, Charles W. *Expository Preaching without Notes and Sermons Preached without Notes*. Grand Rapids, MI: Baker, 1962.

Larson, Craig Brian. "Holding Hearers Captive." Preaching Today, online. Accessed 30 November 2015. http://www.preachingtoday.com/skills/themes/deliveringthesermon/200102.22.html.

Larsen, David. *Anatomy of Preaching: Identifying the Issues in Preaching Today*. Grand Rapids, MI: Baker, 1989.

Lerner, Jennifer S., Deborah A. Small, and George Loewenstein. "Heart Strings and Purse Strings Carry over Effects of Emotions on Economic Decisions." *Psychological Science* 15, no. 5 (2004): 337–341.

Lewin, Kurt. "Quasi-Stationary Social Equilibria and the Problem of Permanent Change." In *The Planning of Change*, edited by Warren Bennis, Kenneth Benne, and Robert Chin. New York: Holt Rinehart, and Winston, 1961.

Lim, Johnson T. K. *Power in Preaching*, revised edition. Singapore: Word N Works, 2005.

Lloyd-Jones, Martyn. *Preaching and Preachers*. Grand Rapids, MI: Zondervan, 1971.

Liske, Thomas V. *Effective Preaching*, 2nd edition. New York: Macmillan, 1960.

Litfin, Duane. *Public Speaking: A Handbook for Christians*, 2nd edition. Grand Rapids, MI: Baker, 1992.

———. "New Testament Challenges to Big Idea Preaching." In *The Big Idea of Biblical Preaching: Connecting the Bible to People*, edited by Keith Willhite and Scott M. Gibson. Grand Rapids, MI: Baker, 1998.

Long, Thomas G. *The Witness of Preaching*, 2nd edition. Louisville, KY: Westminster John Knox, 2005.

Longman, Tremper, III. *How to Read the Psalms*. Downers Grove, IL; Leicester, England: IVP, 1988.

Lowry, Eugene L. *The Homiletical Plot: The Sermon as Narrative Art Form*, expanded edition. Louisville, KY: Westminster John Knox, 2001.

———. *How to Preach a Parable*. Nashville, TN: Abingdon, 1989.

———. *The Sermon: Dancing the Edge of Mystery*. Nashville, TN: Abingdon, 1997.

Luchetti, Lenny. "Connecting with More Listeners: Preaching That Connects to the Diverse Needs of Your Listeners," accessed 9 Sept 2015. http://www.preachingtoday.com/skills/2015/march/connecting-with-more-listeners.html.

Marshall, Lisa B. "How to Communicate Better Using the Rule of Three." Accessed 24 November 2015. http://www.quickanddirtytips.com/business-career/public-speaking/how-communicate-better-using-rule-three.

Massey, James Earl. *Designing the Sermon: Order and Movement in Preaching*. Edited by William Thompson. Nashville, TN: Abingdon, 1980.

Mathewson, Steve. "Outlines That Work for You, Not against You." Accessed 7 September 2015. http://www.preachingtoday.com/skills/themes/structure/200010.20.html.

May, Gerhard. *Creatio Ex Nihilo: The Doctrine of "Creation out of Nothing" in Early Christian Thought*. Edinburgh: T&T Clark, 1994.

McGrath, Alistair E. "The Biography of God." *Christianity Today* (22 July 1991): 23.

McKeon, Richard, ed. *The Basic Works of Aristotle*. Translated by W. Rhys Roberts. New York: Random House, 1842.

McMickle, Marvin A. *Living Water for Thirsty Souls: Unleashing the Power of Exegetical Preaching*. Valley Forge, PA: Judson, 2001.

Miller, George A. "The Magical Number Seven, Plus or Minus Two." *Psychological Review* 63, no. 2 (1956): 81–97.

Nicoll, William Robertson. *Princes of the Church*. London: Hodder & Stoughton, 1921.

Nouwen, Henri. *The Genesee Diary: Report from a Trappist Monastery*. Garden City, NY: Image Books, 1981.

Oettingen, Gabriele. "The Problem with Positive Thinking." *The New York Times* 24 October 2014. Accessed 13 November 2015. http://www.nytimes.com/2014/10/26/opinion/sunday/the-problem-with-positive-thinking.html.

Onoda, Hiroo. *No Surrender: My Thirty-Year War*. New York; Tokyo: Kodansha Int'l, 1974.

Peace, Richard. *Contemplative Bible Reading: Experiencing God through Scripture*. Colorado Springs, CO: Navpress, 1998.

Pennington, M. Basil. *Lectio Divina: Renewing the Ancient Practice of Praying the Scriptures*. New York: Crossroad, 1998.

Pfister, Hans-Rüdiger, and Gisela Böhm, "The Multiplicity of Emotions: A Framework of Emotional Functions in Decision Making." *Judgment and Decision Making* 3, no. 1 (2008): 5–17.

Ramsay, Arthur Michael, and Leon-Joseph Suenens. *The Future of the Christian Church*. London: SCM, 1971.

Ramsey, George W. "Is Name-Giving an Act of Domination in Genesis 2:23 and Elsewhere." *Catholic Biblical Quarterly* 50 (1988): 24–35.

Ranganathan, Vinoth K., Vlodek Siemionow, Jing Z. Lin, Vinod Sahgal, Guang H. Yue. "From Mental Power to Muscle Power: Gaining Strength by Using the Mind." *Neuropsychologia* 42, no. 7 (2004): 944–956.

Reed, John W. "Visualizing the Big Idea: Stories That Support Rather than Steal." In *The Big Idea of Biblical Preaching*, edited by K. Willhite and S. Gibson. Grand Rapids, MI: Baker, 1998.

Robinson, Haddon W. *Biblical Preaching: The Development and Delivery of Expository Messages*. Grand Rapids, MI: Baker, 1980.

———. "Preaching to Everyone in Particular." *Leadership* (Fall 1994): 100.

———. "Strengths and Seductions of Humor (Part I)." Preaching Today, online. Accessed 24 November 2015. http://www.preachingtoday.com/skills/themes/humor/200403.8.html.

Rosenberg, Jennifer. "The War is Over . . . Please Come Out." Online. http://history1900s.about.com/od/worldwarii/a/soldiersurr_2.htm.

Rushton, J. Philippe. "Generosity in Children: Immediate and Long-Term Effects of Modeling, Preaching, and Moral Judgment." *Journal of Personality and Social Psychology* 31, no. 3 (1975): 459–466.

Sangster, W. E. *The Craft of the Sermon*. London: Epworth, 1954.

Spurgeon, Charles H. *Lectures to My Students*. London: Marshall, Morgan & Scott, 1964.

Stanley, Andy and Lane Jones. *Communicating for A Change*. Colorado Springs, CO: Multnomah, 2006.

Stanovich, K. E., R. F. West, M. E. Toplak. "Myside Bias, Rational Thinking, and Intelligence." *Current Directions in Psychological Science* 22, no. 4 (2013): 259–264. Accessed 22 December 2015. http://dx.doi.org/10.1177/0963721413480174.

Stott, John R. W. *I Believe in Preaching*. London: Hodder & Stoughton, 1982.

Streett, R. Alan. *The Effective Invitation*. Old Tappan, NJ: Revell, 1984.

Stuart, Douglas K. *Old Testament Exegesis: A Handbook for Students and Pastors*. Louisville, KY: Westminster John Knox, 2009.

Stuempfle, Herman G. Jr. *Preaching Law and Gospel*. Philadelphia, PA: Fortress, 1978.

Sunukjian, Don. "Sticking to the Plot: The Developmental Flow of the Big Idea Sermon." In *The Big Idea of Biblical Preaching*. Edited by Keith Willhite, Scott Gibson and Haddon Robinson. Grand Rapids, MI: Baker, 1999.

Swoboda, A. J. "Sinners in the Hands of an Angry Preacher." Preaching Today, online. Accessed 1 December 2015. http://www.preachingtoday.com/skills/2014/october/sinners-in-hands-of-angry-preacher.html

Tan, Jimmy Boon-Chai. "Retaining the Tri-Perspective of History, Theology and Method in Spiritual Direction: A Comparative Study of Ignatius of Loyola and John Calvin." PhD diss., Fuller Theological Seminary, 2014.

Trible, Phyllis. *Texts of Terror: Literary-Feminist Readings of Biblical Narratives*. Philadelphia, PA: Fortress, 1984.

Towner, W. Sibley. *Genesis*. Westminster Bible Companion. Louisville, KY: Westminster John Knox, 2001.

Vest, Norvene. *Bible Reading for Spiritual Growth*. San Francisco, CA: HarperCollins, 1993.

Wahba, Mahmoud A., and Lawrence G. Bridwell. "Maslow Reconsidered: A Review of Research on the Need Hierarchy Theory." *Organizational Behavior and Human Performance* 15, no. 2 (1976): 212–240.

Walster, Elaine, and Leon Festinger. "The Effectiveness of 'Overheard' Persuasive Communications," *Journal of Abnormal and Social Psychology* 65, no. 6 (1962): 395–402.

Waltke, Bruce. *Creation and Chaos: An Exegetical and Theological Study of Biblical Cosmogony*. Portland, OR: Western Conservative Baptist Seminary, 1974.

Wardlaw, Don M. "Need for New Shapes." In *Preaching Biblically: Creating Sermons in the Shape of Scripture*. Edited by Don M. Wardlaw. Philadelphia, PA: Westminster, 1983.

Webb, Joseph M. *Preaching without Notes*. Nashville, TN: Abingdon, 2001.

Wenham, Gordon. *Exploring the Old Testament, vol. 1. The Pentateuch*. London: SPCK, 2003.

Wesley, John. "A Plain Account of Christian Perfection." In *The Works of John Wesley*, vol. 11. Oxford: Clarendon; Nashville, TN: Abingdon, 1984–2013.

White, Bill. "Sinning in the Pulpit." Preaching Today, online. Accessed 1 December 2015. http://www.preachingtoday.com/skills/2013/april/sinning-in-pulpit.html.

Williams, James R. "Guidelines for the Use of Multimedia in Instruction." *Proceedings of the Human Factors and Ergonomics Society 42nd Annual Meeting* (1998), 1447–1451.

Willhite, Keith. "Matching Delivery to Content." Preaching Today, online. Accessed 27 November 2015. http://www.preachingtoday.com/skills/themes/deliveringthesermon/200006.11.html.

Willhite, Keith and Scott M. Gibson, eds. *Preaching: Connecting the Bible to People*. Grand Rapids, MI: Baker, 1998.

Wilson, Paul Scott. *The Four Pages of the Sermon: A Guide of Biblical Preaching*. Nashville, TN: Abingdon, 1999.

———. *Preaching and Homiletical Theory*. St Louis, MO: Chalice, 2004.

Wright, Christopher J. H. *Knowing Jesus through the Old Testament: Rediscovering the Roots of our Faith*. London: Marshall Pickering, 1992.

Young, Frances. "'*Creatio Ex Nihilo*': A Context for the Emergence of the Christian Doctrine of Creation." *Scottish Journal of Theology* 44 (1991): 139–152.

Author Index

A

Adams, Jay E. 52, 55, 176, 177
Anderson, Bernhard W. 41, 53
Anderson, Rindy C. 243
Aristotle 22, 24, 33, 133, 216
Arthurs, Jeffrey 237, 246

B

Bechara, Antoine 18
Bockmuehl, Klaus 60, 61, 62, 63
Bockmuehl, Markus 42
Böhm, Gisela 18
Bradley, Margaret M. 135
Bridwell, Lawrence G. 172
Briscoe, Stuart 229
Broadus, John A. 190, 212
Brooks, Phillips 8
Bullock, C. Hassel 47
Buttrick, David 213

C

Calvin, John 63, 152
Casey, Michael 65, 66, 67
Chapell, Bryan 27, 30, 37, 38, 39, 54, 56, 57, 81, 82, 83, 84, 87, 99, 121, 122, 135, 136, 139, 144, 149, 161, 164, 165, 173, 175, 176, 177, 187, 190, 191, 192, 215
Childers, Jana 241
Childs, Brevard S. 53
Cianci, Rebecca 172

Cowan, Nelson 227
Craddock, Fred B. 13, 14, 24, 38, 39, 55, 57, 79, 93, 99, 109, 116, 144, 148, 155, 246
Crum, Milton 98

D

Daly, Patrick 14, 15
Davis, H. Grady 35
Davis, Ken 229
Day, David 96, 100
Denney, Andrew S. 133
Dunbar, R. I. M. 229
Dwight, Sereno 25

F

Farris, Stephen 31, 38, 39, 46, 57, 153, 154
Fee, Gordon D. 43, 47
Festinger, Leon 99

G

Gambrel, Patrick A. 172
Graham, Billy 208, 209
Green, Joel B. 45
Greidanus, Sidney 47, 56, 57, 89, 90, 98, 100, 106, 109, 110, 116, 153

H

Hamann, S. B. 135
Hasel, Gerhard 53

J

Jacks, Robert 231
Jensen, Richard 98

Johnson, Darrell W. 7, 12, 13, 56, 84, 151, 238
Johnson, Val Byron 136
Jones, Lane 29, 32, 177, 200, 202, 224, 239, 240
Jowett, J. H. 33, 34

K

Klofstad, Casey A. 243
Koller, Charles W. 237

L

Larsen, David 132
Larson, Craig Brian 242, 245
Lerner, Jennifer S. 18
Lewin, Kurt 201
Lim, Johnson T. K. 56, 58
Liske, Thomas V. 132
Litfin, Duane 33, 56
Lloyd-Jones, Martyn 24
Longman, Tremper, III 47
Long, Thomas G. 9, 19, 20, 27, 28, 36, 37, 38, 39, 58, 69, 71, 80, 81, 85, 93, 100, 110, 113, 116, 135, 136, 141, 142, 144, 145, 172, 214, 216, 217
Lowry, Eugene L. 98, 100, 102, 103, 104, 106, 143, 175, 181, 201, 239
Luchette, Lenny 80

M

Marshall, Lisa B. 227
Massey, James Earl 81
Mathewson, Steve 83, 86

May, Gerhard 42
McGrath, Alistair E. 132
McMickle, Marvin A. 28
Miller, George A. 227

N
Nicoll, William Robertson 48
Nouwen, Henri 251

O
Oettingen, Gabriele 200, 201
Onoda, Hiroo 7, 8

P
Peace, Richard 65
Pennington, M. Basil 66, 67, 70
Pfister, Hans-Rüdiger 18

R
Ramsay, Arthur Michael 153
Ramsay, George W. 58
Ranganathan, Vinoth K. 200
Reed, John W. 134
Robinson, Haddon W. 27, 33, 35, 39, 56, 86, 93, 94, 95, 97, 98, 121, 122, 127, 133, 134, 138, 139, 140, 141, 160, 161, 172, 173, 175, 177, 199, 200, 201, 212, 228, 229, 231, 235, 236, 241, 242
Rosenberg, Jennifer 8
Rushton, J. Philippe 16

S
Sangster, W. E. 132
Spurgeon, Charles 134, 246, 251, 252, 253

Stanley, Andy 29, 32, 163, 177, 200, 202, 224, 239, 240
Stanovich, K. E. 91
Stott, John R. W. 24, 48, 132, 153, 159, 160, 190, 198, 233, 237, 245, 246
Streett, R. Alan 204, 209
Stuart, Douglas 43, 47
Stuempfle, Herman G., Jr. 172
Suenens, Leon-Joseph 153
Sunukjian, Don 94, 161
Swoboda, A. J. 247

T
Tan, Jimmy Boon-Chai 63
Toplak, M. E. 91
Towner, W. Sibley 41
Trible, Phyllis 58

V
Vest, Norvene 67

W
Wahba, Mahmoud 172
Walster, Elaine 99
Waltke, Bruce 41
Wardlaw, Don M. 89
Webb, Joseph M. 237
Wenham, Gordon 57
Wesley, John 63, 190
West, M. E. 91
White, Bill 247
Willhite, Keith 241
Williams, James R. 240
Wilson, Paul Scott 31, 33, 35, 36, 37, 38, 39, 58, 74, 95, 98, 172
Wright, Chris 53, 56

Y
Young, Frances 42

Scripture Index

Old Testament

Genesis
1 .... 30, 41, 56, 57, 159, 219, 225, 226, 228
1:1–2 41
1:1–9 194
1:1–19 182
1:2 182
1:26–2:4 218
1:31 51
2 .... 57, 159
3 30
12 189
12:1–3 .... 52, 206
12:1–9 49
15 .... 178, 179, 188
15:1–6 201
15:16 54
16:13 58
23:1–20 84

Exodus
6 106
6:2–9 105
20:1 165
32 204
32:7–14 192

Leviticus
25:10 6

Numbers
11:25–29 60
20:1–13 104

Deuteronomy
3:23–28 104
4:1 14
5 14
6:4 86
6:4–5 86
6:5 86
6:6 227
10 14
14 14

Joshua
10 50
10:8 50

Judges
2 89
2:6–15 87

1 Samuel
2:22–26 74
2:30 74
3:9 65
17 .... 86, 87

2 Samuel
12:7 100
22:35 14

1 Kings
19 203
19:19–21 101

2 Kings
18:1–5 177
19 178

2 Chronicles
17:9 14

Ezra
7:10 16

Esther
2:19–36 184

Psalms
1 .... 48, 49
1:2 66
9 38
13 .... 115, 179, 196
13:4 236
13:6 196
23 .... 55, 68, 128, 157, 175
23:4 .... 17, 69
23:4–5 84
23:6 215
80:15 236
88 115
100 .... 114, 133
104 38
119 83
139 156

Proverbs
25:11 224
30 227
30:15–16 227

Ecclesiastes
12:10 224
12:11 233

Isaiah
2:3–4	199
6:9–10	13
7	56
9:1–6	126, 207
30:15–18	74
40:1	17
40:2	9
43	22
43:10	21
45:7	42
46:3–4	143
53	12
58:3–6	152
61	6
61:1	10, 28

Jeremiah
9:23–24	252
20:9	24
31:33–34	60
33:34	31
34:8	6
34:15	6
34:17	6

Ezekiel
3:9	69
17	6
36:25–27	60
36:26	xvii
37	xvi, 12
37:2	43
37:3	43
37:7	xvii
37:8	xvii
37:9–10	xvii
37:10	12
37:14	249
46:17	6

Daniel
7	112
7:14	112
10	45, 112, 113
10:1	44
10:2–19	44
11	112

Hosea
2	235
11	235

Joel
2:28	60

Amos
2	167
5:1–2	110
5:4–5	152
6	110, 111
6:1	224
8	89, 125
8:1–3	97
8:1–7	87, 97
8:5	97
8:6	97

Jonah
1:2	9
3:1–10	73
3:2	9
3:4	9

Micah
6:1–2	110

Zechariah
4:6	249

New Testament

Matthew
3:1	5
4:17	5
4:23	5, 10
4:35	5
5:2	15
6:12	250
6:13	250
6:21	139
6:25	156
6:25–34	52, 173
7:3–5	247
7:24	15
8:4	8
8:18–22	47
9:35	5, 10, 11
10:7	5
10:8	5
10:16	5
11:1	5
11:28	204
13	12
13:9	13
13:14	13
13:54	15
16:15	93
21:12	235
23:13	247
23:37	245
24:14	5, 10
26:6–13	100, 137, 226
26:8–9	137
28:11–15	134

Mark
1:38	5
1:45	8
3:14	5

Scripture Index

4:12 13
5:43 5
6:2 15
6:13 5
7:36 8
8:26 5
8:27–29 93
9 202
9:37 202
10:17–22 96
10:19 96
14:3–9 100

Luke
1:3 57
1:46–55 39
2:10 11
2:14 11
3:18 19
4:18–19 6
5:13 236
5:14 8
5:17 15
7:14 236
8:10 13
8:54 236
9:1–6 46
9:2 5
9:6 11
9:10–17 128
9:18–20 93
9:26–62 128
9:34–35 129
9:37–42 129
9:57–58 128
9:57–62 .... 46, 124
9:59–60 129
9:60 44
9:62–62 129
10:1–12 46
10:25–29 43
10:27 197
10:36 93
11:1 17

15:1–2 57
15:12–13 127
15:20–24 144
15:28–32 57
19:42–42 245
24:48 22

John
4:42 21
8:11 197
8:28 15
10 55
11:35 236
12:40 13
13:17 190
14:26 .... 15, 60
14:27 241
15:27 22
16:13–14 60
17:16–17 146
20:30 22
20:31 21
21:24 21
21:25 22
21:27 42

Acts
1:8 22
2 162
2:17–18 60
2:41 29
5:42 .... 11, 17
6:4 42
8 162
8:4 11
8:6 5
8:29 61
8:35 12
10 162
10:19 61
11:12 61
11:28 61
11:23 19
13:2–4 61

13:32 11
14:22 19
15:28 61
16:6–9 61
17 91
17:16 245
20:21–22 61
20:27 52
20:31 245
22:15 22
22:20 22

Romans
1:16 11
4:17 42
8:9 63
8:11 63
8:14 63
8:16 63
8:26 192
8:28–29 38
10:13–15 6
10:14–17 12
10:15 10
10:17 .... 5, 6
12:1 18
13:13–14 62
15:1–6 195
16:25 11

1 Corinthians
1:10 19
2:4 11
2:14–16 192
4:15–16 18
11:17–34 116
12:13 127
13 62
13:1–3 191
13:2 29
13:13 227
14:24–25 61
14:29 61
15:12 12

2 Corinthians
1:1–11 180
1:3–4 19
5:20 17
7:10 165
9:2 146
12:9 145

Galatians
2:2 10
3:1 247
3:3 191
4:13 .... 5, 127
4:19 247
4:20 247
5 176
5:2–15 .... 171, 183
6:7–9 230

Ephesians
1:3 52
2:3 250
4:1–2 18
4:13 20
5 57
5:18 50
6:12 249
6:18–20 249

Philippians
1:19–21 191
1:27 12
2:10–11 250
2:12 191
2:13 191
2:19 146
2:25 146
3 116
3:17 145
3:17–20 73
3:18 245
4:7 156

Colossians
1:5–6 12
1:10 191
1:22–23 7
1:23 10
1:28 16
3:16 15

1 Thessalonians
1:5 11
2:9 10
2:11 20
2:11–12 18
2:12 20
4:18 19
5:11 20
5:19–21 62

2 Thessalonians
2:16–17 17

1 Timothy
5:23 5

2 Timothy
4:20 5

Titus
2 157

Hebrews
4:15 147
5:7 147
12:4–13 72
12:11 72
12:22 52
13:14 52

James
1:19–20 247
1:22 151
1:22–25 190

4:2 127
5:16 156

1 Peter
1:25 51
3 180
3:8–12 179
4:10–11 191

2 Peter
3:2 52

1 John
1:1–2 22
1:3 22
1:9 250
2:27 15
5:6 22
10 22

Revelation
1:4 227
1:8 227
4:8 227
21:1–5 101

Langham
PARTNERSHIP

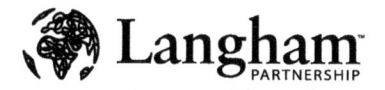

Langham Literature and its imprints are a ministry of Langham Partnership.

Langham Partnership is a global fellowship working in pursuit of the vision God entrusted to its founder John Stott –

to facilitate the growth of the church in maturity and Christ-likeness through raising the standards of biblical preaching and teaching.

Our vision is to see churches in the majority world equipped for mission and growing to maturity in Christ through the ministry of pastors and leaders who believe, teach and live by the Word of God.

Our mission is to strengthen the ministry of the Word of God through:
- nurturing national movements for biblical preaching
- fostering the creation and distribution of evangelical literature
- enhancing evangelical theological education

especially in countries where churches are under-resourced.

Our ministry

Langham Preaching partners with national leaders to nurture indigenous biblical preaching movements for pastors and lay preachers all around the world. With the support of a team of trainers from many countries, a multi-level programme of seminars provides practical training, and is followed by a programme for training local facilitators. Local preachers' groups and national and regional networks ensure continuity and ongoing development, seeking to build vigorous movements committed to Bible exposition.

Langham Literature provides majority world preachers, scholars and seminary libraries with evangelical books and electronic resources through publishing and distribution, grants and discounts. The programme also fosters the creation of indigenous evangelical books in many languages, through writer's grants, strengthening local evangelical publishing houses, and investment in major regional literature projects, such as one volume Bible commentaries like *The Africa Bible Commentary* and *The South Asia Bible Commentary*.

Langham Scholars provides financial support for evangelical doctoral students from the majority world so that, when they return home, they may train pastors and other Christian leaders with sound, biblical and theological teaching. This programme equips those who equip others. Langham Scholars also works in partnership with majority world seminaries in strengthening evangelical theological education. A growing number of Langham Scholars study in high quality doctoral programmes in the majority world itself. As well as teaching the next generation of pastors, graduated Langham Scholars exercise significant influence through their writing and leadership.

To learn more about Langham Partnership and the work we do visit **langham.org**